STUCK IN OUR SCREENS

Stuck

In Our

Screens

Setting Aside Social Drama
and Restoring Human Connection

KATHLEEN P. ALLEN, PH.D

ISBN: 979-8-9923979-0-1 eBook
ISBN: 979-8-9923979-1-8 Trade paperback

Library of Congress Control Number: 2025903299

References and details to industries, events, places, and companies have been changed. Any resemblance of content to actual persons, living or dead, or companies is entirely coincidental.

Book design by Glen Edelstein, Hudson Valley Book Design

First printing 2025.

For
Chloe Joy, Faelyn Rhea, Connor Michael, and Tanner Marie

Contents

Preface

What happens when adults trade maturity for adolescent social drama and teens buy into nonreality? We end up in a mess.

WE ARE IN A precarious place. We have some decisions to make about who we are. We need to rethink our identity and choose a healthy way forward. We are acting like adolescents who are doing identity work and using drama to accomplish this developmental task. Only we are not adolescents, and the drama that we are doing is destroying us and undermining our future and our well-being. It is time for us to be grown-ups.

This book began as an exposé on adolescent social drama. The research I did for my PhD dissertation on bullying among high school students led me to a construct that teens and their educators claimed was *not* the same as bullying. Several published research articles later I began to write a book about adolescent social drama, but two things happened that stifled my creative urges.

The first was a comment by a writer friend. After reading two-thirds of the completed manuscript on adolescent social drama, she said, "This isn't about adolescents; this is about our identity as a society in America.

The second event was the election of Donald Trump to the presidency in 2016, which caused my brain to experience a flash freeze (now amplified by his win in 2024). I found that I couldn't focus on much of anything except the dysfunctional adult behaviors of politicians, the media, and ordinary citizens playing out in real time. Adolescent drama seemed to have lost its relevance as our nation became entangled in adult social drama of national proportions. I was paralyzed and totally consumed by watching public figures, news anchors, celebrities, and otherwise reasonable people behave worse than most adolescents ever did. Prominent and powerful adults were engaging in social drama on a grand and horrifying scale, and it didn't feel like many people were noticing it. It felt petty and small to focus on adolescents doing drama when prominent and influential adults were behaving far worse. Perhaps there have always been adults who acted like immature and poorly developed adolescents, but what struck me was the way these behaviors were being normalized, repeated, and celebrated. It occurred to me that as a society we were embracing drama on steroids.

This is not a book about politics, although politics is ground zero for some of our worst social drama. This book is about human behavior in America in the twenty-first century. It is about how we interact with each other, how we manage conflict and differences, and how bad behaviors have undermined and shifted our individual and collective adult identities.

Social drama for adolescents helps them figure out who they are. It allows youth to explore and develop a sense of themselves, but adult social drama is not an exercise in healthy identity development. It is an exercise in fragmentation and dysfunction. Instead of becoming mature, insightful, rational individuals and members of a developed society, we are imploding. We need to reimagine, re-envision, and restore ourselves individually and collectively, and we need to do it soon.

I hope this effort promotes thoughtful reflection as well as personal and collective growth, and leads to existential change—and a wiser society.

Acknowledgments

SO MANY PEOPLE HAVE influenced the telling of this story. To them, I extend my gratitude.

Emma Rion and Barry Lyons, my editors, Glen Edelstein, my book designer, Maria Sosnowski, my indexer, Marissa DeCuir and her team at Books Forward, my publicists, and Matthew Gorman, old friend, good thinker, and my social media consultant. Sr. Edwardine Weaver, RSM, my seventh grade civics teacher, for her spot-on feedback. She is "my old teacher," and I am her "old student." Eileen Church, dear friend, brilliant woman, and fellow writer, who told me this book needed to be about our whole society, not just adolescents. She was right! I cherish our friendship. Molly Kuhl, good friend who has been with me since the beginning, who made it clear that boys do drama, but that "they just do stupid stuff." Karl, Jerry, Eric, Jude, Erin, Tom, and Amy, friends at Pittsford Mendon High School who helped me see drama as a construct different from bullying and helped me put it on the academic map. Jen, Kankana, Liz, and Essie, my doctoral dissertation buddies, for their encouragement to keep writing. Beth Anson, whose passion for research and gently irreverent sense of humor have always buoyed me. Harriette Royer, a good friend, fellow intellectual, and sensitive soul, who offered to read my manuscript. God bless you. Patti Michalek, long-time friend, fellow traveler on the journey of life, and consummate cheerleader, and her husband, John, whose love, depth, and intelligence are immeasurable. You are both precious gifts. Julie Thaney, thoughtful, generous, and wonderful mother who met with me several times to discuss her take on adolescent drama. Kate Landdeck, dear friend and fellow academic who cheered me on through my dissertation and challenged me to keep working on this book. Amanda Nickerson, who believed in me and gave me a role to play in the academic world. I am so grateful to you. John and Molly Hedges, life-long friends, great parents, and terrific grandparents. My wonderful sister, Mary, and her daughter, Kate, who are kindred spirits and great loves. Thanks for always being there, even when you think I am crazy! My wonderful son-in-law, Mike, who gives me great books that make me think. My "shiny" daughter, Mikaela, who loves The Real Housewives franchise and brought me up to speed on reality TV. My dear husband, Buck, and my daughter, Brenna, for going the long haul with me. I know it feels like forever. Nancy and her daughter, for their generosity of spirit and willingness to share their story. My mother, Norma, who is our rock.

In many authors' journeys there are the scholars, writers, and academics whose research and publications are intellectually inspiring. These are the brilliant, deep thinkers whose creativity, intuition, and vision keep people like me going. Whenever I hit a wall, I seek out, or return to their words, ideas, and conjectures. Some of you, I know in person. Others of you, I have yet to meet. Some of you have passed on. Please know that all of you are with me between the lines and in the pages of this book even if you are not referenced in the notes or bibliography. Thank you for sharing your intellect with all of us, but especially with me:

Dan Ariely, Albert Bandura, Roy Baumeister, Diana Baumrind, Peter Benson, danah boyd, David Brooks, Nicholas Carr, Jonathan Chein, Sarah Coyne, Wendy Craig, Nicki Crick, Dorothy Espelage, Karin Frey, Megan Garber, Erving Goffman, Jonathan Haidt, Susan Harter, Patricia Hawley, Samir Hinduja, Shelly Hymel, Robin Kowalski, Jennifer Livingston, Alice Marwick, Murray Milner, Jr., Justin Padgett, C J Pascoe, Amanda Rose, Howard Ross, Scott Lyons, Laurence Steinberg, Dena Phillips Swanson, Susan Swearer, Henry Tajfel, Richard Tremblay, Jean Twenge, Marion Underwood, Niobe Way, Margaret Wheatley, and Maryanne Wolf.

Prologue

The Drama Debacle

TWO DAYS BEFORE I delivered a keynote address to teachers in my home school district, a crisis engulfed our family. It was 1995, and my older daughter was in the second month of the eighth grade. Mikaela had been moody and cranky for several weeks, but I hadn't really picked up on it. The day before the keynote, I asked her something about her friends, and she shot back at me that she was on the outs with them. I distinctly remember her saying, "Haven't you noticed that no one has been calling me?" Like everyone else, land lines were still the main way we "called" each other.

Her problems began six weeks earlier during the first week of school when she and one of her close friends got into a snit over sharing a locker. Apparently, that was a big deal among middle-schoolers in 1995. Prior to their conflict, Chelsea and Mikaela had been part of a close group of friends. While there might have been more to their disagreement than sharing a locker, what ensued was the wholesale expulsion of my daughter from the friendship group. The girls stopped calling her on the family phone (cell phones were virtually nonexistent) and started a rumor that blasted through school like a Hogwarts howler: that Mikaela was a lesbian. The damage was immediate. Mikaela was a marked person, taunted, and ostracized by a large portion of the class of 250 students. It took several months to figure out exactly what had happened and to theorize why it had happened. We concluded that the "why" was due to a power struggle for control of her friendship group (i.e., it was about status and influence), and that the "how" was to spread a rumor that would ruin her reputation so that they could legitimately exclude her from their group and doom her to widespread social exclusion.

The internet had just been born, but thankfully, social media platforms didn't exist at that time, and as noted, hardly anyone, let alone kids, had cell phones. The horror of her experiences would have been magnified multiple times if the rumors weren't limited to word of mouth.

Discussions about relational aggression had yet to appear in the mainstream press, so it was difficult to put a name on what she had experienced. It was mean and it was a woeful betrayal of friendship. It cut deeply and caused our family a great deal of soul searching, looking for answers to what this was and how it could happen. These were girls who had had sleepovers at our house, had been invited to our cottage in the summer, and whose parents we knew and respected. The best we could do at that time to make sense of what they had done was to label it sexual harassment, which ironically, was the topic of the keynote speech I was about to deliver to the teachers in our school district. My professional and private worlds had collided in a grand fashion. I had been caught off guard and was devastated.

It wasn't until 2002 that two authors, Rachel Simmons and Rosalind Wiseman,[1] wrote books about the type of nonphysical aggression that they claimed girls were more likely to be involved in. They called it relational aggression. It was bullying that used verbal and social strategies to hurt someone's reputation or social standing. It could take someone out without swinging a punch. In fact, most kids who were targeted by relational aggression said they would have preferred a knock-down drag-out brawl over being socially destroyed by a covert aggressor.

One thing I had learned doing professional development for educators over the years was that kids didn't tell adults about sexual harassment or bullying until they were certain that the fallout and retaliation wouldn't be any worse than the abuse itself. At the time Mikaela disclosed to us what was happening with her, she begged us not to talk to the principal about what was going on. So we didn't, and that was a mistake.

Months later when we found out who had started the rumor and theorized why her close friend had betrayed her, she told me that while she was afraid to get adult help because of the repercussions, she had believed that I would do something. "You know so much about this [the problem of bullying and sexual harassment] that I thought you would do something about it. That's why I told you." The problem was that I hadn't done anything about it until we knew who started the rumor. We were surprised that it was her ex-friend, Chelsea, who rather thoughtlessly commented to Mikaela several months after the first round of rumors,

"You know that rumor that's going around about you now, 'that you are a lesbian'? Well, we didn't start it *this time.*"

At that point, it was January, and we went to the principal to tell him what we had recently discovered about the events of September, but the damage was already done. We asked that he require all the girls involved to attend a session on bullying and sexual harassment as a consequence. Mikaela wanted to sit in with them because she thought that if they understood the depth of the pain they had caused her, they would apologize, welcome her back into their group, and all could be forgiven. Obviously, that was not to happen. Instead, the group split in two. Half the girls and their parents attacked us for having gotten them in trouble, and half felt terrible about what the girls had done and apologized to us. But none wanted anything to do with Mikaela, and so there was a secondary round of anguish.

In the mid 1990s, the hot topic in schools was the problem of sexual harassment, with a growing concern about bullying that hit a climax in the early 2000s. "Drama" as a social construct had not entered the academic literature at the time. Research on bullying and relational aggression was mushrooming in the academic journals, but there still seemed to be a gap in our knowledge of what kids were experiencing that was going unnamed.

The missing piece wouldn't arrive until my research on social drama[2] was published almost simultaneously with danah boyd's and Alice Marwick's research in 2012.[3] I had worked with schools developing prevention and intervention policies, programs, and practices dealing with bullying, which included social and relational aggression. I had published articles on some of those issues, but when I began doing research with high school students trying to understand how *they* understood bullying and social aggression, I found that there was something else going on that looked somewhat like bullying and shared characteristics with relational aggression but wasn't an exact match with those constructs. According to the adolescents and the teachers that I interviewed and surveyed, some of what they were involved with that was being called bullying wasn't bullying. It was *drama.* Hence, they helped me introduce a new behavioral construct though not a new phenomenon, social drama, into the lexicon of adolescent social development. The word "drama" had been used loosely in the popular press to describe political behaviors, celebrity behavior, and other conflictual social phenomenon including adolescent behavior, but there was no succinct definition that articulated what my research participants insisted was going on in their social worlds.

Students told me that the difference between bullying and drama was that you could extricate yourself from drama, but you could not from bullying. They saw drama as more annoying and pointless than anything. High schoolers claimed they knew what bullying was, and that they were too mature to engage in behavior as bad as bullying. They relegated bullying to the antics of middle school students, and claimed that by high school, no one bullied anymore. However, many were involved in drama, if not by choice, then by proximity to the main actors.

Most participants said they hated drama but that it presented itself as an inevitable facet of their social lives. They said that some people loved stirring the social pot and producing drama. It provided entertainment and could be quite enjoyable to watch if you weren't caught up in it. Even the teachers asserted that it was easy to start drama. A look, a hairy eyebrow, a sideways glance, and by then, a cryptic or ignored text message, could foment drama. Rumor, innuendo, and gossip were its life blood, and it was often irresistible, if not impossible to watch.

The parallel to theatrical drama was obvious and clear. It seemed a perfect metaphor for how adolescents performed their lives with and for each other. But it also had a dark side if it morphed into the meanness and aggression that could become bullying, or more likely by 2009, cyberbullying, because of smart phones and social media. Most adolescent social drama stayed less serious and was more like breathing air than hyperventilating or having an asthma attack, but the possibility of it was floating under the surface if it got out of hand.

In the end, I concluded that adolescent social drama was more a curse than a death sentence. For a number of youth, I found evidence that social drama was a part of their identity development. It helped them try out behaviors, observe their impact, and for most, learn from their mistakes. Even my study participants acknowledged that they sometimes acquired some wisdom following their inadvertent involvement in drama. For a slice of youth, though, drama was a problem that seemed to have roots in personality development, and we know that personality is relatively hard-wired. These kids were the ones my participants said started drama and relished in it, despite the chaos and confusion they stirred up.

At this point, it's relevant to mention that the teachers, coaches, school administrators, parents, and siblings of drama kings, queens, princes, or princesses, labor under the constant wariness of drama to come, or current drama to get worse. One school social worker told me that "all day long, all I do, is deal with drama." He told me he kept a large spoon in his office that he brought out when he was working with a student who was "doing drama."

In hindsight, my daughter's middle school experience was closer to relational bullying than drama. It did spin off drama that many students who were not part of her friendship group joined in. I'm sure most of these kids would write it off as minor drama, something quite common in their middle school lives. It would be nothing to get worked up about. It was just a part of life .

✦   ✦   ✦

This book is going to examine social drama in depth and attempt to make the case that we have a serious social problem because too many high-profile, influential adults are doing drama on a grand scale. It's a problem of adolescent social drama on steroids, and it is dangerous to our collective well-being. We can give youth a pass on the drama they do that is part of their development, but we cannot survive a future where too many adults are doing drama, routinely and publicly. I'll attempt to connect adolescent social drama with adult social drama, make a case for personal and social soul-searching and renewal, and offer some suggestions for addressing this problem.

This book has been written for a reader who is thoughtful, engaged, and concerned. I, like you, seek information that is factual, reliable, and rational. I have sought to write a book that connects reality-based ideas and generates research-based solutions. Please feel free to send me your thoughts when you are finished reading this narrative. As a social science researcher and thinker, I am always seeking new knowledge and intelligent discourse that move us forward. Join the conversation if you are so inclined.

stuckinourscreens@gmail.com

Introduction

CAN WE BE SERIOUS for a moment? Really serious.

No ideologies. No taking sides. No pointing fingers. No tribalism.

No plugging our ears, no shaking our heads side-to-side and saying, "Na, na, na, na, na."

Somehow our American society has advanced a new template for acceptable adult behavior. Instead of actions that reflect maturity, competence, thoughtfulness, and concern for our collective well-being, we are acting like a nation of underdeveloped and immature adolescents, living moment to moment on smart electronic devices, reacting impulsively, and pretending that life is a reality TV show. It's not a good place for us to be.

Social drama is relatively common among adolescents and is a way for youth to explore their developing selves. It's a way for youth to try on various behaviors and figure out who they are. We call it identity work, an essential part of growing up. Not all youth engage in social drama, but most youth are aware of it. In this book, I define and explain adolescent social drama and then take a dive into the broader world of adults where social drama is taking root, spreading, and infecting our body politic. It's a tragedy that is well on its way to becoming the only way we know how to live. This exposé will consider what can be done to encourage and support those who engage in drama to retool these behaviors that cause so much damage and chaos. Lastly, I tackle social drama on the grand scale and offer suggestions for redefining our collective social identity.

- **Chapter 1** looks at the introduction of screens as a way to consume information, and later to reach out to each other and suggests ways these technologies have changed our behaviors.
- **Chapter 2** defines and describes the characteristics of social drama and helps us identify those who have a "need for drama" in their lives, as well as an introduction to drama addiction.

- **Chapter 3** reviews a case study of adolescent social drama. It reports on the antics of a group of teens that not only turns their world upside down, but also that of their parents, educators, and peers with nasty behaviors and outcomes.
- **Chapter 4** looks at the connection between social drama and personality, with a focus on narcissism, entitlement, extroversion, and impulsivity.
- **Chapter 5** explores reality TV and social media platforms that promote drama for viewers and encourages bad behaviors that get replayed by the masses via online platforms.
- **Chapter 6** interrogates how and why adolescents "do" drama as a feature of identity development, and then explores excessive adult drama and its effects on all of us.
- **Chapter 7** considers how groups of people behave toward the members of their "in" groups as compared to the members of "out" groups with whom they don't identify. It explores some of the triggers that produce nasty behaviors like moral disengagement, revenge, retaliation, and desensitization.
- **Chapter 8** looks at social drama in the world of adults, explores how adults act like adolescents when they "do drama," and considers the origins and consequences of adults engaging in social drama.
- **Chapter 9** reviews the outcomes of too much online time and how it deprives youth of necessary social development, and from learning empathy, boundary establishment, and communication skills.
- **Chapter 10** addresses how adults can parent and educate children to avoid drama and maintain balance in their lives.
- **Chapter 11** considers the problem of wide-spread social drama in an advanced society and the issues that it raises.
- **Chapter 12** explores how we can stop the social drama that is consuming and warping our identities and improve our functioning as healthy human beings in a civil society.

Human beings are capable of solving their problems through cooperation, working together, honest dialogue, and sharing responsibilities.

Living our lives, orchestrating social interaction, and trying to meet our basic human needs through screens has become a serious detriment to what it means to be human. If we are not to be subsumed by misinformation, loneliness, extreme polarization, and the negative outcomes of a future controlled by artificial intelligence, we must take a pause and reconsider what it means to be human in America at this time—and for the near future. We need a frank conversation about who we are and who we want to be. This is serious. We must ditch the drama and become grown-ups.

CHAPTER 1
Why Are We Stuck in Screens Doing Drama?

The First Screen: The Big Ole' Box in Our Homes[4]

VERY FEW PEOPLE TODAY would decry the invention of the television, but Neil Postman cast a skeptical eye on it in 1984. Much of what he predicted came true. Today, those same concerns can be said almost word for word about social media and posting, texting, tweeting, and short messaging on our electronic communication devices.

So, what did Postman predict would happen to us and why? It requires a bit of a history lesson, so hop on and bear with me.

Speaking and talking comes with being human. We are born with a brain and body parts that are specifically designed to help us become mumbling, voluble, blathering, speechifying creatures. As long as humans can hear and have the necessary vocal accoutrements, with a few exceptions, they will learn to speak whatever language is spoken around them. We are hardwired to be talkers. But not so when it comes to reading and writing. There is no human born knowing how to read and write. It has to be taught, but even before that, it had to be invented. Thus, writing, and then reading what has been written, depended on the invention of a system of putting marks on a surface that symbolized speech, such as the alphabet or some form of picture system as exists in many Asian languages.

Before writing was invented, remembering what was spoken was the only way to capture and stay in touch with the past; being able to remember people, events, and important information was necessary to survive. Forgetting that over the mountain was a tribe not to be trifled with was important knowledge to be retained and passed on. Auditory recollection of all things learned and valuable was critical to a society's longevity. But when writing developed, as long as there were people who could read and write the language, a permanent record could be made that lasted as long as the parchment, animal skin, or cave wall they wrote on existed. But those records were fragile and couldn't be consumed by the general population, who couldn't read or write anyway.

Then came the printing press, and voilà: Books could be produced faster, more cheaply, and be more accessible to more people, who now had a great incentive to learn how to read.

At this point it is important to note that writing and print are media. Examples of media are written language, images on paper or a screen, or microphones and speakers that broadcast sounds and words. Media are a way of transferring information to someone else. Media are forms of communication and each kind of media has characteristics that shape the message that can be transmitted in that particular way. The only medium that humans had that facilitated communication until the invention of photography, the telegraph, the radio, and the telephone, was through long, reasoned narrative prose, and if you could draw, some sketches to go along with it. What does that mean?

It means that people wrote their thoughts in letters, essays, articles, books, periodicals, and speeches. Some were published in newspapers, others in pamphlets or simple magazines. Some people kept journals if they had access to paper. This is how the people who founded our country communicated with one another. These forms of expression were shaped by the kind of media that existed at the time. And it created a society where reading, writing, and thinking were sophisticated and often quite complex, because people had time to make sure that their ideas were thoughtful, accurate, and logical. Sentences were long, and people used lots of big words, and the literacy rate in our country was above 90%, unless you were a slave (that's another story). The point is that we were a highly developed and literate group of people back then.

When all we had was print, pens, and paper, we used lots of language to express ourselves, and hence we had great thinking ability. Language and thinking are intricately connected, and there are two sides to this phenomenon. One side is the side we understand when we hear something or read something. The other side is the one where we generate our own speech through speaking or writing the language being generated in our brains. It's this side of language that requires the ability to do complicated thinking. When we think, we link ideas, assess them, draw conclusions, and come up with new insights or observations. When new forms of media and expression arrive, it can change the way we process thoughts and then use the information in those thoughts by speaking or writing them. Television was probably the most impactful form of media introduced to humanity because it only requires that we understand what we see or hear, and even if we don't, there are rarely any consequences. It is a passive medium that requires very little of us.

I've skipped over the complicated effects of photography, the telegraph, radio, and the telephone, because we need to get to the screen, the one in the big box full of tubes (mostly gone today or found in antique shops or landfills that collect our dead electronic devices), or the flat screen hanging on a wall, in just about every room in our home, or the one we hold in our hands.

Postman wrote in the eighties that television is a medium that was designed to entertain, otherwise, people wouldn't watch it very much. Therefore, everything we see and hear from a TV is specially designed to catch our interest and hold it. Long expository speeches don't sell very well. Just check the ratings for some channel like C-span. No one wants to buy advertising on a channel that is so boring that hardly anyone wants to watch it or listen to it if you have satellite radio.

TV was designed to mesmerize and capture our attention. While the news is meant to inform us, the information is delivered in short sound bites, like commercials. The people we see on information TV are attractive, thin, and well-dressed, or we'd probably not spend much time consuming their offerings. So, no matter what we tune in to on TV, it is meant to amuse and entertain us first, last, and foremost. Even *Sesame Street*, despite its educational content, is there to keep our children enchanted (while we fix dinner or fold laundry).

As predicted, most people stopped reading as much as they might have once the television entered our lives. After all (as my husband would opine), why spend the time reading a book when the movie will be out soon. Reading is like any skill that has to be learned. If you don't practice it, the skill gets rusty. Our society became rusty at reading because of television, and when that happened, we lost some of our capacity for deep and creative thinking because of the passive nature of watching TV. After all, the creativity comes out of the screen, but asks nothing of us, and that's about where it stops.

Today, our two-way screens do more than entertain us; they allow us to live in a world of information bytes that get shot at us, to which we often respond in lightning-fast repetition if the context is two-way. Not much is thoughtful, profound, or valuable. In fact, most is trivial, superficial, and shallow. And when the medium only allows for that type of input, that's what our brains get good at doing to the unfortunate demise of intellectual growth and successful social functioning.

So what did Neil Postman see happening in our future and why did he make these predictions forty years ago?

Postman argues that prior to television, our ideas about education, knowledge, truth, and information—all realms of the intellect— were developed, explained, and expanded upon by thinking that was presented to us through the printed word. Developing ideas, knowledge, and truth involved writing and thinking—and maybe consulting other writers and thinkers in the process. Writing down one's ideas took time then and takes time now. It is not lightning fast. It is slow and deliberate. Stating a point or a proposition, and then backing it up with evidence requires thinking, reading, writing, rethinking, and rewriting. Reducing such thinking into sound bites does a disservice to intellectual honesty, and compromises the validity of ideas, and thus, knowledge.

Postman asserts that this process of expository writing lent itself to an "orderly, coherent arrangement of facts and ideas." This method of presenting and debating ideas and knowledge created a public discourse, or general way of having an open and many-sided conversation about a topic, that was mature and civil, and that pushed people to think "conceptually, deductively and sequentially." A high value was placed on reason and an orderly presentation of ideas, coupled with a dislike and avoidance of contradiction, that produced objectivity in thinking.

Fast forward to the entrance of television in our lives. Regardless of the shows we watch, television gives us performance first and ideas later. Well, sometimes TV gives us ideas. What television does best, however, according to Postman, is entertain us. Included in that entertainment is a lot of trivia and distraction. Most of us would agree with that unless you are a heavy consumer of science and history shows. But what Postman says happens next could have been written in the past six months, not forty years ago. "Americans no longer talk to each other, they entertain each other. They don't exchange ideas; they exchange images. They don't argue with propositions; they argue with good looks, celebrities, and commercials.... all the world is a stage..."[5] Oh my! Where have we heard that before?

Ten minutes in a restaurant will confirm that we don't talk to each other anymore. We send text messages and pictures to one another, often when we are in the same room or vehicle. We avoid looking at each other. Our conversations seem to work best when we have them through mediated communication devices. And if we think about his thoughts on good looks, celebrities, and commercials, it is impossible *not* to think of social media, video posting, and the influencers we follow. When television came into our lives, we could watch people with good looks all day long. Now that our media offers us two-way experiences, we are the entertainment for each other.

So what?, you might ask. Do we care about the effects of this latest advance in media technology? Isn't it the latest and the greatest? After all, look at how the world has opened up to us. What's to care about? Postman would argue that we should care for some serious reasons. One of them is that mass amusement can distract people from what is really going on around them. A constant diet of amusement dumbs people down and makes them vulnerable to misinformation and lies. Postman says it best:

> When a population becomes distracted by trivia, when cultural life is redefined as a perpetual round of entertainments, when serious public conversation becomes a form of baby-talk, when, in short a people become an audience and their public business becomes a vaudeville act, then a nation finds itself at risk; culture-death is a clear possibility.[6]

Whereas Postman wrote that about the television and what it would usher in, it describes exactly the place our society finds itself today, but not so much because of TV. As if he had a crystal ball, he foreshadows what social media and the smart phone would do to us, even more so than the television. His words were written some forty years ago, before everyone had a two-way screen in their pockets. His predictions are just as fresh as if they were written yesterday. It leaves me with a pit in my stomach.

I see links between social drama and social media use, and the disintegration of the ability for adults to do the work that moves us beyond adolescence to adults who see the big picture (and I don't mean the picture in the screen). I have this uncomfortable worry that thinking big thoughts and knowing how to express them is a skill that may be more than rusty, it may be on its way to becoming obsolete. Returning to the past is never a good idea, but we've acquired some habits and practices that overall aren't good. We need to envision a future that is different from where we are headed. We are living in screens, doing cultural drama ad infinitum, acting like feckless adolescents, clueless to what we are giving away and to what is being done to us. It's time for adult social drama to get the director's hook. It's time for us to be grown-ups.

CHAPTER 2
Social Drama Explained

DRAMA IS ONE OF those illusive concepts… kind of like pornography, difficult to describe and pin down, but also one of those things that fits the adage: "You will know it when you see it."[7] The use of the word "drama" to describe certain types of interactions and activities is fairly common, but until recently, we didn't have a definition or a description of social drama.

My foray into social drama was part of my experience as a parent, but it wasn't until I did research at a high school that I learned what drama looked like from inside the world of adolescents. My original research question revolved around how teenagers and their educators understood bullying. I had been studying and teaching about bullying for several years and one of the biggest challenges was to get people to agree on a definition of bullying and then apply that definition uniformly to situations and experiences that may or may not be bullying. That, however, tended to be an elusive goal for those of us studying bullying.

I began my research by doing focus groups with students to get a sense of their understanding of bullying, but all I heard about was "drama." When I asked them to define or describe bullying, I got blank stares. So I probed with questions about disagreements, conflict, meanness, social problems, aggression, and gossip. They said that younger, immature kids engaged in aggression and bullying, but that the older and more mature they got, the less this happened. They readily admitted that conflict was a part of their lives, and it could involve talking about people behind their backs, secretly making fun of people, and generally spreading unkind gossip and rumors.

Over time, it became clear that labeling a social interaction as bullying, and making distinctions between constructs like aggression, conflict, verbal arguments, spreading rumors, ostracism, and harassment was difficult, because it was subjective, personal, and nuanced. Everyone seemed to have their own mental template about what constituted conflict, bullying, and drama. Often the differences were quite nuanced, making it difficult to name the problem and to figure out how to address it. So my hypothesis about defining bullying was confirmed, and in the process I came to the conclusion that drama was its own unique kind of social debacle, and my study participants wholeheartedly endorsed my suspicions. Students and school staff members had quite a lot to say, and the following is what they told me about drama.

DRAMA IS ONE OR MORE SOCIAL INTERACTIONS

Drama[8] can't happen without at least two people interacting with each other. That interaction could be face-to-face, such as in conversation, a look, a gesture, a stare, or even a noninteraction, such as when someone ignores a person in a situation that calls for acknowledgment. A social interaction can happen when two people are not physically together but communicate in some form with each other. That can include telephone conversations, email, text, e-chat, or posting to a social networking platform such as Facebook, Instagram, Snapchat, X (formerly Twitter)", TikTok, or one of the constantly evolving ways to connect over the internet through social media. And just as noninteraction in face-to-face situations qualifies for the definition, noninteraction over the phone or in cyberspace qualifies, too.

DRAMA IS ABOUT SOMETHING TRIVIAL, INCONSEQUENTIAL, OR OF INFLATED RELEVANCE

Drama is usually about something stupid. Whatever it is about, it is usually quite unimportant. Drama can be about sex, promiscuity, nasty gossip, telling someone's secrets, cheating, or lying. Whether it's who slept with whom, making up stories about someone, or blabbing someone's not-so-nice comments, the importance of it gets inflated.

DRAMA INCLUDES OVERREACTION

Overreaction is a necessary component of drama because if nobody overreacts, then there isn't anything to do drama about. Strong reactions aren't necessarily a problem, but when the reaction to the situation looks like somebody is "making a mountain out of a molehill," then it's overreaction.

DRAMA INCLUDES EXCESSIVE EMOTIONALITY

Drama is drama because it involves lots of emotion and the expression of that emotion. These emotional expressions are not limited to the person who is the subject of the drama but can spread to others whose feelings are hurt in the process.

DRAMA INCLUDES THE INVOLVEMENT OF MORE PEOPLE THAN SHOULD BE INVOLVED

Drama is most entertaining, dynamic, and outrageous when many people are involved, so drama will often grow to include extraneous others. Drama is like a magnetic black hole that sucks everyone into it.

DRAMA IS PROLONGED IF SOMEONE IS BENEFITTING

Drama is something that should be over and done with quickly, but actors will keep it alive if someone is getting some benefit from it. The benefit might be more attention, more status, or more power, usually of the social kind.

DRAMA USUALLY ENDS WHEN SOMETHING ELSE MORE INTERESTING COMES ALONG

While drama is often prolonged, it can have a short shelf life, especially when it's about something trivial or if its importance has been excessively exaggerated. So the life of a given instance of drama is related to who's directing the show and the rewards that are coming in from the box office.

DRAMA IS PERFORMATIVE AND PARTICIPATORY

Just as the word "drama" suggests, the people who do drama enact, perform, and play a role. Drama involves putting oneself "out there," so that others can watch, comment, and participate. This, of course, is all made very public because participants put themselves out there on social networking sites where they have an eager audience anxious to react to what is happening. Usually there are one or two people who are starring in the drama. Others are supporting cast members, and still others are sitting in the front row eagerly shouting, "Bravo!" when the action gets intense or outrageous. There are even a few wannabees waiting in the wings for a new part to develop so that they can get in on the action and maybe catch enough attention to become a cast member.

Social drama is not new. In fact, it's as old as humans are. Just check out some of the behaviors in the Old Testament of the Bible. Read a few of the stories involving pretty bad behavior and draw your own conclusions about what was being said and done as the events unfolded. Without a doubt those involved and those on the periphery were putting in their two-cents, making things worse, and either gloating or being horrified by the goings-on. Most biblical writers left out the "he said/she said" nonsense. For sure there were always some folks expressing their opinions, taking sides, and joining in the drama, but it seldom made it into the sacred texts (what a blessing!). Today, however, our stories get told differently because we have communication tools that amplify, bolster, distort, and instantly spread the drama to a ready audience through two-way screens.

Before social media and smart phones, social drama was rather contained. Now it is not. Even the old push-button telephone didn't have nearly the power that screens have today. Surely, gossip made the rounds relatively fast on the telephone grapevine, but the annoyance and irritation, plus the damage of social drama were relatively contained. Today, our constant access to each other through technology not only spreads the drama, it can also start it. All it takes is someone who has a need for drama.

DOING DRAMA? TAKE THE TEST[9]

When asked about the traits that people who do social drama exhibit, college students easily identified this lovely list of nasties: easily offended, sensitive to criticism, plays the victim, prone to outbursts, manipulative, exaggerated sense of entitlement, shifty moods, unstable, impulsive, shallow, low self-esteem, blames others for their own failures, judgmental, arrogant, disrespectful, resentful, insincere, compulsive, and scheming.

Using this information, these researchers came up with twelve statements for people to respond to, using a 1-7 scale from strongly disagree to strongly agree. Based on the responses, this group was able to identify individuals who exhibit personality traits that predict their "need for drama."

Do you or someone you know have a "need for drama?"

1.   Sometimes it's fun to get people riled up.
2.   Sometimes I say something bad about someone with the hope that they find out what I said.
3.   I say or do things just to see how others react.
4.   Sometimes I play people against each other to get what I want.
5.   I wait before speaking my mind. *(This item was scored using the opposite of all the others because agreeing with this statement means a person tries to avoid drama.)*

6. I always speak my mind but pay for it later.
7. It's hard for me to hold my opinion back.
8. People who act like my friends have stabbed me in the back.
9. People talk about me behind my back.
10. I often wonder why such crazy things happen to me.
11. I feel like there are people in my life who are out to get me.
12. A lot of people have wronged me

Respondents generated the following statements when asked to describe friends and acquaintances who had a high need for drama in their lives:[10]

She will make life a living hell for anyone who doesn't agree with her on absolutely everything.

He liked to start problems on his own, as if he received pleasure from causing rifts between the rest of the roommates and I.

Every detail of infidelity gets posted on various social networks for the world to see and arguments between her and her boyfriend occur in public places.

Whatever is on his mind he will say it no matter who is around to hear it. He lacks the filter that prevents people from blabbing out something offensive about someone to their face.

Anything bad that happens sends him into a panic where the next half hour is taken up by him complaining… This happens daily and sometimes he will talk about his problems and the people that are responsible for them for hours at a time while working.

Everything is a huge problem. No matter what it is, she acts like it's the end of the world.

DRAMA AS A COPING MECHANISM

Most of us would think that drama is just nonsense, that it serves no purpose for the person stirring the pot, but Dr. Scott Lyons[11] has concluded otherwise, and his assertions are not just based on science, but on his own personal history. Fourteen years after my original exploration of the social drama phenomenon, and seven years after the Frankowski study reviewed above, Scott Lyons published a book on drama and what happens to a person who is heavily involved in it and can't seem to live without it.

Dr. Lyons's definition of drama is "the stirring, the excitement, the exaggeration, the eruption, the unrest, and the battle to feel alive in relation to the numbing of the internal and external world around you."[12] That's quite a statement from someone who admits to being addicted to drama. It's interesting to note that his definition includes much of my original definition. This suggests that what the outside world sees in a person doing drama is similar to what the person doing the drama sees in him or herself... namely, the wild chaos of it all. What Dr. Lyons adds to our understanding is the perspective from the inside of the person doing all the pot stirring. He says that drama is a drug that is sought or manufactured as a coping mechanism to deal with both the internal world of the person and the external place a person finds him or herself in. That's a pretty heavy dose of self-reflection and self-awareness. But there is more.

Lyons links addiction to drama to a dependency on chaos and crisis. This need comes from an inability to manage stress, not just caused by daily living, but from trauma experienced while growing up. For those addicted to drama, rampant chaos, high emotions, and volatile relationships cover up and hide a profound sense of abandonment and loss. When things are calm, boring, slow, or relaxed, the drama addict is unsettled and seeks or creates drama to fill in the sense of internal emptiness. For these folks, joining someone else's crisis, or creating one of their own is a way to fill a void. Chilling out is not something they find pleasurable.

Drama addicts experience a life of extreme ups and downs. Their thoughts and feelings tend to be supercharged and uncontrollable. They will tell you that they feel more alive when they are wound up tight and spinning through the whirlwind of their lives. Many of these people will say that they don't feel like they have any control over their lives, and that during an episode of drama, they feel alone and isolated, as if there is something profoundly wrong with them. In the midst of sucking everyone into the black hole of drama, they seldom feel connected to those flying alongside them, or if they do feel connected it is through major breakdowns in boundaries. One person's craziness becomes the other person's craziness, and they get lost in each other. All of this creates chronic fatigue for the addict and those around him or her.

In the end, drama becomes tightly integrated into an addict's identity, the part of the self that defines who a person is. Disconnecting from drama then becomes an intense process of reconstructing that identity and reinventing how one will live moving forward. Regardless of whether the view is from inside the addict or external to that person and being experienced by nearby friends, colleagues, and relatives, it's an exhausting experience all around. Being addicted to drama is no joke, so anything we can do to help our children, our families, and ourselves avoid its pitfalls is valuable information to have.

Not everyone who does drama has fallen into the abyss of drama addiction. In younger kids, especially adolescents, drama is a well-known phenomenon. For most kids, it's more a nuisance than an affliction, but it can rock the world for anyone embedded in it, both kids and adults.

CHAPTER 3
Teen Social Drama: A Case Study

WHILE MY INITIAL STUDY yielded a definition of drama based on the voices of my research participants, I sought to find real life examples of situations that were labeled as drama. I wanted to see if my thinking could be applied to repeated incidents in real life. Was there something generalizable here? I wondered if I had missed anything, or if there was more to the construct of drama than I had uncovered. The following example of adolescent social drama serendipitously found its way to me and convinced me that I was on to something.

PART I

Vanessa is a strikingly beautiful and charming high school student who is between her second and third year. She is articulate, polite, and self-confident. We are meeting to discuss a series of events that took place during the past school year when Vanessa was a sophomore. As we waited for her mother to arrive, we chatted a bit. I explained why I was interested in her story and how I expected to use the information in my research. According to Vanessa, the problematic events of February began around December 20th. Vanessa is one of six girls who consider themselves very best friends. The girls are all fans of hockey and regularly attend their school's boys' hockey games. During the hockey season, one of them found a Twitter account called "hockeywhorebabes." Vanessa explained to me that the name referred to females who were obsessed with hockey and "hockeywhorebabes" but shortened it to the HWBs."

Another group of girls whom Vanessa describes as "part of our friend group, but girls we're not best friends with," and who "like to start drama a lot" took on the identity of "Pretty Pucksters," and joined the HWBs in a series of tweets that at some point turned hostile. Vanessa couldn't recall what the tweets said, but she remembers them as being "kind of mocking." After some time passed and Vanessa reflected on what they were doing, she told her friends that she thought the HWBs should stop the exchange of nasty tweets with the Pretty Pucksters. However, two of her friends got so angry with Vanessa that the five girls broke off their friendship with her. The estrangement between Vanessa and her five friends continued for the rest of the Christmas break and into the first week of school in January.

The girls ended their conflict at a party where they told Vanessa they were sorry and admitted that they had done "a lot of things that were not OK." I asked Vanessa why she thought they changed their minds and apologized:

> I was keeping my distance because I was like "if you are going to do this to me I'm not going to be friends with you." And then I started hanging out with my other friends like ... that I was friends with before, like a year ago that I hadn't really seen in a while. It was like... "awright. You're going to do this to me, I'm going to hang out with other people." I think they saw that and they realized that they had really hurt me, so they were going to say they were sorry. So I didn't want the drama so I forgave them.

PART II

On February 3, 2012, a series of events began that quickly escalated and triggered attacks against the six girls. The bulk of the hostilities occurred through social media and involved students at their high school. The events revolve around one of the girls in the group of six whose boyfriend had purportedly cheated on her when they were dating.

On that morning, around second period, "We found out that when Sydney and Ian were still together, like the end of January, Ian had sex with a girl named Samantha."

> He told us that the entire grade, even all of our friends knew, but the whole grade had made a pact not to tell us six. We're in school.

It's fourth period and me and one of the girls are like, "What are we going to do?" So we go to the counselor. And she's telling us that we shouldn't tell her in school... that we should tell her after school and everything. But at that point Sydney knew that we were keeping something from her. Sydney was like, "Tell me, tell me, tell me." And we were like, "No... we'll tell you after school."

So Sydney already knew that something was up. And she knew it was about Ian. So it's now the end of fourth period. So I texted all of my friends saying what happened. "We need to talk to Sydney."

[At the end of fourth period] we brought her into the bathroom and then the bell rings and we're going to skip fifth period because we're all going to tell her this. And so we're sitting in the bathroom and we tell her straight up.

"When you and Ian were still together Ian had sex with Samantha." Sydney just bursted [sic] out crying, crying her eyes out. She was honestly a mess. She was not in a state to go to class that entire day, and so we're all crying. When we see one of our friends cry, we're just so emotional that we start crying, because we've seen one of our friends be so hurt. Then we're like, "What are we gonna do? We can't go back to our classes. That's not even a possibility." And so we call all of our parents. "Can someone pick us up? We just need to go home. We need to go to someone's house and talk about things. We just need to be out of school."

So we're trying to figure out everything, who's picking us up. Who's calling us in sick... all these things.

Five of the girls call their parents to have them excused from school, but one girl calls the school impersonating a parent of another girl to get her out of school. At this point, the principal is suspicious and concerned that six girls who are all friends are leaving school at the same time with one mother, so she calls the other five parents to confirm that they have given permission to leave school, tipping one parent off to the fraudulent phone call. This process provoked a great deal of angst and frustration on the part of the girls. The principal agrees to let them leave in the care of one of the mothers. She drops them off at her home and goes back to work. At this point the six girls are alone.

And we're at the table eating and we're just kind of talking about everything. We're talking about how annoyed we are about everything; how sad we are... And so then we get our phones out and we're like, "Let's tweet. Let's just put our emotions right in writing." And so... we're tweeting really mean things about the girl that Ian cheated with. There's about 200 people each following each of our tweets. Some of us aren't private so anybody random can look at our tweets. It's kids in our class and throughout the whole school [who can read their tweets]. Mostly our class but other classes, too.

Then everyone *started tweeting us back, saying "You guys are disgusting. I can't believe... you call each other HWBs." Just really mean things. Like we got back ten times worse than what we did in just those tweets in the last twenty minutes. So I was the one who was like, "Erase all of your tweets. They're not worth it. We need to erase them right now." So we all go on our phone and we erase it. And so then we're still getting tweets and it's like an hour later and people were still tweeting at us such mean things. And so... I was like, "I'm going to delete my Twitter. I'm done. I can't read these." It hurt. It physically and mentally hurt me to read these.*

So I went on the computer and I deleted my account and then everyone followed me and deleted their account. So at that point we had no Twitter. We still had Facebook then. We ... we were even crying because so many people were saying things. I don't even remember it because there were so many people saying things. So after that, pretty much our entire school hated us.

The girls go back to school for cheerleading practice at 2:15 P.M., but before they do, one of them sends a text to the girl who cheated with Ian, telling her they were sorry about the mean tweets, that they regretted what they had said, and that they hoped she would forgive them.

In the following days, the entire cheerleading squad, which included five of the six girls, were booed and heckled by the student body while performing at a basketball game. All the girls experienced verbal harassment in the halls at school to the point where they feared for their safety. Student Facebook accounts contained multiple hostile comments to and about the girls. An anonymous call was made to the cheerleading coach complaining that these girls had bullied her daughter who is a junior varsity cheerleader as well. A group photo of the cheerleading squad that was hanging in the main foyer of the school was defaced. Several of the girls received an anonymous letter via US postal mail that included copies of some of their nasty tweets and challenged the veracity of their claims of being the victims. Several months later, the girls don't know who sent this mailing, and are still upset about the viciousness of the author's comments to them and about them.

Additionally, the girls believed that the father of the girl who cheated with Ian wanted the school to punish them for the tweets that they had sent out. The policy on this type of infraction required a warning first before suspension, so unless the girls did something hostile or aggressive in addition to posting the nasty tweets, the school would not punish them.

On the evening of the initial set of events described above, Vanessa reopened her Twitter account to see what students were saying about them.

> I reopened my Twitter to just look at the things that people were saying because we found out right after cheerleading that someone told the school. Someone showed our tweets to the school... all of the tweets. And so we wanted to get proof that, "Yes, we were the ones that said things first and we did bring these things upon ourselves." So we took pictures. I probably had 300 pictures of tweets of people who wrote us back. So I took pictures of every one of those tweets that... to say, "Yes we did tweet this, but we were not the only ones that did this. People also tweeted things that they shouldn't have. If we're going to get in trouble, I do want to know who actually did things back to us." At that point, we thought... I literally thought I was going to get suspended from school, even though what we said happened outside of school. I thought we were going to [be suspended] because of how bad it was. And so I was like, let me take pictures of every-thing everyone else ... what they said.

PART III

The previous section might by itself, be the end of the story, if new drama hadn't developed during the actual interview. This extension of the story is recounted because it exemplifies the way this group of girls and their parents communicate on social media, and the situation that Vanessa created and pulled me into. By itself, this is an example of drama.

It is 12:45 P.M. on the day of the interview and Vanessa's mom has to pick up two of Vanessa's friends and take them to cheerleading practice that starts at 1:15 P.M. In what I believe is in the interest of time, Vanessa's mom invites me to ride along with them, so that we can continue our conversation after the girls have been dropped off. As she and I are walking to the car, Vanessa is in the house texting her mother. When we get into the car, her mom starts reading Vanessa's texts to me. The transcript of our conversation is as follows:

> **Mom:** *She's afraid that the two girls are going to feel awkward.*
> **Author (KA):** *We won't say anything to them [about any of this]. Is this upsetting her?*
> **Mom:** *Yes.*
> **KA:** *Are you OK with that?*
> **Mom:** *Yes. Will you wait here [at their house]? She feels she's putting her friends in a very awkward position. She told them who you were. She's afraid of them being in the car with you. She's feeling that I'm putting her friends in an awkward position. She agreed to this, not them. That's what she texted me. She's feeling that you being in the car...*
> **KA:** *So you want me to stay here?*
> **Mom**: *Do you mind?*
> **KA:** *Oh no.*

When her mother returned about forty minutes later, she reported that Vanessa had cried all the way to her friend's house. While I was not present for the conversation, her mom said that Vanessa was upset because all the parents "talk behind the girls' backs," and she claims that they have done things that have hurt the girls.

If your head is spinning and you feel a bit scrambled in the brain, that's to be expected. This is what drama can do. Drama unleashes a fog machine hidden somewhere in the theater that coats everything in mist, even the people in the audience watching what is going on. Drama can produce a sense of confusion and unreality, and these events qualify as social drama. This narrative produces personal drama, group drama, school-wide drama, and even interview-drama.

One of the factors that seems to be related to whether a person has a proclivity for drama or not is the individual's personality. This is most evident in adolescence, but also is a factor later in life, when other characteristics manifest themselves. For now, we'll grapple with personality, what it is and how developmental angst can get drama rolling.

CHAPTER 4

Personality and Social Drama

SOCIAL DRAMA CREATES CHAOS and confusion, garners attention and reaction, and provides endless angst and entertainment. It takes a special person to incite such mayhem. Drama puts some explosive personality traits on display. These lovelies include combinations of extroversion, narcissism, impulsivity, and entitlement, often accompanied by high emotions, the inability to let go, and obsessive thinking. None of these cognitions, emotions, or actions by themselves are a match to flame, but the right (or wrong) assortment of these tendencies can lead to drama.

PERSONALITY

Personality is the tendency to think, act, and feel in certain consistent ways across time and situations.[13] It's a combination of genes (i.e., biology), and environment (i.e., experience), and experts have observed that personality changes continue until we are 50 years old, albeit in relatively small ways.[14]

Once someone is into doing drama, these traits contribute to ratcheting up the emotional level, as opposed to scaling it back. In addition to the traits previously mentioned, other traits and behaviors that provide the momentum for drama include delaying gratification, distress experienced empathically within close friendships, rumination, co-rumination, and rejection sensitivity. Understanding these traits and tendencies can give us a foundation for making sense of behavior that looks a lot like behaviors most of us would want to avoid.

EXTROVERSION

Extroversion is associated with being dramatic.[15] For example, a teen creates a video of herself performing a popular song, wearing hideous makeup and a skimpy outfit. She then posts it on social media and it ends up being viewed by a wide-ranging audience of acquaintances and a bunch of people she barely knows, but with whom she is connected on social media. In the moment she thought it was fun, funny, slightly outrageous, and entertaining, and certainly it was. The comments from her "audience" are just what she was looking for. Extroverted individuals are highly sociable, expressive, talkative, lively, energetic, outspoken, outgoing, forceful, enthusiastic, adventurous, noisy, and often bossy.[16] They may also be imaginative, creative, smart, inventive, and likely to show off.[17] Every one of those traits leans in the direction of someone inclined to engage in social drama.

DELAYING GRATIFICATION AND IMPULSIVITY

Delaying gratification is waiting and holding off on something desirable because being patient and waiting will be rewarded in the end with something better than what is available now.[18] It's the old marshmallow test. Can a child stare at one marshmallow that's available for consumption *right now*, so that she can eat two marshmallows in ten minutes? It requires a lot of willpower, determination, and self-control to be tempted thus and not cave in. Waiting ten minutes even when it will yield much better gains and more of the good stuff is a difficult tradeoff.

Delaying gratification requires the skill of self-control, which is sometimes in short supply during adolescence, and for some, even into adulthood. Think of the teen who has a new smart phone, complete with a set of rules for when it can and cannot be used. Suppose it's against school rules to have that device out during class. If our teen is aware of some fast-developing interpersonal drama taking place on social media, waiting until lunch to catch up on its progress is going to require delaying gratification, which requires a good amount of self-control.

Drama tends to be filled with impulsivity.[19] A boy gets a text from his girlfriend ending their relationship. He's upset and deeply hurt. His impulse is to get back, so without thinking, he posts a tweet divulging some private aspect of their relationship that makes her look really bad. It provokes comments, criticisms, and sympathetic moaning au extraordinaire from a wide-ranging audience. It made him feel good in the moment, but the fallout turns into a messy spectacle, indicting him and hurting someone he really cared about. Might he have been more gratified if he had exercised self-control and dealt with his feelings in a different way? Probably so.

Adults struggle with impulsivity as well.[20] Think of the person who posts emails full of invective and ranting. Or the driver who tailgates, cuts other drivers off, and flips them the bird. Real life is full of examples of adults who have limited self-control when it comes to getting what they want when they want it, and their nastiness is a burden to those around them.

Drama invites immediate gratification and slams the door on self-control, triggering some of our basest tendencies to be irresponsible, hard-hearted, thoughtless, and cruel, all undesirable personality traits.

NARCISSISM, ENTITLEMENT, AND PLAYING THE VICTIM

Narcissus was a boy who loved himself so much that he died gazing into a watery reflection at his own beautiful and dashing image.[21] He was vain, self-centered, and quite stupid, as he failed to take care of his own needs and as a result died from self-neglect. Apparently, no one felt sorry enough for him that they insisted that he get a grip, eat dinner, and sleep once in a while. Word has it that not too many people really liked Narcissus or cared about him, as he wasn't interested in anyone but himself. Who wants someone like that for a friend?

Narcissus comes to us from Greek mythology, but if he really existed, and if he were alive today, we would likely find him in the electronic world of social media posting, playing, and performing not only for his own benefit but for his large, admiring audience. He might even have his own reality TV show. But it's certain that he would probably be up all night texting, tweeting, and what have you, and in the morning be unable to raise his handsome frame from the bed and get himself to school because he is too tired.

Narcissism is a personality trait that manifests itself as a sense of entitlement, which is the feeling and belief that one deserves more than others.[22] Narcissists must be first because they are special. Everyone else must be behind the narcissist in line. They see themselves as highly deserving, and when someone challenges their right to get preferential treatment, they get angry.[23] No one is quite as impressive as they are. Just ask them.

Psychologists point to two types of narcissism[24] that share the features of entitlement and hostility to criticism, but while the similarities tend to end there, some research indicates that certain individuals fluctuate between the two types. One sort of narcissist is referred to as grandiose and the other is referred to as vulnerable.[25] These two variations of narcissists give us people with overlapping sets of behaviors, but with different orientations to the world. Both types are high maintenance, but the grandiose folks are a bit more endearing than the vulnerable ones.

Grandiose narcissists are extroverted and outgoing.[26] They usually have high energy. They're talkative, noisy, and often outspoken. They show off with performances that demand attention from whomever happens to be nearby. Modesty is not their strong suit. They dominate the scene. They have opinions that are "right." They can be quite forceful, often using their charm to get what they want. They are bossy in a nice way. They love attention and admiration. However, at times they can be cold and cruel, critical and thankless, and… sneaky. These behaviors come out when they have been criticized, or when they don't get their own way. They may use aggression, of the social kind, to get back at someone who has crossed them. That means that instead of confronting someone face-to-face over an infraction, they go behind the person's back and get even by badmouthing them. They display aggressive tendencies when people contradict their grandiose views of themselves. They value popularity and status and use their influence to remain at the top of the social hierarchy. They hate to lose. They can be manipulative, and they aren't particularly fond of following rules that don't suit them. They have high, but fragile self-esteem.[27]

Vulnerable narcissists can be tense, moody, and touchy.[28] They feel sorry for themselves and can be despondent. They might be called high-strung. They experience more negative emotions than positive ones. They approach the world as if everyone is out to get them. They interpret many innocent actions of other people as being hostile and threatening. These people tend to have difficult relationships because they aren't very trusting and can be quite suspicious. They shy away from intimacy and the self-disclosure that comes with interdependent and healthy relationships. They tend to be introverted. When confronted with evidence that they aren't as deserving as they feel they are, they retreat. They are susceptible to depression or anxiety. They struggle to get on with life in a constructive way. They have low self-esteem.[29]

Regardless of the type of narcissist, they share several characteristics.[30] They crave admiration. They also share the view that they are always the victim. They don't like to take responsibility for the messes they make, and they blame others for qualities and behaviors of which they themselves are guilty.

Of course, the big question is where does narcissistic behavior come from?[31] Unfortunately, that's not a question that has a simple answer. Evidence suggests that parental over-valuing (e.g., spoiling) children may contribute to grandiose narcissism, and that childhood trauma such as abuse, or excessively rigid, cold, and punitive parenting may contribute to vulnerable narcissism.[32]

A bit of self-focus is normal and predictable as kids develop and start to experience life.[33] For many youths, socialization will trim away these overbearing tendencies and transform these obnoxious proclivities into a healthy, but not overbearing, self-confidence. By the time humans are adults they begin to see themselves in realistic terms. People acquire the ability to see the world through other people's perspectives and learn to be empathic.[34] Narcissists struggle with making these shifts, but for most youth who are likely to become more rather than less narcissistic in adolescence, the long-term prognosis is that beyond adolescence, narcissism decreases as people age.[35] That's really good news, but it may not make it any easier to live with a highly narcissistic adolescent. Kids who have a high sense of entitlement and blame everyone else for their problems are a pain, and for those of us who live much of our lives within the shadow of a full-blown adult narcissist, it can be an unpleasant, perpetual balancing act.[36]

Based on the features of social drama, it's easy to see that narcissists are likely to be major contenders for leading roles in drama. For better or worse, they love the attention and visibility, the high-flying emotions, the sense of importance, and the ability to pull people and events into their sphere of action. They know how to put themselves center-stage, assign roles to underlings, and run the show. They also know how to use drama to get back at people who have insulted their sense of superiority. They can use drama to bait people into reacting in ways that shift the blame for bad behavior elsewhere. They can make good people look bad, and bad people look good. They seldom experience self-doubt. They are powerful, and quite happy about it. They have a very strong sense of entitlement, of which they are largely unaware.[37]

EMOTIONS, RUMINATION, AND EMPATHIC DISTRESS

Emotions and emotional expression are a hallmark of personality.[38] Emotions factor into how we react to people, confront challenges, respond to opportunity, evaluate experiences, and generally deal with life. Emotions are strong motivating forces. They influence how we think and act. Emotions are connected to what we like and what we don't like. Emotions can be energizing or debilitating, and learning how to manage them is a major life task, one that is very much associated with the journey from childhood through adolescence, ultimately landing each of us in adulthood.[39]

Everybody has a bad day sometimes, and very often how we react to difficult experiences will determine how quickly we get over them and move on or end up wallowing in them. We all have our own ways of dealing with heavy or challenging experiences and the feelings that they engender. Whether we are successful at figuring out how to soothe ourselves when we are upset will determine whether we let it go or punch someone when we are angry. Successfully coping with painful emotions stands between us and hitting "send" when our response to being hurt or humiliated is to fire off a nasty email.[40]

One of the not-so-healthy ways of coping with pain, frustration, rejection, or other similar unhappy experiences is to ruminate.[41] Rumination is obsessive thinking about a problem or a bad experience that is triggered by the emotions that accompany these situations such as anger, shame, embarrassment, indignation, guilt, or sadness. Ruminators can latch on to a mental script that attacks someone or something, or they can fixate on internal talk that is full of self-criticism and blame. They enjoy playing that tape over and over in their heads, stoking their emotional response. Rumination can make an angry person angrier or a sad person sadder. Ruminators focus heavily on the negative and end up magnifying the problem and amplifying the emotion that goes with it. Ruminators stew: They don't, can't or won't let go of bad feelings. They can end up living life in a perpetual funk.[42]

As alluded to, some rumination focuses on external events or people. This kind of rumination focuses blame and hostility on the person or situation that caused the upset. Ruminative thinking about an insult might sound something like this: *I can't believe she doesn't like my outfit. I spent a lot of money on this and it's endorsed by [X celebrity] who wears the coolest stuff. How dare she be so rude? And she thinks she's a fashion diva? Really! Her sense of style stinks. What a b*tch! I am so mad! I hate her.*

Some rumination, however, goes inward and might sound like this: *Oh my god! I thought I looked great in this outfit. She's always spot-on when it comes to fashion and style. What was I thinking when I wore this? I'm so embarrassed. I don't know how I can show my face at her house tonight for the party because I'm sure she has told everyone how stupid I looked today. I just want to die.*

Recall that for adolescents, a lot of social comparing and intense scrutiny from peers is developmentally appropriate, as is a hefty ration of self-consciousness.[43] This social scrutiny and constant comparison to peers at a time when youth are extremely self-conscious can make teens painfully aware of their shortcomings and turn their lives into a nightmare if the peer judgments are mean and nasty.[44] The increasing realization that they may never be quite as beautiful or attractive as they would like to be coupled with negative peer evaluation can trigger rumination as a coping mechanism.[45] And as psychologists tell us, it's not a very successful coping strategy because it can promote depression.[46]

In addition to individual, internal rumination, there is also a phenomenon called co-rumination.[47] This happens when two friends get together and rehash distressful situations ad nauseam. It can include dredging up old issues, talking about current problems, or speculating about upcoming potentially distressing situations. It's laden with negative emotions like anger, sadness, or frustration, as opposed to reflection that leads to self-discovery and problem solving; it produces emotional distress, not catharsis or closure. Co-rumination creates an intense sense of intimacy and closeness because it involves a lot of self-disclosure.[48] It's something that close friends do, and it usually tightens their friendship, sometimes to the point of suffocation.[49]

Co-rumination has rewards because it contributes to high-quality friendships, but it also can lead to depression or anxiety, especially for girls.[50] Depression and anxiety can have a contagious effect on close friends and co-rumination seems to be one of the ways it happens. Girls especially can get so caught up in their friends' problems that they begin to experience what's called empathic distress.[51] This happens when one friend becomes so emotionally involved in her friend's difficulties that friend number one adopts the same emotional baggage that friend number two is carrying around, and that can become a problem for both girls.

As you can see, co-rumination is a double-edged sword because while it has benefits and can infuse a relationship with intense feelings of intimacy,[52] it can also have drawbacks for girls' emotional well-being. In some cases, all this heavy-duty disclosure is more negative than positive. Boys do co-ruminate, but unlike girls, they don't seem to end up in this downward spiral of emotional negativity and angst,[53] but for girls it's a real risk.

Co-rumination is reminiscent of the "feeding off of each other" that is so common in drama. Co-rumination can lead to overreaction to a problem, too much negative emotionality, and the unnecessary prolonging of a bad situation, all characteristics of drama.

REJECTION SENSITIVITY

While rumination is a cognitive process that goes on inside a person's head, and co-rumination is a social process that goes on between two people, rejection sensitivity is best thought of as a personality trait or characteristic. Rejection sensitivity is the tendency to be anxious about social experiences, to expect to be rejected by others, to perceive that one is being rejected when one isn't being rejected, and to overreact in these situations.[54]

People who are rejection sensitive assume that everyone has or will reject them. They need constant reassurance from their friends that they are OK and that their friendships are secure, which can make them high-maintenance and exhausting. These folks are also, quite naturally, oversensitive to being judged or evaluated, which means that their level of self-consciousness is in the stratosphere,[55] and as we know, the amount of social comparison and peer evaluation that goes on starting in adolescence is frightening.

Researchers have distinguished two kinds of rejection sensitivity: anxious and angry, and both can be problematic in close friendships or romantic relationships.[56] People who are angry rejection-sensitive tend to have a lot of conflict in their friendships and they tend to respond with aggression or complete withdrawal from the situation. These folks don't have good coping or negotiating skills, so they either hang in there and duke it out, or completely exit the scene, neither of which are particularly good ways to maintain healthy relationships. These struggles can, of course, contribute to drama.

Considering the fallout that lands on and around people who do drama, one would naturally ask why anyone would ever think it useful to get involved in these antics. What purpose does drama have, especially for youth? The longer I tried to make sense of what kids and adults got out of doing drama, the more it pointed to identity development, which is what we do to figure out who we are.

One of the most important developmental tasks a person accomplishes is to solidify an identity that answers the question: Who am I? Most of us have a pretty good sense of self by the time we become adults because we have worked it all out as we have grown up.

CHAPTER 5
Social Drama and Identity

IDENTITY

DRAMA IS NOT SOLELY a product of personality traits, self-esteem, or dysfunctional and nonproductive behaviors. For those youth who do drama, it is a process connected to identity development,[57] one of the most central tasks of life. Not all kids find that they must do drama in order to figure out who they are. Many people develop a strong sense of self without engaging in any or much drama, but some folks just can't help themselves. They need to put their struggles out there for others to see. They take their social dilemmas public and put all that angst on the stage for others to consume.

An identity is a representation of yourself.[58] It's a composite of all that you are, that distinguishes us from others. An identity is not something that someone gives us. It's something that we construct or put together ourselves. Each of us makes a "self" that we present to the world. We express identity by how we think, speak, communicate, work, play, relate, and act. In the end, life is a performance of one's identity,[59] and whether we are consciously aware of it or not, there is always an audience sizing us up and giving us feedback. And while identity construction is a project and a process that goes on throughout life, adolescence is a period of development where there is intense focus on developing an identity and seeing what others think of our performance.[60]

How does a person "get" an identity?

A person's identity is formed, shaped, created, recreated, and revised as a person observes other people, imitates behaviors, and then evaluates him or herself in various situations.[61] For youth especially, this involves a fair amount of copying, testing, and experimenting.

Human growth and development happen in relationships.[62] That means human beings come to be who they are through interactions and experiences with other people. These people are parents, siblings, grandparents, aunts and uncles, cousins, babysitters, playmates, classmates, friends, teachers, teammates, coworkers, neighbors, clergy, and so on. People figure out who they are in the interactions that they have with these people. These kinds of interactions are seemingly infinite, but mostly they include being with and talking to others as individuals play, go to school, work, share meals, do chores, watch movies, read, play games, do sports, develop hobbies, vacation, celebrate holidays, worship, recreate, hang out, and relax. Trust is built and bonds are formed. Youth experience acceptance or rejection, solve problems, learn to compromise, resolve conflicts, figure out what they like and dislike, decide what's important, and become part of groups and communities. In essence, interaction with others is required in order to become fully developed people.

Positive, caring, and nurturing relationships are essential for developing into a healthy, well-adjusted adult.[63] Without relationships, we are stunted. Without the experience of relationships, we fail to learn how to engage in basic activities. Relationships to caregivers, parents, and guardians are the most important ones during early life,[64] but as we move toward and enter adolescence, peer associations become vital to human development.[65] It is in these sometimes intense relationships that we explore who we want to be. Adolescence is the crucible for identity development.

SELF-DISCLOSURE, INTIMACY, AND IDENTITY

Talking, sharing deep feelings and aspirations, disclosing secrets, and finding similarities produce intimacy and create bonds.[66] Awareness of mutual interests and experiences builds connections that create close friendships. Females are especially attracted to this kind of sharing and intimacy. Males seek closeness by doing things with their friends. They may not share sensitive, private information as much as girls and women, but they too need the experience of close friends that they can trust and with whom they can be their authentic and vulnerable selves. Identity development and growth is a byproduct of these relationships.[67]

Self-disclosure and close friendships validate kids and support their understanding of themselves.[68] It's part of that feedback loop that helps kids see themselves as others see them. For kids today, a fair amount of the communication that includes self-disclosure occurs via screens and social media.[69] In fact, researchers have found that online communication with supportive peers enhances well-being for teens and further strengthens existing friendships.[70] That doesn't mean that face-to-face communication is becoming obsolete, but it means that mediated communication is as good, or in some cases even better than being physically in the same place.[71] This seems to be because kids, especially boys, who might find it hard to disclose sensitive stuff in-person, are able to do a better job of it when they have time to think about their responses and carefully choose their words as they can with mediated communication.[72]

Experts have recently found that when people disclose information about themselves to another person, the reward centers in their brains light up.[73] This means that telling someone about ourselves makes us feel good. Sharing information about ourselves has the same effect on our brains that taking mood enhancing drugs does. People will pass up money in lieu of being able to talk to someone about themselves.[74] We don't know yet if the same thing happens in the brains of teens, but as they move into late adolescence, it is possible that there is a chemical, feel-good action taking place when they express intimate thoughts with a close friend.

In addition to making people feel physically good, mutual self-disclosure feels inherently safe. The bond that results and the experience of trust that develops can feel euphoric.[75] And in the background, is the implicit understanding that telling each other things that shouldn't get out to the masses is a way of guaranteeing that your dirt is safe with your best friend, because you've got equally bad dirt on her. It's like both sides having the nuclear bomb and because neither wants to be annihilated, there's an unspoken, but tacitly understood pact that deters either party from using their knowledge as a weapon. Knowing that both are facing "mutually assured destruction"[76] is a hedge against either party going rogue and dishing on the other.

Unfortunately, however, this is where the disclosure thing can backfire, and drama is one place where the dirty laundry can get strung across the stage for everyone to examine and gossip about. Self-disclosure makes a person vulnerable, which is a necessary component of really close, trusting, intimate relationships,[77] but it can have its downside. Drama is one of the outcomes of losing control of personal information and disregarding friends' privacy by sharing their secrets, online or off. When trust is destroyed, it can have terrible consequences for either or both parties.

Many kids do keep the faith nurtured in their close friendships. In one study, just under half of adolescents say that they never disclose personal information about their close friendships online.[78] However, for those who are outgoing, uninhibited, extroverted, attention-seeking risk-takers, all that personal disclosure and talk about sensitive and private matters can light a fire that becomes drama, starts rumors, leads to the spread of gossip, and damages relationships.[79]

Today, communication within relationships has become heavily dependent on the use of electronic devices and social media. Consequently, our screens and how they are used have an impact on the identities and perceptions of self that teens, as well as adults, are constructing and performing.[80]

What does it mean to perform an identity?

Who a person is isn't just something that is inside of him or her. It's what a person presents to the world. So in a very real sense, we perform our identities, and who do we perform them for? Ourselves and everyone that we interact with.[81]

Experts who study human development have used the idea of performance for quite a long time to describe and explain what is involved in having a "self" or an identity and expressing that identity throughout our lives.[82] These experts aren't using the term performance to mean playing a fake or pretend role or a part that has been created by a playwright or screenwriter. What these folks mean is that people engage in social performance whenever they engage with another person.[83] In other words, we act out who we are. Or to quote William Shakespeare: "All the world is a stage, and all the men and women merely players."[84] A famous anthropologist named Erving Goffman observed that people go about their daily lives very much as if they are performing both for themselves and for the rest of us as they act, react, and interact with each other and the world.[85] In the sense that Shakespeare and Goffman are thinking of, we express our identity and our understanding of our "self" by performing who we are for our whole lives. In essence, living is a performance of one's identity.

CELEBRITY-ISM

If you were famous in ancient Rome, they put your face on a coin. If you were famous during the Renaissance, someone painted your portrait.[86] If either survived, it's likely to be displayed in a museum or hanging in an art gallery. Today if you are famous, you have millions of followers on X (formerly Twitter)", and your every Instagram post gets "liked" by thousands of "friends."[87]

It used to be that you became famous if you were born an aristocrat or a monarch or did something significant like win a war, invent the printing press, beach your boat on the shore of a "new" continent, or engineer a spacecraft to put humans on the moon.[88] Before movies and TV, newspapers and radio were the primary vehicles for nurturing fame. You got famous by getting in the papers or being talked about over the airwaves. During the previous century, motion pictures and the invention of TV gave us access to famous people such as entertainers, musicians, athletes, politicians, performers, artists, and the like. However primitive radios, movie theaters, and the old grainy black and white TV may seem now, these media tools allowed us to see and hear the performances, interviews, etc., of people we seldom if ever saw in person. They offered a much more intimate connection to people who had become well known and often wealthy. That type of celebrity existence was one way. We could see and experience them, but they couldn't see or experience us. As consumers we couldn't use the TV screen to respond to a celebrity's performance. The only way to give feedback was to pick up the phone, or write a fan letter, and nobody does that anymore, and even if they did send that letter, they seldom got a response from those they admired.

Motion pictures and TV increased our awareness of fame and being famous and created a celebrity culture and industry that has become a multi-trillion-dollar enterprise.[89] Paparazzi chase stars and celebrities photographing them grocery shopping and walking on beaches. Celebrities market everything from cars and candy to shirts and soccer balls.[90] We used to join fan clubs and write letters to our favorite entertainer or movie star. (Yes, the kinds of letters that are written on paper and require envelopes and a postage stamp.) Now we buy celebrities' lines of perfume and shoes and follow them on Twitter, Instagram, or some other recently introduced social media platform. As the tools of media have evolved, our exposure to the rich and famous has increased. Celebrities offer us more to consume: knowledge of their public and private lives as well as the products they endorse. In fact, they themselves have become the products of consumption. And now finally, with the introduction of smartphones that can take pictures and movies, and access the internet, ordinary people have the electronic communication devices to showcase themselves the same way celebrities do.[91] Everyone can at least act like they are famous, and unlike the performances on TVs, today's screens can be two way, making feedback immediate.[92]

Today, we live in a "celebrity" culture.[93] The word "celebrity" is a noun, which means it is more than just a person who is famous. It is used in the mainstream media to describe a category of fame and influence, as in the statements "celebrity has become an essential characteristic and dynamic of our contemporary cultures and societies" or "celebrity has become a valued power resource."[94] As a former English teacher, I struggle mightily with using celebrity as a noun to discuss a concept that doesn't line up with the definition of someone who is famous. Used in the way the word is in the two previous examples from Oliver Driessens's work, "celebrity" is highly awkward, vague, and difficult to understand. In my opinion, the word "celebrity" should be used as an adjective to describe concepts such as "celebrity status," "celebrity influence," or "celebrity capital." It can also be turned into a noun, "celebrification," which means to be made into a celebrity (a person who becomes famous). Apologies for this English-teacher bird walk on parts of speech, but because none of these words or their uses directly addresses a topic so essential in the world of drama and social media use, I now propose a new word: "celebrity-ism," to mean the desire to become a celebrity or at least to behave like a celebrity, seeking fame and attention, and attempting to become more than just ordinary by putting oneself out there on social media for all the world to see, know, and hopefully, admire.[95] Celebrity-ism is strategically using social media to present oneself like a celebrity, to become popular and to feel like one has celebrity status, at least with one's immediate audience of primarily known friends or potential friends who might be able to make the person into a real celebrity by admiring, paying attention to, and fawning over the person in much the same way fans do over a famous person. Even if a wannabee celebrity never becomes a celebrity, he or she can feel and experience what it might be like to be a real celebrity.[96]

Celebrity-ism is encouraged by reality TV shows that voyeuristically peer into ordinary people's private lives.[97] Reality TV portrays a world where anyone can become famous by behaving outrageously in front of a camera that is always on.[98] Using the Kardashians as an example, we see people who become famous and rich by telling and selling their most private thoughts and moments to the media, which are then consumed as entertainment by the masses. It's no longer necessary to be important or to do something important to become famous. If you can strut your stuff online or post a crazy video of some inane stunt, you just might get noticed, and get famous.[99] And if you are good at promoting yourself and/or a product, you might end up being an influencer and make money.[100] Getting a company to hire you to become a face and a voice on a YouTube channel can mean real income.

Famous people and celebrities have promoted themselves in such a way that they aren't just who they are, but a brand to be consumed by admirers, wannabees, and those who will buy items with their names on them.[101] Donald Trump is someone whose identity is (or once was) tightly connected to all kinds of consumer items: hotels, casinos, a personal aircraft, wine, steak, a defunct university, and the motto, "Make America great again."[102] "Trump" is a brand,[103] just like the Kardashians, not just a person's last name. People who have become successful influencers are highly skilled at creating a brand and connecting it to something that the audience is interested in having.

BRANDING

When advertising became a common practice in the marketing of products, the focus was usually on something inanimate such as a brand of toothpaste, dish washing soap, lipstick, or an automobile. As time went on, people began to identify themselves with various brands of products, often ones with high-value and high-cost that speaks to status, wealth, privilege, and prestige. Think of high-end sneakers, electronics, jewelry, clothing, homes, and vacation destinations, and connect this to the visibility of celebrities and their social media presence today. Branding is a planned process that people use to market themselves to others, achieve status, and acquire wealth.[104] It is a form of self-promotion, and it expanded our taste for more goods and experiences.

Now we brand ourselves, our children, and our families.[105] We create these brands by splashing photos, videos, and information about our private lives and personal relationships on social media platforms that we share rather indiscriminately. We put ourselves "out there" to be viewed, critiqued, and consumed. We make an identity for ourselves that gets performed for an audience of hundreds or thousands of followers.[106] In some ways, we have become not only addicted to screens and social media, but we have created personal reality shows where we act out our identities just like celebrities.

Youth are acutely aware that ordinary people like themselves have become internet celebrities by developing a brand that catches others' attention, imagination, and admiration, so much so that they generate money from this constant online presence.[107] These "influencers" who have accomplished becoming a celebrity by creating and performing a public identity have moved beyond being ordinary. They are known. They belong. They are important. They are celebrities. And some of them make a lot of money.

However, two-way screens can be problematic. Unlike the old media world of one-way screens (TVs and movies), feedback can be swift and ugly, and if something goes awry and things start to unravel, maintaining the position of status and prestige can demand a blast of impression management, relationship repair, reputation reconstruction, and damage control.[108] Having a successful internet identity and constantly performing it as a reality TV star or a salesperson can generate a lot of drama that is not just produced, it is consumed by admirers, as well as their detractors.[109]

We live an era where unless we tell our stories for an online audience, we have even begun to question whether it really happened.[110] If I had fun at a park, if I don't upload pictures on social media showing me having fun, I wonder if I really had fun. If my audience doesn't acknowledge my fun at the park, my fun is diminished, or even nonexistent. Multiple moments of life need to be uploaded in a virtual, continuous reality TV show. The real and the unreal have begun to overlap,[111] creating drama of and for the masses.

All of this, of course, is made possible by the fact that nearly everyone has a smartphone in their pocket, ready to take selfies and videos galore and upload them into the virtual world of unreality. We produce an identity with all these selfies and videos that get sent lightning-fast to the world cyber stage for consumption.[112] What you say about others on their Facebook wall is also part of your own identity construction.[113] It is a performance, not just for the person to whom it is directed, but to the entire audience watching, who can make an evaluation of you as a result.

Posting on a social network site is thus a performance, not a private communication between two people. In the same fashion, a "like" is also more about you than about the person you are "liking" something about. It's a performance that contributes to identity construction, and these performances can be celebrated or denounced. Any of this can become drama or worse, with technology amplifying and intensifying the effects.

Social media is a double-edged sword. As smart phones have become prolific, it is not only youth who have gotten themselves into trouble; adults have as well.[114] Using social media to complain, vent, rant, accuse, and lie is much more likely to be seen in adult behaviors than it used to be—that is, before we all lived in a reality TV world. Some of this behavior occurred because early users of social media didn't understand how it worked and didn't realize the reach of their postings. Others adopted some of these less than savory ways to "let it out" and express their feelings without caring how it might affect them or others. Regardless of the motivation, posting and performing on social media is a near universal activity,[115] one that can have negative repercussions for even well-meaning folks. Yet, it is growing in frequency and intensity.[116] Why?

BELONGING, STATUS, AND FOMO

Belonging or being included, accepted, and affirmed is one of our most basic human needs.[117] Belonging and being accepted means you are known and valued. It means you are connected. It means you have relationships. It means you are not alone. It confirms that you have an identity and that others see it and approve of who you are. By the time kids enter middle school it is becoming clear to them and their families that friends are taking on greater significance in their social world. Whereas hanging primarily with family is acceptable in early and middle childhood, peer friendships are taking on more importance in middle school.[118] Figuring out who you are now needs to extend beyond a small circle of a tight family and social circle, and expand to a larger, age-similar crowd. In the real world, without access to the metaverse and a device that connects to it, it's nearly impossible to be part of a group of friends. A smart phone becomes an essential tool in meeting the need to belong.

Belonging and connection are intertwined with identity and self-perception. So too is status. Status is defined as "accumulated approvals and disapprovals that people express"[119] toward things, individuals, or groups. What people think of you translates into status. If you want to change your status, you must change people's minds about you.[120]

Status exists within groups and among groups. Often within a group of friends there will be an established hierarchy or ranking of who is most admired, who is deferred to, and who has more power than someone else. Likewise, groups of friends are often part of a social hierarchy of groups. That means that there will be groups that have more influence, visibility, popularity, prestige, and power than others. Which groups are the most powerful are determined by the values and norms of the entire population. In some societies the beautiful are admired and emulated; in others it might be the smart people, the athletes, or the musically talented. Not everyone can have high status because if everyone had high status, no one would have any status at all.[121] So status means that some people have more of it than others. Or more realistically, there's a continuum from low to high status and all of us fall somewhere on it depending on who we are and what groups we belong to.

Our understanding of our status can be thought of as an indicator of our belongingness and connection that affects how we see ourselves, which in turn affects how we construct and perform our identities.[122] One of the key features of identity development is getting feedback from other people.[123] In other words, creating a sense of self involves evaluation and assessment. We get criticism, praise, or ambivalence from people with whom we are in relationships, and this provides information that helps shape self-understanding and self-perspective. Young people may choose to use this information to change their attitudes, beliefs, or behaviors.

Since status is based on what other people think of us, changes in status can cause self-reflection, and that can then produce growth and change at the individual level. It's an integral feature of identity development and performance.

Lastly there's a phenomenon that has only recently begun to be studied and it links belonging and status together. Researchers are calling it FoMO,[124] which stands for "fear of missing out," and it can be epidemic among adolescents who are in the deep throes of trying to have status and belong to a group of well-regarded peers.

Think FoMO when you are trying to have a conversation with your child and he or she can't look at you because his or her face is fixated on a screen. Your child is terrified that something is happening among her friends that she should know about, and if she's not able to participate, she will be forgotten about, become a less valued member of her social group, and lose status. Teens' involvement with friends is critical to their social standing. There's tremendous pressure to always be "on" so that nothing is missed. That's why some kids sleep with their smartphone under their pillows.[125] They are afraid of missing out on something critical because being in the know and being accessible to everyone is vital to their existence.

A lot of the boring and repetitive communication that youth have, especially online, is what is called "phatic communication."[126] Basically, that means "small talk." Often, it's a ritualized way of starting a conversation, like saying, "Hi. How are you?" It's also a way of acknowledging another person as being in my life with something as mundane as a question like, "What's up?" Or "Off to practice. Later!" Or even more mundane, "Brushing teeth. Going to bed." These exchanges have very little substance because the content is really about the person and the need for the person to belong and be connected. It's not what the communication is about that's important; it's that there is communication with one person being responsive to the other, which confirms belonging. By acknowledging that "we're still here for each other," both parties have a sense of connectedness. This is one of the reasons it is so hard for youth to cut off a series of texts. A failure to have a text returned is akin to being shunned, and it has the potential to create drama. So, many youth engage in constant online small talk because it soothes the fear of missing out.

Fear of missing out can trigger drama when a person sends out one of these phatic "feelers" and nobody responds. To the sender, it feels like rejection, which is anathema to the need to belong. The reasons for these feelers to be ignored could have nothing to do with the status and state of the relationship of those involved, but the person who has initiated the feeler doesn't know what's going on and that uncertainty can lead to drama.

If there's high drama going on, and it involves one's social group, or a group the actor would like to be a part of, getting in on the action is important. Nobody wants to miss the big stuff, so FoMO means that kids can't resist checking their screens for updates, new information, and social pings, and of course, responding to every one of them with comments, feedback, and questions, which leads to a slow but steady trickle of gossip and rumors.

Particularly in the world of adolescent social drama, youth rarely act alone past the first or second volley. FoMO assures that the number of people involved will increase and perhaps take a turn for the worse.[127]

TEEN SOCIAL DRAMA REPRISE

To recap: Vanessa is a sophomore in high school when her story begins. It is Christmas time, and a conflict is brewing between her and her friends. Previously, this group adopted the moniker, "Hockeywhore-babes" (HWBs), which refers to the website of a group of women who follow hockey players. The overall flavor of this website has strong sexual overtones. A separate group of girls, some of whom are friends with some of the HWBs adopt a different name for their own hockey fan club and call themselves the "Pretty Pucksters." Their rivalry becomes a conflict that is played out publicly.

Just before Christmas, Vanessa decides that the whole idea of the HWBs isn't a good one, so she suggests to the group that they drop it. Two of her fellow HWBs are opposed to this and end up screaming at Vanessa. Vanessa leaves their gathering and is still estranged from them when school resumes in January. Vanessa's former friends gang up on her, bully her, and say mean things to her, primarily because she sees the HWBs and Pretty Pucksters fight as immature, and they do not. At some point in January, the girls apologize to each other, and their friendship continues.

In early February it comes to light that one of the girls in the friendship group had sex with a boy who also had sex with another girl while he was dating this friend. The information about the event was known to everyone in their class. Now that this information is out, the girls gather with their friend in a restroom to tell her the bad news about her ex-boyfriend. Things quickly spiral out of control, as everyone begins crying and commiserating with each other over their friend's betrayal. The girls decide that they need to leave school and find a place to deal with the situation. One girl calls in sick for another, while another calls her mom who makes her own call to the principal to get her daughter excused. The principal becomes suspicious and calls all six parents to confirm that the girls can leave school together.

Gathered at one girl's home, and very angry with the girl who slept with their friend's boyfriend, the girls decide to vent their emotions via Twitter. Because they each have so many followers, their Twitter accounts quickly blow up with nasty tweets from multiple kids who are still at school. The result was "that everyone hated us." Harassment of the girls continues when they are heckled during a basketball game as they perform a cheerleading routine, and by verbal insults as they walk the halls at school. Parents get involved. The girls fear for their safety and believe that they are being baited into acting aggressively again so that they will get suspended.

Five months later, at the time of the interview with Vanessa and her mother, Vanessa is still struggling. The mailing sent with their mean tweets is something about which she ruminates. She is tormented by not knowing who mailed the letter and copies of all the screen shots of their mean tweets. She desperately wants to know who did this to her and her friends.

If we deconstruct the elements of this narrative, it becomes apparent that this is an example of classic drama. Any number of participants exhibit personality traits that lend themselves to social drama. There is entitlement. There is manipulation of adults through lying. There is frustration with the principal as he shows concern for what is happening and refuses to let the girls all leave without contacting their parents. Likewise, the students are disgruntled with their parents for not immediately acquiescing to their demands. There is overreaction to events and impulsivity based on emotions. There is group rumination, using one friend's distress to ramp up individual emotional states. Shared intimacy stokes feelings of betrayal, even though it was only one girl who was cheated on. Disinhibition takes over. Screens get fired up, and all manner of venting gets texted and tweeted. Everyone, including the audience, displays elements of shamelessness. Regardless of who is on whose side, there is indignation and righteousness, and a lack of self-reflection and awareness. While the girls recognized their responsibility for the initial volley of abuse, by the end, they see themselves as victims that didn't deserve to be treated the way the general school population responded to their antics, and they were probably right. But that's what can happen in drama.

These behaviors get the girls a great deal of negative attention, which frankly, is understandable. They don't appreciate the truth contained in the anonymous mailing that points out their hypocrisy. Consciously or unconsciously, they commodify themselves for the marketplace of social media, but they overstep the boundaries because their behaviors show them to be hypocritical. They pay the price for being clueless about what the audience will and will not accept from them. Normally their high status might protect them, but in this instance, it probably adds to the overall animosity directed at them.

While it is difficult to accurately analyze the behavior of those who become the audience for the girls' drama, it seems reasonable to conclude that there is a fair amount of desensitization, disinhibition, and deindividuation infecting the audience members (i.e., noninvolved, or marginally involved students), as well as the girls. The collective response from the fans at the basketball game who boo the cheerleaders suggests that the whole school student body has been sucked into this black hole and is out to get the cheerleaders. Whether done by an individual or a group, the recriminatory mailing sent to some of the cheerleaders suggests aroused and widespread feelings. Lots of people are involved, upset, feeding off each other, and behaving quite badly.

If we take a step back, it becomes clear that these girls are playing with identity, branding, competition, and status. These girls establish a brand that they market, not only as cheerleaders, but also when they adopt the HWB brand and appropriate it as their own. They perform an identity that will draw attention to themselves. The pseudo competition with the Pretty Pucksters pumps more juice into the drama, which gets played out on social media, setting the stage for the next act. The audience, which eventually becomes the entire school population, responds as consumers, expressing opinions and taking sides. People are angry, confused, and hurt. Undoubtedly, this is classic adolescent social drama.

One last comment. As with much drama, there is sex and sexual inuendo threaded throughout the narrative. Sex is front and center in much of this conflict. The HWB appropriation is overtly sexual. The discussion of who is having sex with whom and what it means lights up the gossip grapevine. Drama makes public that which is usually private, giving the audience on social media an opening to be involved in commentary. And almost on cue, it is gendered and one-sided. The girl who cheated is publicly chastised, but not the boy who had sex with her. He seems to dodge criticism. These behaviors create the impression that drama is something girls do, and boys do not, despite the fact that a boy's sexual betrayal triggered the conflict and boys are part of the audience of those who comment, criticize, and push the drama further.

In my opinion, this episode of drama is fairly tame in comparison to some of the messes that kids make today, especially when no one is watching what they are doing on social media.

Sometimes things get out of hand and social drama can turn into individual or group bullying,[128] but this isn't a risk that only teens face. Adults face it, too. The spillage from one to many can lead to a dangerous devolution of meanness and cruelty on several levels that feel much like reality TV.[129] If youth don't see enough drama unfolding in their own lives, tuning into the latest version of whatever the genre has coughed up will sate their need. Regardless of what outrageous human exploitation a producer has served up, kids and adults will find marketable entertainment with people behaving quite badly. Interestingly, adolescent social drama feels a lot like what we see on reality TV shows.

CHAPTER 6

Reality TV and Adult Social Drama

IN 2012 WHEN THE girls of a previous chapter were enacting their own personal mini-drama, TV viewers world-wide could tune into an assortment of reality TV shows: *Keeping Up with the Kardashians, Survivor, 90 Day Fiancé, RuPaul's Drag Race,* and *The Real Housewives of New Jersey*. Reality TV is a fixed and enduring genre on broadcast and cable TV, with no loss of popularity in sight.[130] Initially, reality TV appeared as a genre that had its roots in documentaries designed as educational or observational pieces.[131] In these early versions, real people who weren't auditioned or coached became the "actors," but as time went on, reality TV participants were "camera-ready people"[132] performing or "over performing themselves."[133] This development meant that we were no longer observing people acting like themselves as in a documentary, but what we were seeing was professional or semi-professional performers being primed with scripted or controlled events that moved away from authenticity and stretched into the made-up.[134] Of course, producers looked for people who were good at being naturally outrageous and who would be highly reactive to each other in multiple settings.[135] Shows that became successful not only had highly dramatic personalities in them, they also had creative writers and producers who knew ways to push the boundaries.[136]

Now, when it appears that producers can't invent another narrative that exposes our grossest, most disgusting, and most jaw-dropping secrets and behaviors, *presto!* Here comes another reality TV show. We can watch people going on a date wearing no clothing, a pimple popping doctor, two people punching each other in the face until one passes out, and people drinking donkey pee. *Ick!*

Reality TV can turn anything into spectacle and entertainment.[137] If it makes us gasp, look away, or cringe, it is fair game for a reality TV show. There were similar types of entertainment from the past such as *Candid Camera* or *America's Funniest Home Videos*, but that changed in the late 1990s when the content of these shows took a dive into private and unsavory aspects of life, presented to us by nonactors who became actors, or at least celebrities in the process.[138] Reality TV is supposed to be nonscripted entertainment, and some of it is, but producers and directors instigate, trigger, and promote behaviors and story lines designed to capture and keep our attention.[139] Often these behaviors are highly anti-social.[140] Reality TV routinely showcases swearing, sarcasm, threats, yelling, shouting, mean gossip, petty jealousy, and mocking of people's appearance, competency, intelligence, and background.[141] These behaviors then trigger retaliation and provoke greater levels of aggression toward other "contestants" on the show.[142] Most viewers will secretly admit that the extremes of reality TV are ugly, divisive, and a waste of time, but they *are* entertaining, and they are hard to look away from, so people watch anyway.[143]

The other feature of reality TV that is new and different from the old TV shows that showed people doing stupid and funny things is that audiences now participate and engage in ways that were not possible when people had one-way screens.[144] The audience is part of the show now, so theoretically, anyone can become a celebrity. The audience watches, gossips, consumes, and then joins or extends the narrative. The audience becomes vocal fans or anti-fans, who bring the momentum online and act, re-enact, and amplify the messy, mashed up content.

Teens, as well as adults, are avid consumers of reality TV[145] and online "celebrity" social drama, and sadly, some research suggests, predictably so, that there is spillage from the behaviors and attitudes consumed to the lives of the consumers. It seems that narcissism and entitlement are short-term effects for youth, but materialism is a permanent effect of participation in reality TV and online participatory social drama.[146] Researchers explain these differences, citing that narcissism and entitlement make life miserable for the people who are around them, but materialism doesn't. Having and displaying wealth, luxury goods, and expensive experiences are more socially acceptable (apparently) than too much self-love and me-ism. Suzanna Opree and Rinaldo Kuhne think one of the takeaways for youth is that narcissism and entitlement are offensive to their peers; hence, youth recognize these are behaviors to avoid. So, it seems that just being materialistic isn't as bad as being materialistic, narcissistic, *and* entitled. Afterall, liking lots of nice things seems gentle when compared to the number of other unsavory options we upload on our screens.

DONALD TRUMP, *THE APPRENTICE*, AND ADULT DRAMA

At the risk of being too political, it serves the purpose of this book to bring up Donald Trump for several reasons, one of which is his own reality show, *The Apprentice*.

From 2004 to 2015 *The Apprentice* ran weekly on American television. Its main star, and mainstay of the show's success was Donald Trump. The gist of the show was to solicit input from an assortment of potential employees on how to solve a problem posed by Trump, who at that time claimed to be the most successful real estate developer in New York City. Trump had developed a presence in tabloids and capitalized on it in the show. He was brash, unforgiving, and jubilant, ending each show by firing one or more of the contestants. He finished his performance with a ringing, "You're fired!" The last lucky contestant left standing at the end of the season got a job working for Donald Trump.

The show was very successful when Donald was the man in front of the camera, but not so much when others took on the role after he left. Viewers liked his swagger, his arrogance (only minimally disguised as confidence), his (supposed) success in making deals and making money, and his command of everyone and everything around him. Whether he was acting the part or not, no one cared because it was very entertaining. The ratings, something important to Trump, were great. He is claimed to have made $427,000,000.00 from the show.[147] It didn't matter that many things he claimed about himself and his wealth were questionable or even fictitious.[148] It didn't matter if he was rather unsavory, dabbling in behaviors that made some people cringe. It didn't matter if he mistreated people onstage or offstage. He was after all, a reality TV star. It was his show, and he could do and say whatever he wanted.[149] Whether the performance was the real Donald Trump, or an actor who many secretly wished they could emulate in their lives, he came across as the real deal, and according to some, it set him up to run for president. Enough voters saw him as authentic that he became the 45th president of the United States, and as of January 20, 2025, he is president of the United States once again.

Trump is relevant to this narrative for a few reasons. He displayed and cultivated a persona that became solidified as his brand.[150] As part of that brand, he behaved in ways that made enough of us cringe that it was obvious that he wasn't someone we'd happily look forward to having at the Thanksgiving dinner table (or at least most of us). And, taking that brand and everything it entailed as president, he demonstrated that he was the epitome of someone who did drama. His embrace of drama was so complete that it wasn't a side show as so much adolescent drama is; it was the main show. Politics aside, that is why it must be included in this narrative.

Donald Trump's[151] behaviors are jaw-dropping in their similarity to what we see in adolescent social drama, but he outdoes teens by miles. What youth do that we label as drama, is minor compared to what he does. He just doesn't like attention, he craves it. He isn't just occasionally impulsive; he is impulsive much of the time. He isn't just overreactive once in a while. He overreacts all the time. When anyone criticizes him, he takes revenge on them. No one gets a pass. He manipulates people. He doesn't think rules apply to him. He is clearly narcissistic, thinking that he is better at everything than he really is (grandiosity). He is selfish and doesn't care about other people's feelings. He doesn't just leave a few facts out now and then, or tell a fib. He is a liar. He is unable to see himself as he really is, a trait that teens mostly outgrow in adulthood, but he's an old man, and he still doesn't "get it." He doesn't recognize how his behaviors affect people. He is unapologetic about sexual indiscretions and uses them to enhance his reputation. He baits people. Those around him don't survive unless they get sucked into his view of the world and play a collaborative or subservient role in the social drama in which he stars. He is thin-skinned and plays the role of victim in most interactions that criticize him or call him out. When he is wounded, he strikes back viciously at those who are perceived to have wronged him. He never forgets anyone who has wronged him, and he will carry a grudge until he can get revenge. He is entitled, the world is his stage, and the attention must be on him. And he overwhelmingly uses social media, to stir the pot so that he can raise the curtain, make a grand entrance, command the stage, ramp things up, and create chaos. Sadly, Donald Trump's life has been one perpetual episode of high-end social drama.[152]

One problem for us is that powerful people who act like they live in a reality TV universe offer a standard of behavior that sets a pretty low bar for how we engage with each other in public.[153] Of course, when it's nothing more than entertainment, as reality TV is, and everyone knows it is entertainment, it doesn't have the same impact. However, we can't discount the fact that bad behavior performed by those who have high profiles, can have negative effects on people.

MODELING AND ITS EFFECTS

I distinctly remember hearing my daughter talking over our house landline to a friend when she was in her teens during the 1980s. She sounded like a character on Days of Our Lives, complete with the intonation and melodrama of the late afternoon soap operas that my mother and grandmother watched daily from the sixties on. It was almost as if she were auditioning for a part in the show she had just watched. Such is the power of modeling!

Kids watch adults all the time, and how we act and how we respond to problematic behaviors creates norms that youth internalize as they figure out who they are and how they should act. My granddaughter copies almost everything we do. At age one-and-a-half, she copied me throwing the ball for our dog and then pointing to the floor in front of me for Idgie to retrieve the ball and put it right in front of us. Much learning happens through modeling, which puts a responsibility on adults to show kids how to be mature adults.

Research that goes back a long way shows that under certain conditions, kids will imitate aggressive behavior.[154] Albert Bandura first performed the "bobo doll" experiments trying to see if observing another child pound on a blown-up doll would cause the observing child to do likewise. Often enough, that's what happened. Not all children imitate bad behaviors, but it certainly doesn't help when high-profile people, celebrities, and leaders of all persuasions display bad behaviors—and worse, no one calls them out on it.

As a former teacher, I would have been sorely taxed by a child who behaved as Donald Trump does. From his refusal to accept responsibility, to his acting out when he doesn't get his way, to his propensity for blaming others for his indiscretions, he would have sucked me dry. Children seldom display narcissistic tendencies to the degree that he does, but when they do, they are very high maintenance. For those who are unable to exit the spheres where adults with severe psychological issues such as these call the shots, life is confusing, chaotic, and exhausting.

SOCIAL MEDIA PLATFORMS, ONLINE INFLUENCERS, AND CELEBRITIES

Beyond reality TV, there is the cyber world that has its own version of bizarre narratives and behaviors, only it's not found in the world of broadcast or cable TV. This is the online world of video platforms that become spaces for regular, ordinary people to turn themselves into celebrities, or at least try to. Where once most self-disclosure was limited to blogging about oneself and one's life, peppered with some photos, now vlogging (video blogging) allows wannabe celebrities to create videos about anything and post them to their own channels or widely known social media platforms. Once established as a person of influence or a "star," it becomes a new site for doing drama by stirring up scandals, scams, and feuds among competing niche celebrities.[155] Of course, in this world of social media influencers and reality media celebrity wannabees who make money by marketing themselves and various branded items, it can become mean, nasty, and highly competitive.[156] But it doesn't stop there because the online audience is sitting front and center during these dramas, commenting, taking sides, and joining in the chaos, criticism, and dressing downs. What often results is a power struggle where one celebrity or another is taken out, or "canceled." These platform dramas can begin to look a lot like social smear campaigns, where lying, half-truths, and exaggeration are often the main tools for winning.[157]

Just as in the "olden days" of TV and movie stars, people become admirers of the celebrities they see on their screens. We've always known that often these celebs became models for people, but especially tweens and teens. Today that phenomenon includes celebrities who appear on multiple social media platforms, and given the features of these platforms, kids feel much closer to their social media heroes now than we did when we had one-way screens. Researchers refer to the types of affinity that young people have for their celebs as "parasocial relationships." What it means is that fans will feel that they have a close, intimate connection with someone they follow and emulate on social media, even when they might be one of a million or so consumers of their online presence. The outcome of these parasocial relationships that can be quite intense is that youth, in particular, mimic the attitudes and behaviors that these stars put out there for consumption. Some of what is ingested and then promulgated is biased, negatively skewed, or downright false, and it's not just our kids who are wallowing in that world.

WHAT'S REAL AND WHAT'S NOT?

Part of the dilemma of social drama in the adult world is that it toys with what is real and what is not real, and when it is blended with our incessant focus on entertainment that we both consume and are consumed by, things can get topsy turvy.[158]

According to Megan Garber, we live in a massive entertainment environment.[159] What she means is that between our TVs and our smart screens, we can, if we choose, spend our days being constantly entertained, if not by shows on television, then by social media apps like Instagram, X (formerly Twitter)", and TikTok, or the next app yet to be launched. In the social media realm, we become not just the entertained, but the entertainers. We turn ourselves into the performers who are commoditized, or who offer themselves to be consumed as just more entertainment. Essentially, we entertain ourselves by feeding off each other, and encouraging others to feed off us. Sounds like one of Neil Postman's predictions!

In this media universe (metaverse), there is pretending, faking, misinformation, lying, scamming, misrepresentation, and slander.[160] It is not a world that makes many distinctions between facts and fabrication, and the more people consume this kind of media, the fewer the distinctions they can make between facts and lies. Citing shows that are both entertaining and newsy, such as *Last Week Tonight* or *The Daily Show*, Garber asserts that "the news has become entertainment, and entertainment has become the news." Neil Postman would agree with her wholeheartedly.

Another feature of reality TV is the way basic "anybodies" compete with each other. Pretend entrepreneurs can vie for money to launch a business. Novice chefs can compete to see who can come up with the best gourmet dish. Volunteers with the right amount of camera appeal can decide who to feed to the sharks or vote off the island if they don't make muster. Then there are those who have lost their high-profile jobs and end up on dancing/singing/hanging with the stars to make a few bucks so they can pay the rent. The common theme is competition and winning. The other theme is that reality and fabrication get woven together for the sake of entertainment, which is a very popular and lucrative format for the world's television audience. Researchers are exploring a theory that suggests that the more reality TV people watch, the more they "believe that social reality aligns with television reality."[161] Given the fact that reality TV heralds lots of awful racist, sexist, and ethnic stereotypes, plus the normalization of hostile and aggressive behavior, it becomes hard to defend the worst of reality TV as harmless entertainment.

One of the problems with our society's drift toward a world where people conflate and mash entertainment with factual information, is that it becomes easier to sell lies as truth. When information is not filtered through an editor's or a fact checker's lens, we become a society that latches on to conspiracies. The media universe is a perfect host to unleash these kinds of viruses because there is no antidote or vaccine to stop them. Social drama with its chaos and confusion, is the norm for the metaverse.

There is no coincidence that performative adolescent and adult social drama live in the same world as reality TV, and that in fact, they overlap.

WHERE DO ADOLESCENT SOCIAL DRAMA AND REALTY TV OVERLAP?

Reality TV and social drama of the adolescent sort, have that "ick" factor that seeps in under our armpits when too much information and intimacy is on display. Both push or smash boundaries to the point that we feel as if we are voyeurs who are dismayed by what we see, but cannot look away; hence, the feeling of being sucked into something distasteful or at least awkward, but also entertaining. As the audience gets pulled in, people take sides, which adds to the sense of surprise and anticipation regarding what will happen next, and the million-dollar question, "Will it get worse?" The answer is "Yes," of course it will get worse, because the behaviors get worse as the numbers of actors increase. All that desensitization and loss of inhibition sets off a panoply of awful behaviors: meanness and cruelty, disregard for decency and integrity, lies and half-truths, manipulation of people and circumstances, narcissism, entitlement, selfishness, co-and group-rumination, FoMO, and moral disengagement.

It's worth noting that this is true for both males and females, but the messages sent about females are arguably more damaging. Jennifer Pozner, in her book from a decade and a half ago, writes about the images of women in many reality TV shows. They reinforce the worst possible stereotypes: women are nasty and not trustworthy (especially when it comes to other women); women are dumb; women are incompetent; and women are out to find a rich husband. In light of the power of adult modeling of behaviors, it's not surprising that girls themselves post selfies imitating the worst behaviors of their favorite reality TV stars.

Adolescent social drama and reality TV make people into celebrities, feel like celebrities, or act like they are celebrities. They are about identity: Adolescents developing identity; adults enacting and performing an identity. Both involve the performance of lots of high emotions, conflict, and competition. The most egregious examples of reality TV tend to be a repudiation of adult norms and values. It is like giving authority the middle finger. It's awful. Most people refer to it as a waste of time that produces unnecessary and debilitating chaos that spills over into real life.

SOCIAL DRAMA AND PLAYING TO THE SCREEN

Social drama provides a multitude of opportunities for participation. There are several roles that routinely get filled as the drama begins between an antagonist and his or her protagonist. After all, social drama is a performance, facilitated and amplified with the help of social media. The more people who have access to the set (social media platform), the greater the opportunity to join in the saga.

Usually there is a villain who said or did something wrong or stupid. Then there's the injured party. There's the one who defends the villain saying he had every right to do or say the dirty deed. There are the supporters of the aggrieved, who take on the pain and suffering of the wounded and amplify it, often under the guise of "wanting to help." There are observers who choose one side or the other, add their two bits worth of criticism, and keep the information flowing through the vast network of tweets, texts, and posts. Sometimes adults get involved in their children's drama, in part because many parents stay in constant contact with their children through texting, tweets, Instagram, and the like. Kids will assert that when their parents get in on the drama, whether solicited or not, things can get even more out of control. Parental perspectives and motivations might be quite different from those of the teens involved, and depending on what adults do, they can push the drama to a whole new level and increase the potential for more players and greater chaos.

Not all drama reaches this level of emotional pique. Some feels like run-of-the-mill social life, especially during adolescence. One teen told me that her close friends ended up starting drama when they tried to "help" her deal with issues she was having with her boyfriend. She confided in someone that she and her boyfriend were having some difficutlies, and that person reached out to someone else to see if there was some way that friends could intervene to facilitate a resolution. At that point, the teen lost control of the situation with her boyfriend and the situation got worse. While she eventually worked things out with her boyfriend, she said that things would have gone much smoother if everyone had stayed out of her business.

As it turns out, drama is the opposite of staying out of other people's business. Doing drama is a sure way to get involved in someone's life and potentially manipulate some of what is going on. Drama allows people to acquire a false sense of intimacy with someone because during drama, people's private thoughts, actions, needs, or wants, tend to be exposed.[162] A teen might not be in a popular clique, but if drama is being enacted in a public forum that she has access to, she can begin to feel close to someone and be involved in his or her business when she really is not that intimate with him or her in real life. So drama can create a sense of intimacy with someone when intimacy is imagined but not real. It's a bit about pretending there is a closeness, but because it's a one-way relationship, the intimacy is false. [163]

Drama fits nicely with the concept of "feeding off each other," which occurs when people have lost a sense of boundary and control, and the result is likely to be chaotic, disruptive, and disturbing, or exciting, energizing, and empowering, all depending on the role the person is playing in the drama. What gets "eaten" is someone's privacy, and possibly their dignity. Feeding off each other can feel like a frenzied game or competition that has taken on a life of its own where no one can stop what is happening. So drama can be a game where people are trying to outdo one another or beat one another. When I consume you, I have won, or at least I've garnered some share of the attention, which is what drama is all about.

During these feeding frenzies people experience a wide range of emotions that often depend on what role they are playing. If an adolescent is being humiliated by what is being seen and heard, then the emotions are going to be anger, sadness, or outrage. If a teen is gaining attention and influence because of possessing valuable information and spreading it around, then it's going to feel exhilarating. Those in the audience find it entertaining. As one person is trying to do damage control or get even with someone else, another person is trying to capitalize on being in the spotlight and prolong the drama, all to the enjoyment of those watching.

Needing drama past adolescence or emerging adulthood is a sign that something is amiss. Advancing maturity should be a place where drama of the extreme sort should be viewed as a sign of ill health, be it personal drama or society-level drama. Most normally developing adolescents will carry some of the tendencies to do drama into adulthood, but it won't cause the kind of havoc they previously inflicted on their families, teachers, and peers.

We contribute to social chaos and confusion when we excuse, and worse yet, celebrate and exalt adults who engage in social drama that reaches far beyond the boundaries of entertainment as they live their lives. Teens, however, get a pass because their social drama is often an attempt to figure out who they are and who they will be. It's identity work, a normal and necessary part of growing up. It can be tough to manage, but it's doable because youth are working these things out as they develop into adults. After that, we have a much larger challenge.

The longer we live, the more our world view solidifies, and if we have bought into reality as entertainment, we are likely to have become enamored of social drama. Good people can fall into the trap of bad behavior when they lose control of their emotions, when they lose their moral compass, or when they are in a group that is ramped up and out of control. In the next chapter we examine moral disengagement and its enablers: desensitization, deindividuation, and disinhibition, and consider how these tendencies contribute to social drama and bad behavior.

CHAPTER 7
Feeding Off Each Other

ONE OF THE FINDINGS from my own research was that drama and conflict can easily produce bullying when it becomes intentionally harmful and causes hurt, when it is repeated or carries the threat of repetition, and when it exploits a power imbalance.[164] In essence, bullying is behavior that is harmful, intentional, repeated, and abuses power. Conflict can turn into drama, and drama can turn into conflict. Neither by itself is bullying, but either one can become bullying when the conflict or drama becomes aggressive, mean, repeated, and targets a person or group that is less powerful. Bullying is an attempt to control people, suck up power, get even, destroy people and relationships, and in too many circumstances can be wielded with impunity. That means the bully is never held accountable—no punishment and no consequences. It means that meanness becomes normative.

ADULT BULLYING AND DRAMA

Adult bullying is nothing new. Just ask a woman who's been battered and beaten by her partner. That woman will tell you all about the misuse of power, the intimidation, the repetition, the uncertainty of when the other person will lose it and blow up, and the constant presence of fear. It is soul crushing. Sometimes all it takes is a little bit of conflict followed by a hint of drama, and then…wham!

There are also the child abusers who take advantage of a person who is weaker, less powerful, has few resources, and whose knowledge of the world is limited. There are the swindlers who steal from or abuse the elderly or the gullible. There are those who mock people with disabilities. And there are those who abuse and exploit the marginalized who are not able to defend themselves. In these situations, having power and using it to hurt someone is key to bullying. One researcher even suggested that there is a personality disorder titled "adult bullying syndrome,"[165] which reflects wide-ranging psychopathological tendencies, not just a pattern of mean behaviors. In other words, adult bullies may not be just nasty, they may be sick.

In the workplace, conflict that goes unaddressed has been shown to lead to bullying.[166] As I have proposed in my own research on drama, conflict can become drama, drama can produce conflict, and either can become bullying. Conflict and drama are siblings in the same family, and sometimes look like identical twins, but run-of-the-mill drama doesn't always produce conflict and disrupted relationships. When the workplace is balanced and populated with enough people who are resilient, mature, upstanding, mentally healthy, and able to let minor slights go, drama just goes by the way. Curtain closed. Lights out in the theater. There is no more drama.

However, some workplaces can be horrific. The field of nursing is well-known for its peer bullying.[167] Nurses are said to "eat their young," which would seem to be a contradiction for a profession known for its compassion and caring. Even in nursing schools, peer bullying is included as a topic in the curriculum so that those joining the workforce can recognize and be prepared to confront peer bullying and aggression.

Nursing may be prone to workplace bullying because there is often an informal hierarchy that can exist outside the normal chain of command. Cliques can form and become "ingroups" that misuse their power. Younger nurses, or ones who are new or outside the informal power structure can end up being abused. Nursing involves performing some rather distasteful tasks, and when there is a power imbalance among the staff, these tasks can be foisted unfairly upon those who don't have status or influence. Because nurses need to work with each other as members of pairs or teams, the angry and hostile ones can manipulate workloads, badmouth those who don't submit to their tyranny, silence the outsiders, and poison the work environment.

Adult bullying in the workplace has received less attention than bullying among youth, but interest is increasing because of the number of people speaking out.[168] These folks have suffered greatly, often in silence, because of the fear that they will be terminated or blacklisted. They have limited choices and little support from their peers or their supervisors, either of whom might be the one responsible for the bullying.

Adult bullying is not limited to the workplace. It happens in every sort of organization that humankind creates. This includes volunteer organizations.[169] It's amazing how much drama and bullying go on in PTAs, volunteer fire departments and ambulance corps, homeowners' associations, amateur performing groups, "Friends of the_____," (fill in the blank with any not-for-profit outfit: Library, Museum, Environment, Poor, and on and on). How about the Rotary and Lions' clubs, the retired "whomevers," and the organization for the protection of the "you-name-it?" Formal and informal organizations, with large budgets or no budgets can be the sites of power struggles that devolve into drama, conflict, and bullying. The difference between organizational bullying and workplace bullying is that it is easier to leave with fewer scars and one's mental health in better shape. It just depends on how much is invested in being part of that group.

Most adolescents who engage in drama will tell you that they hate drama; that it is unnecessary; that it is a waste of time; and that it serves no good purpose, but that at times it provides life lessons on how to handle conflict more effectively.[170] Over time, most adolescents will back away from drama. As youth become mature adults, they don't need drama to help them figure out who they are and how they want to be. There will be the few young adults who develop full-blown personality disorders or an addiction to drama, and who will continue to foment drama.[171] However, as adults, most of them will not "do drama" anymore, and only those who suffer from serious psychopathy will chronically use bullying to get what they want.[172] Those individuals who do exhibit dangerous and damaging behaviors destroy relationships, organizations, and lives. Their bad behaviors wreak havoc.[173]

MORAL DISENGAGEMENT

Long before adolescence, children begin to develop a moral sense of themselves.[174] We teach our children what's right and what's wrong and we let them know when they've done something bad, and hopefully we've also praised their actions and efforts when they have behaved well.

Children are first motivated by external factors such as punishment and rewards. They do what they think we want them to do so that they don't get punished, and they do what pleases us and makes us happy so they can get rewarded by our pride in them. Eventually feelings such as guilt and pride begin to develop in children, and they become less externally motivated to make good behavioral choices.[175] When they have done something that they know is wrong, they will feel guilty, which has an inhibitory effect. In other words, if a child knows he will feel guilty after doing something that we've taught him is wrong, the expected feeling of guilt may help him make a different choice. Likewise, if a teen knows that a certain behavioral choice will make us happy and that she will experience a feeling of pride because of it, she may be able to make a better choice, even if it's difficult, so that she'll feel proud of herself.

Guilt, embarrassment, empathy, and pride are moral emotions. As part of developing a moral identity,[176] moral emotions become motivators to choose behaviors that match up with a youth's self-image as a good person. Empathy, the ability to see the world from someone else's vantage point, is a major inhibitor of aggression because when kids can see how much their actions are hurting someone, they are more likely to stop or not do it at all. Being able to experience someone else's pain is a good characteristic because it helps a teen treat people with care and respect. So from a kid's perspective, if making a parent/guardian/teacher feel bad is going to make her feel bad too, she's less likely to ditch her moral code when she makes behavioral choices. However, sometimes this process gets derailed. How does this happen?

One way is what is called moral disengagement.[177] Moral disengagement is a process where a person justifies actions that are generally believed to be morally wrong, by shifting the responsibility for his or her actions to the victim or to the peer group. It is a way of shutting down the normal inhibitory effect of guilt, so the person doesn't feel bad for being mean and hurting someone.[178] Interestingly, younger children do less moral disengagement than teens, perhaps because they are more heavily influenced by family and siblings than by peers. In adolescence, kids often hang with kids like themselves, and one trait that they can share is the ability to morally disengage.[179] It goes something like this: *If everyone else is doing it, it must be OK.* It's classic peer pressure.

Another way that kids sometimes get involved in poor choices has to do with their beliefs about aggression and meanness. If moral identity development takes a direction where the self is always placed above the needs or rights of others, youth may see aggression, meanness, and hostility as acceptable and even desirable.[180] We might call this way of looking at the world stinking thinking. Some of these kids are popular and well-known but not always well-liked. They are usually charismatic and fun to be around, but also tough on their friends when they are challenged. They can be aggressive and mean, but also attractive, powerful, and sometimes sneaky and two-faced.[181] They make terrific friends and terrible enemies.

Most people carry around a picture of themselves that reflects an authentic, honest, forthright, caring person.[182] Woven into most people's identities is a person who has noble values and acts in accordance with them. In other words, as human beings we seek to behave in ways consistent with an image of someone whose actions are in congruence with being an honorable truth-teller or a caring person. When individuals act in opposition to these values, they generally feel guilty and experience dissonance or discomfort, unless of course, they suffer from severe psychopathology.[183]

One of the backstops that keeps people from tearing each other's throats out, or from turning every dramatic incident into a Greek tragedy, is morality. Morals are internalized norms or standards that allow people to self-sanction when they are inclined to act on their worst impulses to strike back,[184] take revenge, or hit the "send" button after writing a horrible email to someone. However, there are people who don't feel these inhibitory emotions and act in despicable ways toward others. Consider the person who sends that vulgar, hateful, dishonest tweet to someone who just did something to hurt the sender's feelings.[185] Good moral functioning is what can keep the black hole of drama from getting bigger or from increasing the gravitational suck that pulls everyone in, but that requires a strong moral self and the ability to resist the tendency to retaliate and exact revenge.

The inhibitory force of wanting to be a good person can be overrun by circumstances. In these instances, kids (and adults) may lose their ability to act in a moral way because they can talk themselves into believing that it's OK to do bad things. It's called moral justification.[186] When people back away from the logic and moral reasoning they have used to make sound moral judgments, they can begin to act inhumanely, but still believe in their own inherent goodness.[187] This in turn leads to moral hypocrisy and is apparent when we see people claim their intentions and actions reflect goodness and righteousness but then do that which contradicts what they espouse.[188] This process is much more developed and sophisticated in grown adults, but the seeds of these behaviors can be sown in childhood, as we see with youth who have no compunctions when it comes to being a bad actor and taking on the role of an aggressor.[189]

REVENGE AND RETALIATION

There's a type of kid who is enamored with aggression because it gets her what she wants, although she is disliked for being aggressive.[190] While this approach works well enough for these kids, it still gets them into a lot of trouble and often leaves them on the social margins. Regardless of which type of stinking thinking is swirling in their minds, instead of feeling guilty or embarrassed when they aren't nice, they might feel indifferent or even proud of what they've done. They either haven't developed a set of good morals, or they have disengaged from them.[191]

There's one other trait that is related to the way kids think and this has to do with how they understand and interpret other people's behaviors. There are some kids who are afflicted with what psychologists call "social information processing deficits" and "hostile attribution bias."[192] All this jargon means is that these kids think that other kids are being mean, nasty, hostile, or dismissive when they really aren't. These kids perceive the meaning and intention of others' behaviors as being disrespectful when they aren't at all. Youth who are prone to thinking this way often respond badly to innocuous behaviors, and as a result, they can feed into drama by misreading social cues and overreacting. They get it wrong, and then they make it worse. They may not have made a moral misjudgment; they've made a social one.

So where do these personality and cognitive tendencies lead youth? It makes them more susceptible to responding to being hurt, insulted, embarrassed, or shamed with retaliation and revenge. Whereas the morally mature individual, in possession of some prosocial skills, might have ways to cope that don't necessarily do damage to self and others, teens who are prone to drama often react to these negative feelings with hidden or overt aggression. They retaliate; they get even. Instead of trying to resolve and reconcile, they seek revenge,[193] all of which spices up drama and ensures that the chaos, confusion, and conflict will go on longer than it needs to.

DESENSITIZED, DISINHIBITED, AND DEINDIVIDUALIZED

Moral sensitivities and good judgment can take a big hit when the three "Ds" come into play. This triad affects both individuals and groups. Individuals can become trapped in these unconscious states and not realize that their emotions, reasoning, and behavior have been hijacked.

Desensitization[194] occurs when a person is so overwhelmed by their exposure to negative experiences and the distress that it produces that they lose the ability to feel empathy for another person who is in pain, understand that their thinking has become distorted and warped, and realize that their behavior is no longer guided by what is right or moral. Desensitization is automatic and unconscious. A person doesn't know it is happening. Desensitization can be a precursor to behaving aggressively. Because drama can involve so much ramped up emotional hype due to conflict, meanness, and aggression, desensitization can overcome those involved. This means that rules about how we treat each other respectfully get the ax without anyone's awareness that it's happening. That can lead to some nasty behavior.

Close to desensitization is disinhibition,[195] which is the tendency to lose one's sense of what is appropriate in a given situation, become less constrained, and act in ways that violate social boundaries. In other words, disinhibition factors into outrageous, obnoxious, and immature actions. People spill their guts to strangers or say awful things to people they know. Disinhibition increased when online communication usurped face-to-face synchronous interaction (conversing in person or over the phone to a real human).[196] Disinhibition is attributed to several factors. People behave as if they are anonymous in online communication. They also believe they are invisible and invincible, and act accordingly.

When there is no social group or person in front of us who gasps, cries, or punches us when we behave badly, we feel as if we can do and say whatever we want.

Deindividuation is what happens when individuals become desensitized and disinhibited.[197] In essence, to become an un-individuated person, is to lose one's identity as an individual. It usually manifests in situations where people are under the influence of a strong and passionate group. Once a person is sucked into that kind of experience, they can lose their self-awareness and their ability to self-regulate. They become part of the mob, and we know mobs do things that individuals would never think of doing, from ignoring someone who is being stabbed on the street, to hitting a police officer with a rock. All sense of responsibility evaporates, and people become irrational, impulsive, and regressive. They identify with the ideology and behavior of the group, while subverting some of their own personal identity to the group.[198]

Drama is loaded with desensitization, disinhibition, and deindividuation because individuals lose their sense of selves and take on mob-like characteristics. So while personality is key in fomenting drama, it is also the behavior of people in groups that can light the fire under the rocket of drama and send things into outer space.

GROUPS BEHAVING BADLY

It's been known for decades that people behave differently in groups than they do when they are alone or with one other person. In 1954 there was the Robber's Cave experiment.[199] A group of campers were placed in two randomly assigned groups. On their own they developed strong affiliations within their assigned group even though they had come to camp with someone who was a friend from home who ended up on the other team. The ingroup connections turned into bias against the other group that eventually became competitive and then conflictual.

In 1971 there was the Stanford Prison experiment.[200] A group of undergraduate volunteers were divided into prisoners and prison guards. They were given free rein to play their parts and because they did it so well, they had to shut the experiment down after six days because of the brutality the "prison guards" inflicted on the prisoners. The conclusions led to an understanding that good people as individuals can do dastardly things in groups that they would never do or sanction on their own.

People look at the members of their own group more favorably than the members of outside groups and find fault with outsiders in ways that are more negative than they are with members of their own group. [201] Kids are the same way as adults, but not from birth. Children embrace everyone as part of their group until around age six, when they begin to demonstrate "othering" behavior toward some children. They will begin to exclude other children, objectify them, and think of them as an outgroup or the "other." Unfortunately, humans stay that way throughout their lives, and this trait has led to terrible behaviors by many people. [202]

Consider the countries that have had civil wars, often due to ingroup-outgroup hatred. Just a few of these countries include: the United States, Syria, China, Ireland, the United Kingdom, Myanmar, Somalia, Argentina, Russia, and Cuba. Civil wars are fought for multiple reasons besides ethnic or social conflict, but in every case it becomes a question of which group will have power and how they will use it.

Besides civil wars, there have been groups where ethnic and religious conflict has existed since practically the beginning of recorded history. Jews vs. Gentiles. Hindus vs. Muslims. Muslims vs. Jews. Shia Muslims vs. Sunni Muslims. Catholics vs. Protestants. Christians vs. Jews and Muslims. Chinese vs. Uyghurs.

And the worst form of ingroup-outgroup hate rears its ugliness in the form of genocides, where one group attempts to kill off an entire outgroup. Genocides have taken place (or continue to occur in some places) in Rwanda, Cambodia, China, the Sudan, and Russia. Specific outgroups that have experienced genocide include Ukrainians, Bosnians, Armenians, Native Americans, Jews, and Muslims.

The genocide of World War II prompted social psychologists to find out how people who purported to be of high moral standing could join in group behaviors that treated people they had known as individuals so horribly. [203] While the reason behind such organized violence against groups is complex, one discovery was how people perceive the members of "their" group versus the members of the "other" group. Researchers call this ingroup favoritism or love, and outgroup condemnation or hate. [204] This phenomenon is apparent in thousands of examples from two teams playing volleyball against each other to one dominant ethnic group exterminating a different ethnic group. Groups that are provoked for some reason by an "outside" group or force tend to see their "in" group as special, better, superior in comparison to those in the other or "out" group. People's individual characteristics disappear and what is emphasized by each group is how much better they are versus how much worse the other group is.

One factor that generates this type of group dynamics is the problem of stereotyping,[205] which is a generalization about a group of people as a group, based on limited information that is negatively skewed or biased. Jane Elliott, an elementary school teacher, illustrated how easy it was to divide her students into ingroups and outgroups by using eye color as the determinant of who was good or bad, privileged or oppressed.[206] Using her influence and authority as a teacher she told her students that children with blue eyes were smarter and better than students with brown eyes. Following her lead, the blue-eyed children mistreated and excluded the brown-eyed students. The next day Elliott told her students that she had lied and reversed the meaning of eye color. Blue-eyed students were now bad and brown-eyed students were allowed to oppress them and treat them badly.

The takeaways from this two-day "experiment" were far-reaching. She demonstrated how the suggestion from a respected authority that something was bad about a group of people based on a characteristic shared by everyone in that group became a negative stereotype. And when a person of respect says it's OK to mistreat that group and models that kind of behavior, good people can do bad things. The genocides that have been committed in the last century make it clear that adults are capable of doing the same.

One outcome from Elliott's experiment was that the children began to understand prejudice and discrimination. Of course, Jane Elliott was not in everyone's good favor after this episode. Some people, including the children, said it was a great way to help kids learn about racism, prejudice, discrimination, and injustice. Others, however, saw her experiment as abusive, damaging, and unethical.

The point is that humans are prone to favor those who are like them, or who share similar ideologies, values, norms, and opinions. And those folks are prone to look down on or think negatively about those in the outgroup with whom they differ on ideologies, values, norms, and opinions. Looking down on a group based on negative stereotypes can spin out of control and lead to hate speech and then violence, especially when they or someone in leadership tells them that the outgroup is evil and is responsible for the travails of their own group. When this happens, traits such as deindividuation, moral disengagement, and desensitization become group emotions, not just individual emotions.

Groupthink[207] is exactly what it says: people in a group all thinking the same way. That can be great if the ideas and decisions are good ones, but too often the influences of peers get everyone sidetracked barreling down a path of bad choices. The ideas get wilder and wilder, and no one seems to notice. Like the common cold, powerful emotional germs get absorbed and spread to other members of the group, leading to some poor or dangerous decisions. As members of the group get caught up in stinking thinking, they lose themselves as individuals; they de-individuate. The norms, beliefs, and values that may reflect traits such as open-mindedness, courage, self-respect, honesty, and compassion can get sidetracked in lieu of other traits such as self-interest and dishonesty. The higher the emotional arousal, the more a herd mentality takes over. People are more apt to believe gossip, rumors and out-right lies about the outgroup. The ability for individuals to think rationally and logically, which might require contradicting the position of the group, gets swamped by excessive emotion and fear of being rejected by the ingroup. Self-reflection is nearly impossible, and perhaps even dangerous. Some of the worst inclinations and traits get mixed into the toxic stew: arrogance, narcissism, a sense of having been wronged, entitlement, fear of rejection, the need to belong, extroversion, and impulsivity.

PSYCHOPATHY

Psychopaths and/or sociopaths[208] are in a drama category all their own. They are often successful, or at least view themselves that way. They have little or no ability to self-reflect, so people often see them much differently than they themselves do. If you are trying to come up with a metaphor to create a picture of such a person, think of the children's story, "The Emperor's New Clothes." In this tale a traveling salesman convinces the emperor that he can provide him with the most beautiful, stylish, and exquisite attire ever warn. The problem is that the salesman is selling him nothing. As the salesman and the emperor stand in front of the mirror, the gullible emperor sees himself as naked, but believes the salesman who is telling him how great he looks in his new duds. Word goes around the kingdom that the emperor is going to show off his new wardrobe in a parade. Of course, as he proudly canters through his kingdom naked, no one except a small child dares state the truth: *The emperor has no clothes on.*

Fortunately, psychopathy of the extreme and dangerous kind is quite rare. Clinicians and researchers have spent years working on the development of accurate profiles of people who suffer from psychopathy. One trait that seems particularly frightening is the ability to hide behind a mask of charming sanity. These individuals seem normal and are quite appealing, yet their relationships with most people are shallow and opportunistic.[209]

Psychopaths may also demonstrate fearlessness, callousness, disinhibition, arrogance, meanness, self-assuredness, invulnerability, cruelty, dishonesty, manipulation of people and situations, impulsivity, lack of remorse, and criminality.[210] It's quite a list if we are looking for the perfect villain to star in a stage play or film, but hellish to deal with in real life. When a person has no conscience, no ability to feel another person's pain, is cold-hearted, and is also smart, attractive, and bold, the only action necessary for stirring the pot of drama is a challenge, a snide insult, or personal criticism, and then everything gets chaotic all over again. Few children behave like psychopaths, but the tendencies can be evident early on, especially as kids enter adolescence.[211] Worst of all are the adults who display the traits of psychopathy, and a frightening number of practitioners believe their numbers are increasing.[212]

CHAPTER 8
Our Society Has a Personality Disorder

PERSONALITY DISORDERS[213] **ARE SETS** of behaviors that a person exhibits that make it difficult for that person to function successfully in relationships with people and the environment. In other words, these people tend to be a problem for themselves and for society in general. There are ten or so categories of personality disorders. Several of the characteristics that contribute to personality disorders are closely related to features of drama and the behaviors people engage in while doing drama. These are the personality factors thus involved: the tendency to interpret other people's motives as malevolent, eccentricities of behavior, impulsivity, excessive emotionality and attention-seeking, narcissism, grandiosity, need for attention, lack of empathy, and hypersensitivity to negative evaluation.[214]

By the time adults are entrenched in the behaviors we see in adolescent drama, they have personality disorders.[215] There are narcissistic personality disorders, histrionic personality disorders, anti-social personality disorders, passive-aggressive personality disorders, and obsessive-compulsive personality disorders.[216] The one thing about the folks who have these personality disorders is that they complicate our lives and add complexity and stress to our relationships.[217]

Should we be worried about adults who "do drama" in excess?

The answer is an emphatic *"Yes!"* We should be very worried about adults when they display these behaviors. This conclusion comes from research on adults who bully alone and in groups, who cause drama in the workplace, who are narcissistic, who may engage in criminal activity, and in some cases, are psychopathic leaders.[218] There is no direct line between adolescent social drama and adult social drama, but there are enough clues to see what happens when adults display the types of behaviors that qualify as adolescent social drama. The contexts tend to be different, but the nature of the beast is essentially the same, only with much more serious outcomes. When the narcissistic, power-hungry performer draws large and unruly crowds (is charismatic and aggressive), when the performer and the performances get more outrageous and extreme (telling and believing lies), and when the performer wields significant power over people and the media (exhibits demagoguery), we are at serious risk of social upheaval and chaos. Irrationality, disbelief in truth, denial of reality, rejection of the outgroup,[219] and chaos, all potential components of adolescent drama, are on display when powerful adults do drama on a national scale.

Adolescent drama causes adults in their lives no end of headaches. Kids who thrive on drama are high maintenance. They are exhausting. They leave those around them with emotional hangovers, but so do adults who do drama.

PERFORMING ADULT IDENTITY

Adults perform identities just as youth do.[220] Those identities are the stuff of which each self is made. It includes roles that we play in the various relationships that involve multiple contexts such as intimate partnership, nuclear family, extended family, neighborhood alliances, work life, religious affiliation and church membership, civic/volunteer/charity work, and political party affiliation. In the relationships that develop in all these contexts, we perform identities that signal who we are, what we believe, what we value, and how we see the world. While our performances may require somewhat different behaviors depending on what is called for, we act out a basic integrated, consistent, and predictable person. That is, we act as we do if we have developed into a prosocial, mature adult, not one with a severe personality disorder.

As with youth, adults perform various identities, often on social media, which is put out there for others to consume. We see it when parents post photos of their babies and children doing everything from smiling cutely, to having a massive temper tantrum or wearing birthday cake all over their faces. We post photos of our vacations, birthday parties, family gatherings, holidays, and celebratory events like weddings and graduations. We boast and brag, inform and elucidate, and expect "likes" as much as teens do. While Generation Z may be addicted to the selfie, so are adults from the millennials to the boomers.

Adults have identities that display the way they think and what they believe, just as adolescents do. But adults are supposed to have stable, mature, and evolved identities. Adults are supposed to demonstrate rational thinking and decision-making. They are supposed to be able to regulate their emotions. They are supposed to be able to recognize facts from fiction. They are supposed to be able to understand other people's points of view, even if they don't agree with them. They are supposed to be able to take responsibility for their mistakes. However, as noted previously, people behave differently in groups than they do as individuals, and one of the factors that affect how we act in groups is called collective narcissism.[221] Narcissism is no longer a trait of individuals; it has infected groups of people, and it is spreading to the point where it is beginning to feel like an epidemic. It isn't a biological virus we are battling—it is each other, and societies skate on thin ice when this happens.

COLLECTIVE NARCISSISM

Jean Twenge and Keith Campbell[222] wrote a book describing a Western world where a social epidemic of narcissism was growing. Their book was published in 2009, but the data that were collected and cited within the book was gathered before that time, when not everyone was in possession of a smartphone. Today, everyone from tweens to older adults carry electronic, computerized, communication devices on their person. In the fifteen-years-plus following their book publication, many of the problems they detail around society-wide narcissism have only increased in quantity and scope. I would assert that our society has developed its own version of a personality disorder.

As more people spend more time focusing on themselves and their own needs and wants, less time is spent observing, recognizing, and addressing the needs and suffering of others. One of the benefits of participating in civic and social service is that youth are taught to notice people around them. Guidance from mature others helps us raise children who will have a sense of responsibility for how others are faring and put their own self-interests aside to help others, at least some of the time. This sense of civic responsibility has waned as our cultural messages have told us that we are more important than the guy next to us or the girl behind us in line. In this crush to make sure we get what we want despite others around us, we no longer care about taking care of each other. After all, isn't life short and aren't we supposed to get all we can out of it? Many young people today do public service, not so much because they really care about helping other people but because they can put it on their college applications. Of course, not everyone is like this, but the numbers of narcissistic and entitled individuals is growing.[223]

Another problem with living in a society where everyone is out for him or herself is the lack of perseverance and commitment to do things that aren't easy, fun, glamorous, or publicly noteworthy. Achieving something that is hard is too often viewed as not worth the time or the effort, yet being the best or getting the most is everyone's goal.[224] So, what does this mean? We cut corners, cheat, get someone else to do the hard stuff, fake it, or lie. Again, not everyone exhibits these traits all the time. Helping people we don't know during times of climate catastrophes or horrible disasters, like hurricanes and tornados, does show people's compassion for others who are hurting, but that kind of empathy comes and goes with the tide.

The last point from Twenge and Campbell's book that is worth mentioning is the quality of relationships when everyone is a narcissist.[225] Narcissists make lousy friends or partners because the zip and zing they come in with fizzles out when the relationship experiences strain. As noted previously, narcissists have high but fragile self-esteem. Their sense of entitlement means they shy away from commitments that take work, time, or sacrifice. Twenge and Campbell make the point that it is often people who have lower self-esteem who make good partners and friends because they are less likely to vacate a relationship when the going gets rocky, and they don't always have to be center stage. Unless these types suffer from depression, they can make wonderful friends. Thus, the authors cast doubt on the adage that you can't love someone else unless you love yourself. Instead, they suggest that "if you love yourself too much, you won't have enough love for anyone else."[226]

If we are looking at behaviors that reflect collective narcissism, what we won't see is caring, grounded relationships where people are able to engage in self-sacrifice. We won't see people putting others in front of themselves. We won't see much kindness unless it produces accolades for the doer, and we won't have the kinds of personal or social relationships that make us a strong society.

COLLECTIVE VICTIMHOOD: "OH, WOE IS WE"

One of the hallmarks of social drama is "victimhood."[227] Consider that students who find themselves on the negative end of drama, despite having started it, cry, "Victim!" In some instances, these same youth began the drama by dishing out their own ration of pain to someone else. However, if it backfires and the sympathy for their plight wains, they may find themselves the recipient of some justifiable criticism and backlash. It is a paradox that the very teen who is guilty of bad behavior that victimizes others uses the very boundaries that have been breached to demand protection from suffering the predictable and legitimate backlash from those first victimized. This doesn't justify violent retaliation, but it seems hypocritical at the least to expect to get off scot-free when there is culpability to be assigned.

While adolescent drama turns individuals and sometimes small groups into victims, a phenomenon called collective victimhood has influenced how adults behave in groups and toward groups, both within the groups where they claim membership, and toward groups they see as adversarial.[228] Researchers have found that ingroups made up of people who share narcissistic characteristics often engage in aggressive behaviors toward outgroups that they feel have not shown them enough respect or appropriate attention.[229] Thus, it is no surprise that ingroups like this claim to be victims and lash out at others. Groups of people who don't share this narcissistic entitlement function much differently. They are not threatened by disagreement or criticism. However, when the net number of people in our society are increasing in narcissistic tendencies, the number of groups that are threatened by other groups is increasing. Grown-ups are not behaving as grown-ups should. It's because we have a society-wide personality disorder.

There are certainly individuals and groups who have been victimized, and are entitled to make their claims, speak their needs, and have them redressed. However, in the past few years, there has been an explosion of claims of victimhood that are basically false. The 45th president of the United States modeled false victimhood in multiple ways and was able to slide out from underneath any responsibility for the criticisms his fake victimhood provoked.[230] Doing drama and performing the role of someone who has been wronged and who deserves special consideration is great theater. It attracts attention and most importantly, sympathy from friends and sympathizers caught inside the unfolding drama.

Everyone has experienced some harm or devastation that makes that person entitled to claim victimhood. Some forms of harm may never be redressed and may be worthy of sympathy in perpetuity. But those who cry "victim" today are often not these folks. Today, just about everyone has a reason to claim "victimhood." Whether it's a genuine plea for sympathy, a ploy to surreptitiously manipulate, or just a way to get attention, it has taken a toll on honesty and authenticity in our public interactions. We have become a nation of whiners.[231] This has damaged our connections to each other, become an impediment to agency and acting on our own behalf and embracing the collective, common good. Aggrievement has outlived its usefulness and is sucking us all down.

Anger, frustration, and stress give way to impulsivity, incivility, and aggression. We see it in adult cyberbullying, road rage, intimate partner and domestic violence, child abuse, workplace shootings, protests that trigger violent reprisals, and rampage shootings. This is not to suggest that the problem is due to more crime. It's due to our impatience, fear, isolation, distrust of each other, insecurity, and loss of perspective. It's because we are unsure of who we are. Our hope for something remotely like a sense of collective solidarity is under assault from within, and many of us are oblivious to it.[232]

We are not a society or country that possesses a single, unitary identity. Some may argue that it isn't necessary to have a collective identity, especially if we share a few core values, subscribe to similar ideas about what it means to be an American, and respect and apply laws equally. But individualism that manifests itself in entitlement for me and to hell with just about everyone else puts a society at risk for disintegration. Adolescent drama may be entertaining because it is usually a phase, but when drama becomes a normalized behavior that defines a collective identity, the adults are in trouble.

BULLYING, PUBLIC DISCOURSE, AND DRAMA

The political events of the past decade or so have done a job on us as Americans.[233] Our populace is numb, exhausted, off-kilter, and damaged to the point where we can no longer engage with each other and work together for the common good. Political social drama on steroids has damaged and fractured our identity as Americans, in serious and problematic ways.[234]

Politics has always been performative, and brutal. What we see in politicians is not always what they are. Sometimes their words and actions are genuine and truthful. At other times, they obfuscate, mislead, and resort to deceptive theatrics, but very few politicians are like that all the time.

Donald Trump[235] and those around him are a phenomenon that has exerted profound influence on America. As a persona, he has presented himself as someone who behaves in ways that most of us would not want our children to behave. His followers find him enamoring, irreverent, attractive, and appealing. They love the way he gets by with being outrageous. They hunger for his ability to speak disparagingly about individuals and groups that they secretly resent and even hate. They admire his law-breaking tendencies and how he slides away from being held accountable. They envy his ability to trash people, destabilize institutions, and denigrate people who are far more mature and morally sophisticated than he is. The former president, who will also be our president for another four years, starting in 2025, is a seriously flawed individual whose behavior has set a new low for how adults behave in a civil society.[236]

Those who favor Donald Trump's antics and imitate his modus operandi display the same behaviors that are jaw-dropping in their similarity to adolescent social drama. He craves attention. He is very impulsive. He is vengeful. He manipulates people. He doesn't think rules apply to him. He is clearly narcissistic, thinking that he is better at everything than he really is. He is selfish and doesn't care about other people's feelings. He is a liar. He is unable to see himself as he really is. He doesn't recognize how his behaviors affect people. He is unapologetic about sexual indiscretions and uses them to enhance his reputation. He baits people. Those around him don't survive unless they get sucked into his view of the world and play a collaborative or subservient role in the social drama in which he stars. He is thin-skinned and overreactive. When he is wounded, he strikes back viciously at those whom he has perceived as having wronged him. He is entitled, the world is his stage, and the attention must be on him. And he overwhelmingly uses social media (or did at one time until he was blocked), in the very same ways that adolescents do to stir the pot so that they can raise the curtain, make a grand entrance, command the stage, ramp up the drama, and create chaos.[237]

Certainly not all adolescent social drama hits this level of bad behavior. Youth may stretch the truth, boast and brag, and lack the ability to self-reflect, but most realize that drama isn't really real. It's just that: play acting and figuring out who they are. It's reality TV played out in real life.

The bad behaviors of some powerful leaders and celebrities go well beyond adolescent play acting. Their behaviors include incessant lying, serious bullying, willful ignorance, cheating, bragging about bad behavior, and accusing others of the same faults and behaviors that they have engaged in, but refuse to recognize in themselves. Rarely do we see adolescents take drama that far. Kids who do drama may make a lot of noise, but rarely does it reach the scope and scale of the behaviors that have spilled into the public square.

Too many of the sounds we hear from some of these grown-ups feel like hatred, contempt, cynicism, and derision. Our public discourse has become hostile, insulting, and screechy. Everyone seems to want to be heard, but no one seems to want to listen. There is a lack of seriousness and an excess of irrelevance in our public conversations. When adolescents do social drama, we might be amused or frustrated, but when it is the way we live and communicate as adults, it's unsettling and frightening.

The Trump[238] trance has led a good number of people to believe that if he can get away with acting like a two-year-old, then they should be able to as well. When people buy the Trump brand and adopt it as their identity, we end up with a surge of immature behaviors, even from some people who would consider themselves serious and knowing adults, and the more cachet these adults have, the more damage they can do to our social fabric. I am particularly concerned about the political power that some religious groups have garnered when it comes to encouraging bad social behaviors that generate conflict and social discord.

RELIGION AND SOCIAL DRAMA

Discussing religion in polite company, or even in a book on social drama is dicey. The purpose of this section is to offer a perspective that is seldom publicly presented when considering how we function as members of a society represented by dozens of religious ideologies. The ideas that I offer fold into the discussion of social drama and the role that religion can play in increasing bad behavior and destroying our connections to one another.

It's important to begin by acknowledging the positive role that religion plays in the lives of people all over the world. Practicing a faith in God or a higher power is one function of organized religions, but another function is bringing people together in community. In these communities, untold amounts of good work and service to others occurs. Not only do members minister to each other, but they often reach out into the community to help others, not of their own faith communities, when there is a need. People in faith communities often forge bonds of friendship that last for years, and as children grow up, and spouses and partners die off, it is these relationships that can stave off loneliness in old age. So while organized religions provide spiritual connection and moral guidance, they also provide relationships that are crucial to helping enhance and sustain our humanity.

The downside is that religions are social organizations, subject to the challenges of all organizations when it comes to social drama. Hence, we see all the aspects of organizational dysfunction in religious groups and communities, too: conflict, drama, harassment, bullying, abuse, narcissism, demagoguery, and all the other problematic behaviors of which we humans are capable. In itself, this is just the way things go. Living in any community comes with its own set of tensions, but in the case of religious organizations there is often a sense of infallibility and an attitude of "I'm right and you are wrong" on a host of topics including abortion, the death penalty, educational curriculum, and what should be the purview of government or a religion. Because the dictates of God are deeply woven into so many positions on controversial issues, religions can have a divisive effect on how individuals and groups interact with each other on a society-level, and when these conflicting perspectives become part of our political policy debates, big drama can unfold.

In some cases religion has been weaponized or co-opted to push political agendas that are anything but benevolent. This is evident in terrorists' use of Islamic principles to kill people, as well as right wing militia members use of Christian principles to justify their attempt to capture, try, and execute politicians in the United States such as happened to Michigan governor, Gretchen Whitmer.[239] Religions, some of their dogma, and some of the stances their leaders have taken, have contributed to the dangerous place in which we find ourselves.

I recently was discussing this book with a Protestant minister, sharing my take on social media when he jumped to the issue of transgender children. He asked me what I thought about the effect of social media on youth and their desire to be a sex other than the one assigned at birth. I replied that I was personally aware of one little boy who knew he was a girl as soon as he understood that our society was divided into boys and girls; for him, this was when he about three years old. He insisted on a new name. He began wearing "female" clothes, playing with "female" toys, and demanding to be allowed to do the things girls do. He had never encountered social media that suggested that some boys wanted to identify as girls and vice versa. I gave him a few other examples of anecdotes that I was aware of that didn't seem to implicate the influence of social media in the increase of children wishing to have gender reassignment.

When I got home I started looking into peer-reviewed research on the numbers of people who have regrets after having gender reassignment surgery, which the minister had brought up seeming to think it was a common and/or serious problem. I found that to the contrary, very few people have regrets about having gender reassignment surgery, and the few that have may not have been counseled long enough and well enough to make sure the decision was the right one.[240]

The minister expressed to me that he believed that transgender youth were influenced just the same way youth have been "influenced" or "recruited" in the past to be gay or lesbian. At that point I suggested to him that gender, much like sexual attraction, is on a continuum, as opposed to the way we frame these issues as binary, meaning it's one or the other, and can't be a bit of both, or neither. I explained that society has imposed strict "male" and "female" characteristics on humans that just don't fit the model of gender expression in our populations. I then said that it's a lot like who people are attracted to sexually. The same binary is false here that is also false when we think about gender. On one end we have purely heterosexual individuals and at the other end are people whose sexual attractions are fluid and even inconsistent.[241]

Of course, this knowledge contradicts the religious beliefs and world views of many people, and is one example of disagreements that cause drama, conflict, anger, aggression, and even war in some parts of the world. This information was not consistent with his beliefs or religious ideology, but he listened respectfully, and this part of our conversation ended leaving us to move on to another topic of discussion.

Opposition to ideas about gender and sexual fluidity is not to dismiss the faith traditions of many religions. However, it must be stated that religions that promote dismissal, condemnation, or hatred, persecution, and discrimination of people who don't fit binary gender or sexual norms are contributing to human suffering and division. I left my conversation with the minister thinking about people who curse, condemn, or reject others based on binary ideas about sex and gender, and what their own children or congregants must experience when their gender and sexual identities are forbidden, disparaged, or labeled as sinful. When faith leaders draw uncrossable lines in their dogma, some followers will interpret this rejection as permission to hate. We are living in a world where conflicting religious beliefs have undermined the social fabric of our society because some believers think that their religious beliefs should dictate how everyone should live, and this has contributed significantly to the divisions in our country and bad behavior along with it. Religious leaders need to assess their motives and how they use their influence when it comes to giving their followers tacit approval to act on hate for their fellow citizens.

The mixing of religion and politics is volatile and destructive, both for religion and for our society. Intolerance of other religious beliefs and ideologies contributes to ingroup-outgroup conflict and social upheaval. Tim Alberta, a journalist who is the son of an evangelical minister, has written eloquently about his personal and public battle with his fellow evangelicals.[242] He has drawn a line between Christianity that is faithful to the message of Jesus and Christianity that has wrapped itself in the quest for power, money, and social domination. Some within this religious sect advocate for their version of a Christian state replacing the secular state. These groups have little tolerance for other religious traditions and would seek to base all our laws on their interpretation of Christian laws. Alberta is not alone in his critique of a religion that wishes to replace our constitutional order with a Christian nationalist one. *New York Times* opinion writer David French[243] echoes Alberta's concerns, and Kristin Du Mez [244] has offered her own take on how religion has added to our social and political polarization. The voices of these clear-eyed thinkers, who are themselves Christians, should alarm us because if the "all or nothing" believers get their way and try to overturn the United States constitution and create a Christian nationalist country, our problems of ingroup-outgroup hatred will get much worse. We could easily have discord, chaos, and social drama on a nuclear scale.

Howard Ross, who writes about bias, stereotyping, and beliefs, emphasizes that beliefs are not facts.[245] Believing something is true, doesn't make it true.[246] When people insist their beliefs are facts, and when knowledge has been developed that contradicts their religiously supported beliefs as universal realities, we will not escape conflict that can lead to terrible horrors. It is the rare society that can escape atrocities of this nature. Religious beliefs can be a double-edged sword that can spread goodness, well-being, and happiness, but they can also do the opposite. Insisting that one's religious beliefs are facts that everyone should see as truthful information contributes to argumentation and social discord. Separation of church(es) and state makes good common sense and reduces social drama. *Amen.*

Identity is something we act out every day of our lives. Identity is influenced by age, gender, race, ethnicity, life experiences, and a variety of ideologies including religious beliefs and practices. People know who we are by what we say and do, and because we have a society-wide personality disorder, what we say and do has become a problem. We are a bit too narcissistic, entitled, righteous, greedy, selfish, fearful, and anxious, and because of this we are struggling to define how our multiple collective social identities mesh with our identity as citizens of our country. It has always been a challenging task, but it's gotten harder and it's why we have so much social drama.

COLLECTIVE SOCIAL IDENTITIES VS.
A NATIONAL IDENTITY

People who live together under the flag of a country usually think of themselves as citizens united by certain common values, beliefs, goals, and characteristics. The acceptance of these beliefs, the adherence to these values, and a recognition of these characteristics comes together in a national, overarching identity.[247] In older countries where many citizens trace their ancestry back hundreds of years, part of this identity is related to language, ethnicity, culture, and a shared history. In the United States we are not bound by a national identity generated by a common ethnicity, religion, or race, as are other nations in the world. We are a group of citizens with very diverse ethnicities, cultures, and histories, so defining a national identity is more complicated for Americans.

In other countries, identity is shaped through shared language, customs and traditions, religious beliefs, ethnicity, and race, character-istics which are not found in the American melting pot or tossed salad (pick your preferred metaphor). While we have some shared customs such as celebrations of national holidays like the Fourth of July, Ameri-cans speak other languages besides English, practice religions other than Christianity, and come from many different races and ethnic backgrounds. The idea of America is that we can build connections despite our multiple differences and live up to a set of ideals that we accept as a national identity. But this is difficult because not everyone is comfortable with the way our citizenry changes over time. Thus, it seems like our identity is in flux.

Deborah Schildkraut offers some thoughts on how we answer the question: What does it mean to be an American?[248]

She has formulated four approaches that have influenced our development of a national identity over the course of our history. She begins by discussing the one that is most embedded in our founding documents: the Declaration of Independence, the Constitution, and the Bill of Rights. The main principle linking these documents is our right to be free as individuals. To be able to pursue life, liberty, and happiness with little interference from government in whatever way the individual chooses. It is the one that grounds our individualism as sacrosanct and inalienable.[249]

The second principle that she describes is what she refers to as civic republicanism, which encompasses the responsibilities that are necessary in order to have a society that is free. It means attending to civic matters, joining organizations that support the common good, voting, following laws and honoring the institutions that uphold them, respecting other people's rights while not forfeiting one's own. Obviously, these first two strands of our American identity work to tone down the other from getting out of hand.[250]

The third element is the belief that America was and should continue to be defined by white, male, Christian predominance. This perspective is called ethnocentrism and corresponds to what we would call white Christian nationalism today. This perspective sees anyone else as less than and seems to contradict the first principle that she describes where everyone who is a citizen has the right to pursue life, liberty, and happiness.[251]

The fourth component is the understanding that all of us from the first colonists on are immigrants in this land, and the diversity of our immigrant heritage should be honored and respected. This line of thinking includes people who double identify with a race or ethnicity and also as an American. Examples are Irish American, Asian American, or African American.[252] It aspires to the nostalgia and pride we feel when we focus on the Statue of Liberty and the lines inscribed on it:

> "Keep, ancient lands, your storied pomp!" cries she
> With silent lips. "Give me your tired, your poor,
> Your huddled masses yearning to breathe free,
> The wretched refuse of your teeming shore.
> Send these, the homeless, tempest-tost to me,
> I lift my lamp beside the golden door!"[253]

What it means to be American is a paradox because it is easy to see that these four different ways of defining what it means to be an American are not always consistent with each other. Some people will appropriate bits and pieces of these four threads as an explanation of what it means to be an American, even if their own opinions and behaviors are sometimes at odds with their belief in a national identity.[254] At the very least, I think that being American connects us to a place (the land we inhabit), to ideas about what and who we are right now (a hot mess), and what we aspire to be based on personal and collective social identities, that include our aspirations and ideals. Regardless of one's description of a national identity, what we know is that people have multiple social identities and some of these inform their ideas about what it means to be an American.

Social identities develop based on how people see themselves as similar or different from one another. Social identities are ways that we differentiate ourselves into groups that share commonalities. Most of us have several social identities that speak to our identification as individuals, but also our involvement, and hence identity, with others. These might include family identity, religious identity, professional identity, political identity, etc.[255] While by itself this kind of self and group differentiation is not remarkable it can lead to what has turned us into a fractured populace, the "ingroup" vs. "outgroup" phenomenon.[256] When our ingroup-outgroup differences override our sense of connection as citizens of a state or country, we can find ourselves experiencing high conflict.[257]

Our ingroup-outgroup disdain for each other is making it harder to see ourselves in each other, and this has pushed our ideas of a national identity to the brink. Our multiple and conflicting social identities have nudged us closer to intolerance of many whom we do not view as like us. And when this happens it is a quick leap from intolerance to objectification, dismissal, and even hatred of that other group.[258]

We need a pause, a reset, and maybe a few sessions of national group therapy so that we can reconsider what it will take to put us back on track for a future where we can connect and disconnect, and agree and disagree with each other in ways that preserve each others' dignity.[259] We need to shake the personality disorders that are turning us into pretzels, making us run from reality, and sending us down the black hole of drama.

One of the things we know is that our children are watching us, and they are dismayed. The amount of anxiety and depression in youth has reached the level of a five-alarm fire.[260] Families often reflect in a microcosm what is happening in the macrocosm of our society. Catherine Steiner-Adair[261] wrote a wonderful book ten years ago about how the digital world has insinuated itself into our families. Since that writing, smartphones and the social media they usher into our lives, have continued to impact children, families, and society as a whole, and not in a particularly good way. What Dr. Steiner-Adair told us ten years ago remains true today: Children need much more from us than a two-way screen connected to the internet to amuse them while we are trying to pick up the pieces of our world.

CHAPTER 9
Kids, Parents, and Screens

AS A NEW GRANDPARENT, I have had a front row seat to how infants and toddlers react to screens. Within days of my granddaughter's birth she was drawn to the large TV screen in her parents' living room. It was bright, colorful, noisy, and constantly changing. As she got older it was clear that she was often more interested in the TV than the faces of her mom and dad.

Within the first six months of her life, she became enamored of her parents' cellphones. She wanted to touch them, mouth them, and when her eye hand coordination got good enough, she would poke them. She preferred a cell phone to practically every toy she had and got very upset when she wasn't allowed to have a phone in her cute little hands. Living several states away, her parents would often FaceTime with us, and I began to be able to tell when she was engaged in my face, voice, and movements, and when she was more intrigued by the phone and the screen transmitting our interaction. I could tell when she was paying more attention to the screen than what she was observing on the screen. Of course, this tale is anecdotal, not a phenomenon that I have researched, but since the birth of two more grandchildren while writing this book, I can see the same things happening, and this is with parents who are making enormous efforts to keep their children away from screens as much as possible.

THE SOCIAL MEDIA DILEMMA: PROS AND CONS

Research on social media use tells us that there are some really good things about screens, messaging, posting, sharing, and connecting virtually.[262] We can reach more people more quickly when there is an urgency.

We can be creative, using images, photos, memes, and videos to express ourselves and entertain our friends and family. For the elderly, those who have limited mobility, or for youth who tend to be marginalized (e.g., LGBTQ+), social media can be a life-enhancing mechanism for avoiding isolation and loneliness. Social media is a way for friends and families to support each other. Social media allows us to explore information from multiple sources and have access to ideas and knowledge previously held in obscurity. Social media can build bridges between people who are different from each other and may never meet in person. Social media has the potential to build strong, vibrant societies.

On the other hand, we also know that the amount of time spent looking at screens creates problems for youth and for adults.[263] When we are looking at a screen, we aren't physically active, and we are often oblivious to what is going on around us. That means that we are somewhat absent from the actual physical space that we occupy. Another thing that can't happen when we are fixated on a screen is first-rate social interaction with the people around us. The more time spent on screens, the more weight we gain, the fewer social skills we acquire and the rustier the ones we have become. Our social and emotional life skills atrophy and we get worse at communicating and interacting with each other in person.

Devorah Heitner,[264] who teaches and speaks on growing up in the digital world, catalogues the issues that have come up when social media use interferes with healthy development. Parents tell her that they worry that their children are creating fake online personas that are nothing like who they really are. They question why their kids feel the need to do this and what the long-term effects might be. She reports that parents see social comparison to other kids and people warping their child's sense of identity and seeding dissatisfaction with who they are.

In the end, however, it's not the amount of time spent on social media that by itself is a problem, it's what a child or adolescent is doing on social media that can be detrimental.[265] So while just being on a screen has some potential negatives, the other part is that the activities being pursued can affect mental health in unfortunate ways, as well as the content that they encounter.

For some teens, too much screen time and social media use can contribute to depression or anxiety.[266] There seems to be a line here, however, that points to the type of social media use that can cause depression or anxiety and the kind of use that has neutral or positive effects on youth. Researchers have determined that there are two types of social media use.[267] Remember, we are referring to apps like YouTube, Instagram, TikTok, texting/messaging, and X (formerly Twitter)".

When a user passively consumes internet content, it can contribute to sadness, depression, or anxiety.[268] Passive consumption includes mindless scrolling, curating other people's feeds, watching videos, and staring at pictures of beautiful and talented people. Passive use of social media means perusing others' social media pages without interacting with the person who created the page. When media consumption encourages constant comparison of oneself to people in perfectly posed pictures and flawlessly shopped photos, it can turn into a downer that leads to depression.[269] This is particularly true of adolescents.

Active consumption is a different way to engage with social media.[270] It includes posting one's own material, not just looking at others' posts. It means making fun videos and sharing them with trusted others. Active consumption involves reciprocally sharing messages and messaging with friends and families. Active users are less prone to being negatively impacted by socially comparing themselves to the gorgeous and gifted, and this is particularly true for adolescents who are self-conscious about how they look and appear to others, especially girls.[271]

Technoference

Researchers, among other types of academic folks, have the great fun of inventing new words. A recent example of such words is *technoference*. This delightful word was given to us by three researchers, Brandon McDaniel, Jenny Radesky, and Sarah Coyne, and it means technology's interference in our lives.[272] In other words, technoference is when you are talking to someone and they stop talking to you and look at their cell phones. Or it means, someone is trying to talk to you and you are oblivious because you are floating around in cyberworld using your cell phone, iPad, or computer. It drives most of us crazy, but unfortunately, it rarely stops any of us from doing it to someone else.

Technoference is apparently pretty common between romantic partners, parents, and parents and their children.[273] Research gives us multiple examples of its effects on our interactions with each other, and it starts early in life. Infants get agitated when their mothers curtail social activity with them to respond to a text message.[274] Repeated interruptions between children and parents due to technoference seem to increase young children's acting out.[275] Additionally, parents have less patience when addressing a child's misbehavior if they are on their phones.[276] By acting out, we mean restlessness or hyperactivity, easily being frustrated, and having temper tantrums. But kids can also respond with what is called internalizing behaviors and these include behaviors such as pouting, sulking, and easily having their feelings hurt.[277]

We have known for a long time that little kids who watch a lot of TV can have delayed language development.[278] We also know that parental technoference interferes with children's language development, too.[279] This can happen when parents pay more attention to their phones than their children when they are engaged in daily routines such as eating, bathing, dressing, playing, and preparing for bed. And, not surprisingly, when parents are on their phones and ignoring their children, children are more apt to misbehave.[280] Apparently, kids want our attention and will become troublesome when they don't get it.

People feel most snubbed[281] when a person responds to a ping or call on their cell phone as opposed to a tablet or a laptop. This is because people currently associate tablets and laptops with work obligations and cell phones with personal relationships. So when a friend takes a call on a cell phone, it feels like being dissed in favor of someone or something more important. When parents routinely phub (phone snub) their teens it correlates with adolescent anxiety, depression, and involvement in cyberbullying.[282]

Social Media Multitasking

Human beings think that they are fabulous at multi-tasking. Some of us even put it on our resumes as a celebrated work skill. The truth, however, is that we suck at multitasking. Researchers have proven that when we try to do two things at once, we generally do them both poorly.[283] About one in a million of us or so can really do two things at once with 100% success at both. So the bad news is that someone or something gets short shrift when we are multitasking, engaging with social media and doing other tasks at the same time.

One of the first functions that takes a hit when we engage in social media multitasking is the quality of our thinking.[284] Our working memory shrinks. Working memory is the ability to hold something just immediately learned in the mind while continuing with a task that is already in progress. It's like hanging on to two thoughts at the same time, which is important to be able to do when we are thinking about complex ideas or problems. Additionally, our attention falters and we lose the ability to filter distractions. In other words, multitasking, with one of the tasks being social media use, creates attention problems.[285] It also reduces our ability to perform sophisticated and complicated thinking. Brain scientists call this skill executive functioning, something critical to making sound decisions and well-thought-out choices. Perhaps this is why heavy multimedia use and multitasking impairs cognitive control, academic performance, and social behaviors, like making friends. Researchers found that children ages four to six had trouble being patient and making friends at school when they spent high amounts of time in front of screens.[286] And a study of children in a museum environment indicated difficulty moving from a social media experience on a screen to a social interaction with a peer.[287]

Kids with ADHD who were prone to having problematic social media use before COVID-19, experienced worsening symptoms when they spent too much time on social media.[288] That means their attention spans got even shorter, they became more anxious, their executive functions became more impaired, they exhibited more oppositional defiant disordered behavior, and their behavior negatively affected the home environment.

Online Gaming

Screen time was once thought to be an equal opportunity nuisance when it came to youth and social media. That is not so. The one activity that doesn't contribute to depression or anxiety (unless it involves cyberbullying) and doesn't take a toll on visual attention, working memory, or task switching, is online gaming.[289] Online gaming is an active pastime. It involves critical thinking, good decision-making, attention to detail, and is not something usually done while surfing the internet or posting selfies. Too much time in the cyberworld slaying dragons or chasing criminals can cause weight gain and loss of physical well-being, but that's because of its sedentary nature. One must do it sitting in front of a screen.

That doesn't rule out all the problems connected to screen time, like technoference, sleep deprivation, or even eye strain, myopia, or dry eye. And it can also result in addiction to social media, a problem that needs to be studied much more, because unlike abstaining from alcohol or smoking, it's nearly impossible to stay off the grid forever.

Addiction to the Internet and Social Media

Scientists have concluded that social media has been designed to suck us in and keep us there.[290] Our brains easily become addicted to the pings, flashes, enticements, and juicy bait that dangle prettily before our eyes and ears. Researchers have developed a number of scales or assessments that are intended to bring attention to behaviors that indicate an addictive relationship to social media. The questions below capture many of the dimensions of the problem. This one is from work done by Nazir Hawi and Maya Samaha.[291] Check yourself out with the following social media addiction scale or think of someone close to you (like a child or a partner) and answer for them as best you can. Just answer "yes" or "no" to each question:

1. I often think about media when I'm not using it.
2. I often use social media for no particular reason.
3. Arguments have arisen with others because of my media use.
4. I interrupt whatever I'm doing when I feel the need to access social media.
5. I feel connected to others when I use social media.
6. I lose track of time when I am using social media.
7. The thought of being unable to access social media makes me distressed.
8. I have been unable to reduce my social media use.

Anyone who answers "yes" to all of those statements may want to check into a social media addiction rehab program, which probably don't exist today, but in the future, surely will.

Internet addiction can have adverse effects on teens' physical, mental, emotional, and social development.[292] Risk factors for becoming addicted to the internet offer a terrifying list of negative life circumstances: poor academic performance, depression, suicidal ideation, and living in a chaotic and disorganized family.[293] Demographic factors include being male, being in a higher grade in school, having parents with a lower education level, and parental use of restrictive and autocratic practices.[294] While screen time and social media use don't seem to affect academic performance for most kids,[295] addiction and problematic social media use do negatively affect academic performance for some of these vulnerable kids.[296] For some youth, their demographics, life circumstances, and excessive internet use are a recipe for disappearing into a black hole and never resurfacing.[297]

Not all children, however, are at risk of getting permanently sucked into the whorl of drama, and not all parents are thoughtless media zombies, but there is enough evidence to raise concerns about children and families. How we parent is influenced by multiple factors including our personality traits, educational background, social class, finances, where we live, religious beliefs and practices, culture, and our own childhood experiences.

Dial Down on Screens

Over time, society has learned how to successfully integrate new technology into our lives so that it doesn't dominate or control us. That has been true of the printing of books, inventions like the television and the telephone, and now mobile communication devices. There is always a sorting-things-out transition during which we figure out how to use these tools in ways that are good for us and for society.

The World Health Organization (WHO) and American Academy of Pediatrics (AAP) recommend very limited screen time until children are well into toddlerhood.[298] WHO guidelines advocate for no screens until age two. AAP recommends screen time of no more than one hour per day for children who are 18 months old to five years old. And, of course, this is for high quality programming. Besides encouraging physical activity and nonsedentary time, these guidelines promote time for face-to-face interaction with live humans, a critical need for developing minds.

Screens became a lifeline for education during the COVID-19 pandemic, but it is critical to remember that learning from tablets and television delivers 50% less learning than real-life experiences with people and objects around them, especially for younger children.[299] Finally, as kids become adolescents, the research tells us that it's not so much the quantity of screen time, but what teens are doing when they are on the internet.[300] As we've said before, active consumption is far better than passive consumption and may have no negative effects on youth. However, one factor that affects every child's engagement with social media is personality; those prone to drama are more likely to get in trouble with social media than those who are not, and the more time spent on social media, the more the potential for experiencing harassment and online bullying.[301]

Virtual Reality and the Next Screen

Technology marches forward and new tools for communication, entertainment, and learning will continue to enter our world and shape our lives. Virtual reality (VR) is a form of computer simulation that provides a three dimensional visual and auditory experience.[302] It requires wearing a headset that is attached over the face and ears and secured to the head. Several technology companies have mass produced them, making them more readily available to the public. Virtual reality headsets block out real sights and sounds and replaces them with a simulated experience that comes very close to real life, minus the smells and until recently, the tactile features of the place where a person is located. Entering a virtual reality environment is like being *in* a movie, not just watching it. You feel like you are moving along with the people, vehicles, and plot, not just observing actions at a distance. It can be quite absorbing and intense.

Research on the effects of the virtual reality headset is scant to nonexistent. In looking for information on this topic, it became apparent that the medical field may have been the first to realize the value of virtual reality experiences for patients who needed to undergo painful medical treatments.[303] A scan of the extant articles indicates that encouraging patients to don a virtual reality headset can be used for all kinds of treatments for conditions like cancer, cerebral palsy, ADD/ADHD, severe burns, pre-medical-procedure anxiety, and fear of needle injections.[304]

The virtual reality experience is an effective way to help someone manage a medically helpful, but painful physical or emotional condition or procedure.

Another valuable use of virtual reality is in the realm of education. Virtual reality headset content is being tested and employed for training purposes including teaching children to treat each other with kindness and respect instead of using aggression or violence.[305] One study specifically focused on using VR to increase knowledge about the environment in order to promote more sustainable environmental attitudes and practices.[306] A meta-analysis (a review of the findings of multiple studies on the same subject) by Dr. Zhonggen Yu[307] concluded that education may be the field that can benefit the most from VR. He cites that VR experiences in the field of surgery show promise where procedures can be observed in a three-dimensional setting that doesn't involve a real human. Yu's meta-analysis also found evidence that when VR was coupled with other teaching methods, like video, lecture, or reading, there is a higher quality learning experience and better outcomes for the student.

So, with all of this good news about using virtual reality to improve our lives in the real world, what could be the downside? Research hasn't begun to answer this question in any comprehensive way, but there are a few hints here and there, and a few lessons from the past that can point to what the future might bring.

Today's VR headsets are rather heavy, so too much use can lead to temporary neck and shoulder discomfort. There is even a condition called simulation sickness or cybersickness which can include head or neck pain, eye discomfort, headaches, nausea, or motion sickness.[308] Porter and Robb solicited information from adults who regularly used VR headsets regarding symptoms that can develop after more than one hour's use on a daily basis. These aftereffects mostly involved depth perception confusion, vision issues, and a loss of body ownership in the real world. All of those in the study reported that the symptoms disappeared after continued use of VR.[309] Thus, it seems that initial problems went away for adults and their bodies adapted. Bexson and her colleagues investigated the effects of VR use on children, and while they didn't find much suggesting that VR caused problems for kids, they did say that the effects of VR use need more research around the possible long-term effects on well-being and behavior.[310] One study they cited loosely mentioned a potential problem experienced by a child. The young fellow wore a headset for an hour a day for an extended period and experienced nose deformity because of the weight of the goggles on his face. It seems that some of the VR apparatus may be a bit heavy or ill-fitting for the heads of children.

One novel use of the virtual reality technology is to invite people into a virtual store where they can purchase real items.[311] Imagine that shopping on Amazon allows you to enter a virtual reality sales environment. (If I were to guess, I'd bet that Bezos is already testing this technology out, so by the time you read this, this could all be passé.) To get the best shopping experience you don your VR headset and strap a band to your arm (similar to a blood pressure cuff). You log in, pick the type of items you are interested in buying, and quick as a nanosecond, you find yourself in a store that feels real and has many of the items of interest to you. A shopping assistant comes up to you and welcomes you to the store and touches you on the arm during her greeting. Magically, you feel her touch as pressure on your arm, just as you would in real life. However, she's not real nor is her hand on your arm, but you experience both as real. The arm band, designed to simulate human contact, creates the sensation of having been touched.

The study that describes this type of VR shopping experience was conducted to find out if being touched on the arm virtually by a virtual sales associate would get a shopper to enjoy the experience more and to spend more money.[312] Such shopper-sales assistant interaction in real life has proven to get people to buy more than if the person were not touched on the arm. Zhao and colleagues found that the virtual touch on the arm was as successful as the real touch on the arm in getting people to have a good time shopping and to buy more stuff.[313]

It is hardly surprising that we may all be shopping this way soon, but what is shocking is that we have begun to cross the line where people can experience human touch without being touched by a human. The technology is there. All that is needed is a body suit with scads of motorized pressure points and we can feel like we are being hugged when there isn't a person within five miles of us. I suppose this will benefit someone, but on the grand scale of our humanity, it doesn't feel like progress. It feels regressive. It is disturbing. I'm not certain if this type of technology is supposed to be entertaining or soothing, but it feels isolating and depressing to me.

Returning to what is not yet in the research on VR use, is just what we've touched on (pun intended). When a person chooses a virtual experience, the world and the people around that person, if there are people there, are all blocked out. I experienced it myself when our university held a small roundtable on VR and offered us the chance to demo the unit under discussion. I found the experience to be pleasant, but since I was the last person interested in trying it, I found myself all alone in the room when I took the headset off. I had hoped to discuss my thoughts on the experience with the others when I was done, but they had all left. No one was there because watching me jive to the music was of no interest to them. They were bored. I was the only one having fun and they were not part of it. It was a huge letdown for me to find myself deserted. The takeaway was that VR would isolate us even more than fixating on our hand-held screens has already done.

Our kids don't need this form of technological entertainment (unless they have some desperate need for distraction like having a burn wound redressed). I predict that when we have found kids who are living much of their real lives in a virtual reality, perhaps even wearing the aforementioned bodysuit, we will discover kids who are badly educated, socially inept, emotionally depressed, civically disengaged, and even possibly physically ill. We just don't need to subject our children to anymore entertainment that takes them away from us and has the potential to diminish their humanity. And a cautionary word to adults: We don't need it either.

So what are the downsides of too much screen time, social media exposure, and living one's life online? Why has the surgeon general of the United States taken a firm stand on reducing social media use for youth?

USE OF SCREENS AND THE DOWNSIDES

In a nutshell, there is an arm's length list of problems that can occur when kids, teens, and adults spend too much time on their two-way screens. Some of it is just common sense and probably not too serious, but some of it is downright scary especially when it comes to our youth: loss of focus and concentration, cranky behaviors and irritability, anxiety, weight gain, depression, and addiction. And this list doesn't include the physical dangers of texting or scrolling while walking or driving.[314]

As noted previously, technoference is a real problem. People acknowledge that our electronic devices and screens have inserted themselves in our lives to some pretty detrimental outcomes. Any parent will tell you that their kids' behaviors deteriorate when the parents are distracted by a two-way screen. They jump around, tug at their parents, and often get into mischief. A study done with small children looked at how screen time affected their ability to delay gratification (hold off getting a small reward now for a bigger one later) and how screen time affected their behaviors with other children.[315] They found that kids were less able to have self-control and were more impatient with their peers during social interactions. In other words, more screen time can make four- to six-year-olds grumpy and anti-social, and results in difficulties making friends at school.[316]

A decade ago, we found out that when we took cell phones away from kids when they went to summer camp, their social behavior and relationship skills improved.[317] Kids got better at understanding nonverbal facial cues. Since then, media-free or media-reduced summer camps have increased in number. And when it comes to cell phones in the classroom, some states are prohibiting them outright.[318] This is in the hopes that it will improve academic learning and reduce certain types of problematic behavior, not to mention students' social interactions. I can tell you that as a teacher, cell phones in the classroom are a nonstarter, even at the college and adult professional development levels.

Not surprisingly, a new social anxiety disorder called nomophobia is on the rise.[319] Nomophobia is a psychological condition whereby a person gets anxious when they don't have access to a cell phone that is connected to the internet. I once took a college student's cell phone away from him during class and put it on my desk where he could still see it. Notably, it was only five feet away. He couldn't take his eyes off the phone, and he became visibly fidgety. While I don't think he was paying attention when he was looking at his cellphone screen, unfortunately I don't think his focus improved when I took it away from him either.

The list of problems that can impact mental health continues to expand. This includes a psychological affliction called selfitis and is described as an urgent need to take selfies.[320] The worse it gets, the more the person cannot resist the desire to post selfies on social media. It comes in three stages: borderline, chronic, and acute. I'm not sure what to think about this one except that it does sound like it could be a feature of a narcissistic personality disorder. And of course, posting selfies has the potential to create drama because the posts may be ignored by people we hope will respond, or it may invite comments that are unflattering. Either situation can make the poster upset and that can be the trigger that sets drama in motion.

I'm certain that many of us have had the experience of going to a family event and seeing everyone between the ages of five and 20 sitting silently in a room together staring at their electronic pads or smartphones. Trying to interact with these youth is tantamount to shouting from the top of a mountain to people six miles away. The screen world feels incredibly impenetrable, and I can't help but think it is really bad for our kids. Long before researchers began to study social media and screen addictions, I had a feeling that something potentially addictive was going on. Fifteen years ago or so, a father at a presentation I did on bullying and cyberbullying told me that when he took his teen daughter's cell phone away from her she acted like an alcoholic forced to go cold turkey.

Depression and anxiety are the really troubling effects of too much social media exposure and two-way screen time.[321] We know that not all kids who spend time on social media get depressed or anxious, but it is a problem, and a serious one for some youth. One of the issues has to do with comparisons of the images on the screen to the reality of the child looking at the screen.[322] When kids compare themselves to the perfect bodies, perfect lives, and the personal wealth that is often portrayed by people and celebrities online they can become depressed, especially for girls who are more likely than boys to be affected negatively by all the images that reinforce the need to be beautiful and perfect.[323] The more time youth spend sucking up these unrealistic and damaging portrayals of fake lives, the more they question their value and feel inadequate.[324] So it's not surprising that kids who spend excessive amount of time on social media feel as if they have lost control of their lives.[325]

Other problems instigated by too much screen time include exposure to cyberbullying and a sense that one's peers are having more fun and more excitement.[326] We know that social media is often one way of experiencing ostracism.[327] It's disheartening and sad to be the kid who gets left out and sees peers or former friends out and about socializing and having a good time, all because it's posted online—while sitting alone on the other side of screen.

HOW ARE KIDS DOING?

In 2001 a group of researchers authored an article entitled "The Kids are Alright." It was a study that looked at youth as they moved from adolescence into adulthood and considered their personality development. They found that almost all kids matured smoothly and became well-functioning adults. Their words were "many adolescents became more controlled and socially more confident and less angry and alienated"[328] as they got older. A few years later when I started collecting data for my dissertation, I agreed with Brent Roberts and his colleagues. I saw lots of research that said that kids were doing OK. Researchers said that the stereotype of adolescence as a time of "sturm and drang" (storm and stress) was more about media hype than a finding based in fact.

Older folks have always seemed to have a blind spot when it came to remembering what they were like as kids.[329] Growing up, I got the sense that adults often took a dim view of young people. I experienced it as a child myself. I remember adults saying insulting things about kids right in front of us. It felt demeaning. I recently had this discussion about youth and the state of our world, with a relative who is the same age as I am, and she said the same things about kids these days that were being said about us when we were kids. Things haven't changed much.

Fifteen years ago, I started looking into the research on moral panics that focused on kids.[330] Moral panics usually happen at a time when there is a sense of fear about changing social norms. They often zero in on youth and behaviors that are disturbing to the establishment. That includes all kinds of phenomena, from what kids wear to gender reassignment surgery. More than a dozen years ago, I concurred with the conclusion of Roberts and colleagues that kids were nothing like what the old folks thought they were, and that they were in much better shape than the consensus of most adults.[331] Most of the time moral panics are a lot of hype laced with too much emotion, about something not very important. Sounds like drama to me.

But now, 20-some years after the Roberts's publication, I am not so sure. I am worried about youth and so are some other people, including teens themselves.

In 2017 Jean Twenge published a book titled *iGen: Why Today's Super-Connected Kids are Growing Up Less Rebellious, More Tolerant, Less Happy—and Completely Unprepared for Adulthood.*[332] Dr. Twenge is a data expert. She takes the forty-thousand-foot view, crunching information on thousands of people to see what kinds of trends are moving along in our society. She is particularly interested in huge data swings that occur in short periods of time, and she found one in 1994-95. What she saw was alarming because it had to do with youth, the kids born at a time when the internet and the almighty smartphone would be in their lives pretty much every moment of their lives. She called this generation of youth iGen. Today they are also called Generation Z.[333] These are the kids who spend significant amounts of time on smartphones, who connect virtually with friends as opposed to face-to-face, and are more likely to experience mental health problems than any generation before them. Twenge was not the only person to be concerned.

Jonathan Haidt is a social psychologist who studies and writes about issues that trouble us, divide us, and cause difficult social problems. He thinks a lot about morality, emotions, and culture, topics that also pop up when we consider social drama. In his most recent book, he expresses concern about an "epidemic of mental illness" affecting youth, which is part of the subtitle of his book.[334] The causes of this trend are multiple. He cites the issues of too much screen time, too much time on social media, too much time living in the virtual world, too little sleep (because of cell phones), too much surveillance (helicopter parenting), not enough free and independent childhood play, not enough face-to-face interaction with peers, not enough exercise, and too much fear of physical, emotional, and psychological risk. This generation is slow to grow up, afraid to take chances, and are at risk for mental health problems.

Lauren Greenfield, a film maker, wondered what life was like for this generation, the teens who have always had access to smart phones and social media, the same kids that Twenge and Haidt worry about. She found a group of older teens, kids who lived part of high school through Covid-19 and online learning and are moving into late adolescence. She asked if she could follow them in school for a year and at the same time, give her access to the content of their cellphones. Her five-part docuseries, *Social Studies*,[335] aired on FX in late 2024.

In the film, she talks to students about what kinds of content they have filmed of themselves and what they have done with it. All of the students had posted clips that went viral, meaning their videos were viewed thousands of times, which Greenfield explained was the Holy Grail of social media, because it made them famous, and able to claim celebrity status. What was most interesting about these kids who live through social media was how naïve they are. One girl, who admitted to having a sex video ready to go, spoke admiringly of Kim Kardashian. She believed that if she put her sex tape out there, she "could become a multi-millionaire, buy a giant company, and become famous like Kim Kardashian." This young woman claimed that "She's (Kim Kardashian) all set up with her whole family. She got famous for her sex tape on platforms like TikTok. Anyone can get famous."[336]

Lauren Greenfield agrees with Jonathan Haidt that smartphones, social media, and the internet have stolen childhood from these kids. She states that these kids suffer from "algorithm pressure," not peer pressure, and because they have been exposed to horribly graphic sexual content, they lost their innocence long before the end of high school. Another participant in the docuseries observed that the more time she spends on TikTok, the more anxious she gets.[337] No wonder… being in their screens is what they do all day long.

Not only are adults concerned, so are teens themselves. When adolescents talk to therapists and social workers they speak as if they are facing an apocalypse, as if the world is imploding, that everything is hopeless, and that they can't envision a future.[338] These teens see the dreadful political and social polarization in this country and question what kind of life is coming their way. They see adults around them unhappy and struggling and question their own identity and their purpose in life. Not all youth struggle this way, but enough of them do that being a parent today has become a highwire act. So how can parents get the support and help that they need?

CHAPTER 10
Parenting in the Digital Age

PARENTING HAS NEVER BEEN easy. Each generation faces some of the same challenges of previous generations, but also some new and often perplexing ones. Certainly, the digital age comes with its own set of problems. Children born after 1994 have never known a world without the internet,[339] and since most youth have a smart phone on their person or within hand's reach during and beyond waking hours, parents have to accept the reality of the permanent presence of electronic communication devices in our lives.

All is not lost, however, because we know what successful parenting looks like, and it's not that difficult to understand. Researchers have known that human beings do best in environments where their experiences are both supportive and loving, and at the same time structured and regulated. So what does that mean?

Children especially need to know and feel the love and caring from the adults who take care of them. They need to see smiling faces looking at them, preferably not through screens, but face-to-face. They need to be talked to and invited to speak back. They need to be held and hugged and told they are good and worthy. Their goodness and good behavior need to be noted and encouraged. At the same time, though, they need to be taught and held to behavioral standards that are caring and respectful. Our modeling of those behaviors is critical. The norms that support those behaviors and attitudes need to be specifically taught. In other words, we need to help them form an identity that is moral, and by moral we mean knowing what is the common good and acting on it. Identities are both individual and collective, and parents need to help children cultivate both.

Diana Baumrind[340] described three types of parenting: authoritarian, authoritative, and permissive. Unfortunately, the first two types sound a lot alike, and this makes it confusing. But they are very different styles. Starting with the last type of parenting, being a permissive parent is akin to helicopter parenting. This involves too much involvement, too much monitoring, too much rescuing, and too much of everything so there is never disappointment or frustration. The first type of parenting, the authoritarian style, is rigid, cold, demanding, and exacting. "Authority" is king, and the children have none. Children need autonomy to take risks, make mistakes, and learn from them, but in autocratic, authoritarian families, risks and mistakes are punished. The middle type of parenting is authoritative, and that means that kids are involved in their own development, that parents give kids leeway and help them recover from bad choices. It means getting second chances but being held accountable. In authoritative families, people are responsible for what they do, and face consequences (not harsh ones) and get second chances after bad behavior.

Overvaluation of a child is detrimental, but so is an absence of love and harsh, unforgiving treatment. Love should never be conditional. Conditional love is associated with certain behaviors instead of being inherently fixed and permanent and directed at the whole child, not the child's behavior. Conditional love comes with strings attached. Kids develop best when we love them no matter what, but still hold them responsible for the unfortunate things they may do.

While personality has a genetic component, genes are not destiny. Environment also plays a role, and we have a lot of influence over environment when our children are little. We can discourage the personality traits and characteristics that feed drama. All the nasties like entitlement, narcissism, and selfishness can be counteracted by how we respond to our children's behavior. Encouraging generosity and sharing, and learning how to recognize and interpret the feelings of others can be taught early on and reinforced over and over as children and their thinking becomes more sophisticated. Learning how to be kind is just as important as learning to do math or to read.

Part of counteracting too much "me-ness" in our children is reframing how we view competition. We need to coach children to understand that winning isn't everything. We shouldn't use competition to pit youth against each other, nor should it be what makes them think their talent or success is what makes them worthy of love from us. Of course, for many of us, the need to come out on top every time is baked into our psyches, but it really has contributed to the problems of ingroup bias and outgroup hatred. We need to help children accept loss graciously. Youth need to understand that everyone loses sometimes and it's OK. There is *always* going to be someone out there who is better, smarter, more attractive, or more talented than any given child. My child needs to know that I think he or she is the most wonderful child in the world, but it stops there. Except for grandparents and a few other close relatives, kids shouldn't expect all the other adults around them to hold them so dear and treat them like a little prince or princess.

PARENTING AND THE SELF-ESTEEM DEBATE

In June of 2012 at the Wellesley High School Graduation ceremony, an English teacher from the school had the audacity to tell the graduates that they were not special.[341] David McCullough, Jr. told them lovingly and affectionately that they had been "pampered, cosseted, doted upon, helmeted, and bubble wrapped." With great humor, he exposed the truth of our era. That grades are inflated and standards for greatness have been relaxed. That appearances are more important than substance, and that when everyone gets a trophy, trophies mean nothing. He had the temerity to tell these young people that there are a whole lot more kids on the planet just like them. Despite their success at graduating from high school, they were not special.

When McCollough's speech went viral, the "self-esteemers" went crazy and made a big stink. They said that comments like this would damage students' self-esteem and were contrary to everything we know about children's successful development. David McCullough's words touched a nerve that had been fertilized by years of media attention to a research construct termed "self-esteem." That nerve was the belief that more than anything, enhancing and protecting our children's self-esteem was critical to their developing selfhood and competitive edge in the world. Bad or low self-esteem was the death knell of making it in the world.

Self-esteem is defined as how a person evaluates him or herself.[342] It is thought of as a trait or characteristic that is more or less stable but can be influenced by daily events. Self-esteem is a person's feelings about him or herself as either positive or negative. If a person has positive self-esteem, he sees himself as worthy and capable. He likes himself. In such a case, on a self-esteem "test'" that person will be designated as having high self-esteem. If a person's feelings about herself are negative, she will see herself as unworthy and incompetent. On the self-esteem "test," she will score in the range that reflects low self-esteem. In other words, she doesn't like herself very much. Self-esteem is integral to one's identity and self-concept.[343] So, it would seem desirable to think highly of oneself.

That's the way the nonscientific world interpreted the research world's discussion of self-esteem. The takeaway was that if our children didn't have high self-esteem they would become bullies, slackers, cheaters, academic failures, losers, and friendless, violent criminals. This position, which by the way is completely false, led to parenting and educational practices that were designed so that children never felt pain, failure, or disappointment.[344] Repeatedly, in preschool, Sunday school, and just about every activity they joined, they were told, "You are special." The principle at work here is based on the assumption that if a child never feels bad, she'll have high self-esteem, and therefore, a child must always feel good so she'll have high self-esteem.

The problem with this approach is that it led to parent overvaluation of children, which contributes to narcissism.[345] Parenting practices have been studied with regards to how they factor into the development of a narcissistic child, and it's been determined that kids do best when we have high but realistic expectations of them, love them unconditionally, hold them responsible for mistakes and bad behaviors, and support their efforts to do well for the sake of doing well.[346] Good parenting is responsive, but not indulgent. It doesn't rescue kids from the consequences of bad choices, mean behaviors, or various kinds of failure. Good parenting helps kids understand these events and how they affect people, but they don't helicopter them out of the situation and make the discomfort go away. Overvaluation and permissiveness seem to contribute to grandiose narcissism.[347]

However, as noted previously, there is another kind of narcissism referred to earlier as vulnerable narcissism.[348] This type of narcissism is connected to life experiences that are damaging or abusive such as physical, sexual, or psychological abuse, traumatic and painful childhood experiences, and rigid, cold, and demanding parenting. Abusive parenting can result in a myriad of bad outcomes for their offspring, and a narcissistic child with fragile high self-esteem, or low self-esteem is one of them.[349]

Confusion regarding whether aggressive behaviors are due to low or high self-esteem has perplexed professionals and experts for years.[350] Some of these folks, "Group One," believe that people who are aggressive have low self-esteem, basing this on the belief that only people who don't like themselves would have a reason to be mean, aggressive, or violent. The other group of experts, "Group Two," sees it differently. They say that aggression is not caused by low self-esteem; it's caused by people who have high self-esteem, as they are the type that lash out when they get angry. In order to reconcile the views on this controversy, Group Two contends that all high self-esteem is not equal. Instead, they believe that grandiose narcissists have high, but *fragile* self-esteem, which is different from the vulnerable narcissists who have low self-esteem and are *not* aggressive.

What makes grandiose narcissists different from other people who have a healthy and high level of self-esteem is that theirs isn't the "fragile" type.[351] These nonnarcissistic people have authentic, realistic, and high self-esteem. They are not aggressive. These people like themselves too, but they can handle criticism, accept failure, and see the world from other people's perspectives without having a meltdown.[352] Not so with fragile, high self-esteem folks. And to make matters worse, a few experts believe that some unique narcissists can flip back and forth between being grandiose and being vulnerable.[353] For sure, these folks *are* special! They keep their world and everyone around them spinning out of control. It's drama on steroids.

As we will discuss later, self-esteem that is solid, authentic, and high is acquired by living with life's difficulties, picking oneself up after debacles, learning to share and care, being able to put other people ahead of oneself, and being able to honestly say: *I don't know. I need help. I'm sorry. I was wrong.*[354] Sadly, the number of people who can utter these words are few and far between for narcissists.

Being told you are special from the day you are born does not give a person healthy self-esteem. It turns him into a narcissist. So what does this have to do with anything? Well, in today's world, when narcissism is on the increase, it also seems that other problems are increasing, too. For some youth, self-esteem is entangled in the problem of narcissism, as is an increase in anxiety and depression. And something that may influence all of it is social media and living through our screens.

PARENTAL PRESENCE BUT NOT TOO MUCH

Parenting is one of the most difficult jobs any of us might ever undertake. Yet, it is probably more important than most jobs we ever sign up for. Considering the challenges of raising children who are inclined to do drama, we need some ideas to help us redirect the instincts that lead kids down that path.

The downside of too much excessive parental monitoring is that it is counterproductive.[355] Too much vigilance and oversight curtail freedom, creativity, and self-expression. It may sound contradictory, but today's children are more surveilled than any other generation, and the result is a fair number of youths who don't know how to grow up and function like adults. Kids have become comfortable and complacent letting parents handle the big stuff. They are risk-averse and would rather be safe than take on challenges.[356]

Kids used to be able to do fun and risky things away from the prying eyes of adults, but now they don't have that luxury because many adults are in panic mode.[357] That's because a few young people have broadcast the bad things they do either by discussing them on social media, tweeting about them, or worse yet, videoing them and posting them online. Parents live in "fear mode," so they helicopter their children's comings and goings. This excessive surveillance didn't just begin recently; it's been going on for a while. It is prompted by things like calls for universal sexuality education, fear of the corrupting influence of certain books, or promoting the well-being of all children including those who don't identify as strictly male or female. The difficulty of this adult fear that turns into too much surveillance is that it denies reality and results in children who aren't sure how to identify with each other or their society. When we don't tell kids the truth and let them take some chances with it, we deny them the ability to develop an authentic identity.

Excessive surveillance also appears to create anxiety in kids.[358] For several decades, parents have micromanaged their children's lives, often connected to fear for their children's safety and well-being. This manifested itself in too many lessons, too many games, too many rehearsals and practices, and too much adult supervision. Kids' lives were so structured that they never had any time on their own to take chances, make mistakes, and get themselves out of messes. We've raised a generation or two of kids who are afraid of the physical world because we taught them that the world was a dangerous place, and constantly reinforced it by the restrictions we placed on them.

There is a growing movement to relax our rules when it comes to kids doing things on their own. Things like playing outside without being watched, going to a friend's house without being driven or accompanied by an adult, riding a bike to a new neighborhood, or taking a bus or subway to an activity. Several psychologists and social psychologists have critiqued the current state of childhood and suggested that children need more freedom, more privacy from adult surveillance, and more responsibility.[359]

When I was 11 years old, my youngest sibling was born. We lived three blocks from a small plaza that contained a grocery store. Our family only had one car and my mom was unable to haul four of us on foot to the store for groceries. I had shown responsible tendencies and was quite capable of going most places in our neighborhood alone. So, she wrote a grocery list, including the prices of the items, gave me an envelope with the correct amount of money, and sent me off with our Red Flyer wagon to buy groceries. The trip was successful, she didn't get a visit from child protective services, and the only mistake I made was buying cabbage instead of iceberg lettuce.

For sure the world is different today, but not such that we have to imprison kids in their homes so they don't get hurt. Becoming self-sufficient and learning how to do things is a great confidence booster, and child psychologists are telling us now that this will reduce kids' anxiety. Most kids are far more capable than we give them credit for, and when we teach them how to navigate the physical world, they just might spend less time living in their screens, with all the negatives they may confront there.

Lenore Skenazy[360] has spent over a decade promoting independence for kids. She recognized that her son was far more capable of navigating on his own than those who adhered to extensive parental hovering and protectiveness. At age nine she let him ride on the NYC subway by himself, of course after much preparation and practice. He did fine as she knew he would. What he gained was independence and an increase in self-confidence and agency. Jonathan Haidt,[361] a professor at NYU and a recognized authority on social trends, wholeheartedly supports Lenore's efforts to promote independence for kids. He believes that a childhood spent on a smartphone has terrible consequences for our children's development, and that coupled with too much parental helicoptering are part of the problem. He has concluded that one of the primary reasons for the high levels of youth anxiety today is the way that cellphones and social media have changed childhood. To counteract the negatives of too much screen time, he advocates for phone-free childhoods. *Hear! Hear!*

Recently, researchers have discovered that Diana Baumrind's exposé of parenting styles meshes with the challenges that social media has created in our families.[362] While this may sound contradictory to an all-out ban on smartphones for kids, it appears that if excessive and rigid oversight is how parents approach screen time and social media use, kids end up being targeted by or engaging in cyberbullying. Kids also report that they feel better about themselves and have better mental health when parents don't helicopter or overregulate their social media use. That said, too many kids get smartphones too soon and without much parental oversight. One of my friend's young adult family members echoes the sentiments of many kids, "My childhood ended when I got a smartphone."

Youth do much better when parents approach social media and its use from the "authoritative" perspective.[363] This involves a few, underlined, *a few*, reasonable rules that are age-appropriate and negotiated with the child. For example, no cell phones in their bedroom at night. Or, no phones at the table during dinner. This also includes active discussion and monitoring of the apps and media content that children are using. It means that kids share with parents what they are seeing, doing, and experiencing on social media. It's an open dialogue that builds kids' knowledge and parents' trust. Youth appreciate and respond positively to parents when they are taken seriously and feel parents understand them. Not so when the monitoring is rigid, inconsistent, or nonexistent.

One of the best ways to support our children in developing successfully is to put some boundaries into place that are reasonable, and both protective and freeing at the same time. This sort of parenting means that we construct and follow rules, establish routines, and outline and adhere to roles that are suitable for each person. When kids are young, we establish these roles and practices for them, but as kids get older, they become part of the discussion where these family boundaries are negotiated. Rules, roles, and routines offer guidance, structure, and predictability to life, and complement kids' abilities to think critically, make good decisions, support developing self-confidence and agency, and avoid drama.

Some youth have no wisdom, which means no perspective and little ability to notice the world around them (i.e., to pay attention). In addition, many have undeveloped critical thinking skills. They have loose boundaries. These kids post their less-than-stellar behavior, getting involved in bullying, cyberbullying, and horrible behavior captured and posted online. Our job as parents is to coach them in relationship and communication skills that reflect responsible and sensible social media use, and to know when to turn the phone off, do some mindful deep breathing, take a walk in nature, learn something without processing it through a screen or taking a picture of it, and just marvel at the world beyond the screen in the moment. And if possible, ditch your child's smartphone for a flip phone.[364]

Today's youth live in a world where their physical activity is overly and endlessly surveilled and restricted, but their cyber world is completely unregulated and unmonitored. Getting kids out of the cyberworld and into the real world of physical living is becoming more of a mandate than a fluffy idea. We need it so that they can develop into successful human beings.

HOW DO WE RAISE CHILDREN TO AVOID THE TRAP OF DRAMA?

Whether we love or hate Donald Trump[365] he is the perfect picture of a child no one wants to parent because he was and still is a star in the world of social drama. His horrible behaviors beg the question: How can we bring children into the world who will avoid the trap of drama?

Unfortunately, Donald Trump[366] was the recipient of parenting that was abusive and damaging. He didn't become a narcissistic bully all on his own. Others have written about his absent mother, and rigid, domineering, brutal, and dishonest father. His lack of positive characteristics seem to be connected to his childhood, adolescence, and early adult life experiences. He was encouraged to behave badly by his father, and then allowed to continue in these behaviors because he never faced any consequences. No one has been able to hold him accountable for the drama that he so skillfully foisted and continues to foist on anyone and anything within his reach—and with his success in the 2024 election, it appears he will never be held accountable for any of the crimes, alleged or otherwise, that he committed during his first term in office. He is a master maker of chaos, as are youth who indulge in high drama. One of the ways, perhaps the most important way, to deter this kind of behavior is by teaching youth how to think critically.

Critical Thinking

Drama often gets its juice from lying, manipulation, and egocentricity. These nasties infiltrate actions when people disengage from their moral compass, assuming they had one in the first place, of course. The antidote to moral disengagement is critical thinking, and we need to understand it, practice it, and teach our children how to do it.[367]

Critical thinking is defined as "the art of thinking about thinking while thinking to make thinking better."[368] Now that should make your head spin, but if you can make sense of it, you are likely a pretty good critical thinker. No child much younger than 13 or 14 is likely to be able to make common sense of the definition, but that doesn't mean kids that age and even younger can't learn some basic principles and develop some rudimentary skills that lay the groundwork for becoming a good thinker. Thinking and self-reflection skills need to be cultivated throughout life, but the foundation for these important abilities begins early on. That's where parenting and education come in.

Critical thinking requires the ability to reason and figure things out. It requires the ability to be fair-minded, which means being honest and truthful about what is and is not right or factual. It requires the courage and ability to put oneself in another person's shoes and view the world through that person's eyes, even when we don't see things the same way.

It means being able to identify emotions and recognize when they are biasing or skewing thinking.[369]

Drama is often based on stinking thinking. Here are some examples:

I'm always right. My gut is all I need to make a good decision. If I believe something, it is a fact. I know everything I need to know. It's true because I believe everything [x] says. It's fair because I say it's fair. I can do whatever I want to get what I want.

One of the ways that parents can help students involved in drama is to help them make sense of it. We can deconstruct it so that kids see the effects of their own and others' behaviors. Ask and answer these kinds of questions:

Why is this happening? Was I being fair when I said that? Did I stop to consider any other perspective besides my own? Is there another way of looking at this? Did I misunderstand someone's intentions? Was I blinded by my own sense of righteousness or entitlement? What choices would have precluded drama from developing? Were my instincts off on this situation? Did I overreact? Am I obsessing? Am I justifying bad behavior and blaming others for my circumstances?

To answer these and other questions about drama, we need to be able to think and reflect on what prompted it, fueled it, and kept it going. A major part of critical thinking is the ability to self-reflect. It is a coping mechanism that helps a person stand in someone else's shoes and study the effects of actions and reactions. It is closely related to the ability to empathize and understand how our actions impact others. It is also sometimes referred to as self-awareness.

None of this means that we shouldn't validate our children's emotions. Nothing is more discouraging than having someone you love tell you that you shouldn't feel the way you feel. But we can't let our kids jump into the world thinking that their feelings are more important than anyone else's, nor can we allow them to jump all over someone who has made them feel terrible. We need to respect and honor our children's feelings but teach them not to feel entitled to harm others when they feel hurt, angry, or jealous.

One of the greatest coping mechanisms of all time is a sense of humor. Being able to step out of your own pain or embarrassment, once it has been acknowledged and respected, is truly a gift. When the frustration, anger, and the desire to blame someone has passed, looking at the other side of the issue can be redemptive. That said, we should not rule out teaching kids how to stand up for themselves without using violence. We want our youth to be able to stand up to abuse and call it out. Standing up for yourself is not the same as taking someone out.

One of the major challenges for kids who do drama is to learn how to manage the tendency to ruminate on difficult experiences and the emotions that go with them. It's that process of not letting things go and letting feelings become dominating and overwhelming. Once kids can think about their thinking (i.e., think critically), we can help them process and understand what they are doing and how rumination can keep them in a funk. Having a conversation that starts with the question "What are you thinking?" (not the sarcastic version of this question) is a good place to begin. Talking through the situation is helpful, but after that we need to help our kids learn how to clear their minds and change the subject, at least for a bit. Helping them with a mindfulness activity can be a great coping technique. It would sound something like this:

> Close your eyes and begin by taking some breaths. I'll do it with you. As you breathe, think about breathing. Think of what it feels like in your body when you breathe in, breathe out, and then pause before you start your next breath. If your mind starts to focus on your emotions and what is causing those emotions, look at the darkness of the backs of your eyelids. Whenever you start to think thoughts, alternate between thinking about your breath and looking at the blackness behind your eyes.

Critical thinking helps us see contradictions, tell the difference between facts, opinions, and lies, make sound judgments, make choices based on reason, and recognize half-truths. It helps us avoid the incivility traps of moral disengagement, desensitization, disinhibition, and groupthink. Critical thinking is one of the most important skills our youth need to learn.

Most drama starts and is fueled by allowing emotions to take over one's thinking. It is related to selfishness, narcissism, and egocentricity. It puts the self in the center of every action and interaction. Ultimately, the way we think affects how we act, and this reflects our identity. Thus, thinking and learning how to manage our thinking are critical to who we are and how we behave; it communicates our identity to the world.

Boundaries

Drama thrives on the elimination of boundaries. Consider what can happen when a friend posts another friend's intimate or private information, shared in confidence, on social media. It may have been done innocently, or it may have been a deliberate attempt to exercise power over the friend, but regardless, it triggers hurt, anger, and probably some drama.

Research tells us that boundaries within relationships, social groups, and even whole societies are important for the health and success of relationships in those contexts.[370] Think about how we teach little children about physical boundaries. Hitting, kicking, pushing, and biting are unacceptable behaviors. We discourage these behaviors and teach kids to "use your words" to address frustration, anger, and hurt. We teach kids that they have the right to bodily integrity and to be able to understand and give consent to how others interact with them, both physically and socially.

Another form of boundaries are emotional ones.[371] Emotional boundaries are the ones that help us protect ourselves from too much of another person's angst. If we don't have boundaries, then we struggle to maintain our own emotional autonomy. Without emotional boundaries we can get sucked into someone else's feelings to our detriment. Boundaries of any kind help us know where we end and someone else begins. This might be fairly easy to determine when we are talking about physical boundaries, but not so when we are looking at emotions. If we have weak emotional boundaries, it is easy for others to blame us for their problems, make us take responsibility for the pain they inflict on other people, and feel responsible for their feelings.

I recently discussed boundaries with a friend who tended to have strong emotional reactions to upsetting situations when she was young. She indicated that she was not good at stuffing her emotions and that she expressed them, regardless of the setting or context when she was growing up. She told me that her family didn't set boundaries around expressing emotional responses, so she was accustomed to letting it all hang out. Admittedly, she was big on drama, not because she wanted to have big emotions, but because that was just who she was. This friend struggled as a youth with what kinds of emotional expressions were acceptable at home, at school, and with friends. She learned the hard way that what might be tolerated at home might cause problems at school, and cause drama with friends. She regrets that her family did not give her good coping skills to deal with emotions in socially appropriate ways.

One of her most painful life experiences was to be told that she was "exhausting" when she was being dramatic. For her, that was an outright rejection of what she was feeling and how she was communicating her feelings, and because it was her family who was dishing criticism, she felt excluded and rejected. Sadly, her family was unable to extend acceptance of her tendency to do drama and help her learn self-protective coping mechanisms to manage her emotions.

This woman also describes how the loose and permeable boundaries within the dynamics of her family made her a vulnerable target when someone was angry with her. Because she lacked self-awareness, she didn't push back when someone close to her was hurting her. Now she has boundaries around herself that protect her from these types of people and experiences. She draws lines and asserts them when there is the possibility that others will overstep their bounds. She knows when and how to hit the pause button, hold off for a bit, and avoid unnecessary and exhausting drama.

Boundaries are closely tied to identity, so it is easy to see how doing identity work might produce drama. Learning secrets and sharing them with the wrong people via social media can damage close relationships and teach us the hard way what a breach of confidence is for those we care about.

Often the best way to tackle a problem with drama is to address it head on in a kind, understanding, and thoughtful way.

Imagine having a conversation with a child who is upset and highly emotional about something. You may even want to immerse yourself in the social drama of the adolescent case study we've been exploring in this book. Think of yourself as one of the parents of the girls involved in the events. Consider asking these questions and discussing these topics:

Are you really upset for Sydney, or are you just enjoying being part of the action? Do you really care if Ian slept with Samantha when he was dating Sydney? It happened several months ago. How is anyone benefitting by digging this up and turning it into a three-ring circus? Does it actually matter now? Are you in this because you want to be or have you been dragged in because everyone else has been pulled in? Are you in it because you are afraid to miss something and get left behind? What kinds of boundaries should exist around problems that involve sex, dating, and relationships?

Is this group gnashing of teeth necessary to be in a popular group of kids? Or is there an ulterior motive? It's OK if there is, but let's be honest about this. This whole thing is much ado about nothing. It's regular, run of the mill adolescent nonsense. Adults are giving you a pass because they are afraid that somebody will do something crazy, and they will be held responsible. But the emotions are way outsized for what really happened. We need to have some perspective here.

Could any of you have responded differently to what happened and is happening? Would there be better responses for dealing with this? Can anything be done to end this and move on?

Maybe we should talk to our kids about real authentic feelings and feelings that we perform for our audiences, one of which is the close friendship group. Kids may be so attuned to knowing what reaction is the best one for getting everyone ramped up that they have lost touch with how they really feel about something. Reality TV is a perfect example of extreme overreaction. If kids think this is how people are supposed to react to situations that are mildly distressing, then what's to be expected when the situation is truly catastrophic (e.g., someone got hit by a train and is dead)?

I don't think this is as out of the ordinary as it might seem. Somewhere in the social media world kids learn that they can garner attention when they overreact. There are just so many examples floating around in our over-entertained internet experiences.

Not being a fan of reality TV, I've had to do some distasteful homework to finish this book. I can see the entertainment value of reality TV. People do funny and stupid things. But they also do mean, selfish, craven, horrible, violent, ghastly, and dangerous things, usually to other people. They engage in behaviors that we try to discourage in small children as they are being socialized to become citizens of the world.

They encourage behaviors that are at best nasty, and at worst, criminal. It's not surprising that so many reality TV contestants have experienced mental health problems when their show was over.[372]

If behavior is identity…holy moly! When so many people who are supposed to be serious are doing these things, we are in trouble.

We need to draw a line between serious and stupid, because reality TV that normalizes stupid, destructive, and abhorrent behaviors is very bad for us. Unfortunately, we've sold it to our kids who are now experts on commoditizing themselves online with outrageous behaviors because they fear that if they don't have a "brand" that is celebrated by thousands of followers, then they don't exist, and they have failed.

One other possibility for helping kids work through authentic vs. fake emotionality is to teach them about degree. Is the rain coming down just a little bit of rain, a medium amount of rain, or a lot of rain? Do you like spinach a little, a lot, or not at all? Do you feel a little sleepy, somewhat sleepy, or really sleepy? When Joe didn't share his toy with you, were you a little upset, more than a little upset, or very upset?

Then we can talk about what to do with feelings that are just "little," such as let them go. We can talk about "in the middle feelings" and discuss ways to either let them go or do something about them. Then we can talk about the feelings that are big and strong, and call for action because we are very hurt or very upset. And all of these discussions need to help kids figure out how to tamp down feelings that are on their way to taking control of them and come up with a response that doesn't send anyone to the emergency room.

I wonder if in our worry over not being responsive enough to our children during their various upsets that we haven't gone too far in the other direction. I don't think there's a research answer to this debacle, but I fear that doing social drama, performing every little upset for the world, and expecting a response, has set us up for relationship challenges. After watching Teresa Giudice of *The Real Housewives of New* Jersey flip a table over in front of friends, guests, and lots of cameras, and put on a tantrum that would shame a perceptive two-year old, I'm concerned that we've gone off the deep end on this one.

Boundaries and Our Phones

We tend to think of the need for and the protection of boundaries in situations that involve people and interactions, but there is another way we can get caught up in not knowing where our person ends and things that are not physically us begin. We're talking about our stuff, here. Specifically, but not exclusively, our smart phones and tablets.

Years ago, I came to the conclusion that if evolution works as it is theorized to, children would eventually be born with a smart phone in their hands. This is, of course, a joke, but it doesn't seem totally unrealistic because once children get smartphones, they rarely leave their hands. In fact, I have heard parents describe honest-to-goodness reactions from kids that sound a lot like withdrawal from alcohol when a parent takes a smartphone away from a child. Kids get grumpy, sullen, whiny, angry, and hostile, and all of those emotions and behaviors go away when the phone is returned to the child!

On a serious note, humans have begun to act as if there are no boundaries between themselves and their phones, along with the social media platforms they frequent. We don't own the phones; they own us. They have become more than just part of our identity; they are fully integrated into our identities, to the point where they are changing us in fundamental ways. Humans have always had a propensity to become owned by their stuff, instead of them owning their stuff. What we have and own is often an extension of who we are, but no invention in the history of people has had this profound of an effect on who we are.

When boundaries are loose and permeable, when private and personal slide into our public and professional lives, there's the chance that someone will get upset and that can trigger drama and conflict, which of course can turn into aggression. Aggression can be minimized when people are able to be empathic because it helps them understand the "why" between someone's behavior and their intentions. Empathy is like a lubricant in our interactions with each other.

Empathy[373]

Empathy counteracts too much me-ness. We have known for a long time that empathy is a personal quality that can go a long way to reducing aggression. Behaving empathically is not something that everyone is naturally born knowing how to do, but it can be learned, and the benefits of teaching our children to be empathic are enormous.

Empathy helps us have perspective. It gives us the ability to see a bigger world than the one we physically inhabit. It pushes us to have compassion for those who may not have the opportunities or gifts that we may possess. It helps us understand why other people do and say things that we find annoying or disturbing.

Empathy is an inhibitor of aggression. It works like this: When a person does something that is hurtful to another person in a face-to-face situation, and the recipient reacts by becoming upset, the aggressor who is empathic feels the other person's pain, discomfort, or sadness, and is moved to feel sorry for having inflicted pain on the other. It's the old "walking in another person's shoes" idea. Empathic people feel remorse for having hurt the other person, and are moved to stop the behavior, and apologize if appropriate.

Empathy can be taught. It begins by treating children with empathy and expressing acknowledgment of their suffering. Kids learn so much from modeling, and when we demonstrate empathy on their behalf, or on the behalf of other people in their sphere, they are seeing it and experiencing the positive effects of it on others. Empathy smooths over the rough spots in social interactions, and learning by seeing and then imitating the behavior, increases children's capacity for positive peer and adult relationships.

In addition to modeling, empathy, like many positive human qualities, can be learned through conversations about it. We can point out the effects of hurtful behaviors and help children read the social clues that say "You just hurt my feelings." Clues like tears, frowns, and sad eyes can be pointed out to children. Parents have a right to tell a child, when they are old enough to understand, that their behaviors have hurt, angered, or seriously frightened the parent. Of course, it needs to be done in a nonaggressive way, that communicates concern for the child, but also nudges the child to think about how their actions have affected a parent. Such empathy can lay the groundwork for mutual respect and better communication. It's OK to tell our children that this is how they have made us feel in an effort to help them see our perspective of things.

One of the ways that empathy is learned is through reading. Maryanne Wolf's research on the reading brain makes it clear that when children read about the suffering or the plights of others, they learn compassion which is what empathy triggers in our psyches. Thus, another reason for fewer screens and more print media for our children.

One of the problems with our screens is that they allow us to communicate without having to experience the reaction of the person with whom we are communicating; hence, empathy isn't activated if we aren't seeing someone's reaction to our post. Of course, combined with disinhibition, desensitization, deindividuation, moral disengagement and all the other nasties, empathy gets deactivated, and we lose that innate mechanism that promotes civil interactions. Even when we see each other through screens in real time, the visual clues are less obvious than they are when we are in each other's physical presence. Hence, we have limited exposure to the nonverbal clues that tell us that someone is upset or in distress. The result, of course, is that the ability to be empathic diminishes when we communicate through screens.

Empathy is also one of those personal qualities that allows us to share in other people's joy, even when we ourselves might be sad. When competition and winning or losing are part of the experience, empathy can help us be glad for the other guy, while also being sad that we didn't win. It brings to mind the aggressive behaviors of both players and fans when a competition of any sort erupts in verbal or physical violence. As a society we are less and less capable of empathy, so it would figure that our children are experiencing the same deficit, and the result is more aggression. Feeling another's suffering makes us better humans and shapes behaviors that are prosocial, as long as we recognize boundaries, and avoid the pitfalls of empathic distress.

One other feature that contributes to bad behavior on many levels for youth and for adults needs revisiting, and that is moral disengagement. As we become more narcissistic and less empathic as a society, the guardrails that keep our bad behaviors in check as well as supportive behaviors like tolerance, acceptance, flexibility, understanding, generosity, and kindness, weaken. These traits and behaviors complement the lubricant so necessary to a functioning and healthy society. These attributes grease our interactions with each other. Religious or spiritual practices can help cultivate these ways of being. Learning to be grateful is also a route to seeing ourselves in each other. Regardless of the method, families and communities are an important source of these kinds of experiences that all youth need, and that all adults should try to model for our children, even the ones that aren't members of our immediate families.

NO-DRAMA DRAMA, OR "BOY" DRAMA

I must confess that I don't think everything that is called drama fits the definition offered thus far. Having talked to a number of adults and thought about the kinds of behavior that contribute to drama, I believe there is a type of drama that lacks a few of the characteristics so far described.

With an eye to critics who will say I am perpetuating gender stereotypes, I pose the question: Is there such a thing as "boy" drama that is different from the definition offered previously? There might be, but it's not determined as much by gender as by personality.

I go back to my friend Molly who said that "boys do stupid stuff," and gave the example of boys who captured a baby deer and then brought it into one of their homes. Molly's example makes me think about a young man who decided it would be fun to moon the fans at a college basketball game. Or another fellow who thought it would be nice to do a lawn job at the home of someone who had ticked off his parents, but then managed to lose the car's license plate in the front yard while ripping up their grass. Big mistake! Or the little guy who broke his arm thinking he could jump out a second story window and fly because he was wearing his Superman cape. In every situation the parents and adults in charge would posit that these actions precipitated a lot of drama.

But girls have similar stories. When I was a child, I recall turning our basement into a skating rink by pouring water and lots of laundry detergent on the floor and then using my dad's golf clubs to smack balls all over. Then there was one of our babysitters who thought it would be fun to climb out on the roof of our garage from a bedroom window, at the urging of the little girl she was taking care of. Had there not been leaves on my daughter's bed, I never would have known.

There was also the time a group of teen girls started talking to guys they didn't know. The stupid part was that they were in separate cars driving in a 65-mph zone. Despite not knowing these fellows, the girls decided to invite them to their home for dinner. They introduced the guys as "friends" to the host parents, even though they were total strangers. It was years before the host parents ever found out the truth about the escapade. Dumb thing to do, but not malicious, and ended up being harmless all the way around. The fact that their parents never found out probably saved them from a lot of drama.

Chaos. Confusion. Cluelessness. But not meanness, manipulation, or deception. Stupid? Risky? Yes—all of it, but with a qualitative difference, and certainly no "feeding off each other." There is something missing in these examples that are present in our case study. If there is deception or hiding something in these no-drama dramas, it is likely to be after the fact, when the actors are trying to dodge the mess they made, rather than being used to manipulate events and people in the thick of the nonsense.

I would propose that there are two versions of drama, one where there is deliberate intent to manipulate, deceive, and exploit, and one that lacks intent to do those things, but still includes the chaos, confusion, cluelessness, and high emotions. The first kind of drama includes meanness, deception, manipulation, and intentional stirring of the pot. There's a knowingness that there is likely to be some harm delivered to someone. The second kind of drama is innocent of those intentions. In some situations, it may not be possible to distinguish between the two, but in fairness, it doesn't appear that all social drama should be lumped under one heading. One kind reflects narcissism; the other reflects immaturity, lack of foresight, and a shortage of wisdom.

"ALL KIDS ARE OUR KIDS"

Years ago, I participated in community training on information referred to as "developmental assets."[374] I remember thinking at the time that knowing about developmental assets would have been all I needed by way of child-raising information when I was a young mother. Years later and an advanced degree in human development in hand, I pretty much still agree with that conclusion.

Beginning in the second half of the last century, the Lutheran Brotherhood of Minnesota began work on helping families and communities create the kinds of environments that would promote what would come to be called positive youth development. By the late 1990s, the Lutheran Brotherhood had founded the Search Institute to develop a framework based on research in multiple disciplines, but focusing closely on what humans need to develop into happy, healthy, productive, and successful people.[375] At the time, I had not yet returned to the academy to get my doctoral degree in human development, but I was raising two elementary school–aged daughters, and this information struck a chord with me.

Developmental assets are defined as "a set of interrelated experiences, relationships, skills, and values suggested to enhance a broad range of positive youth outcomes and are assumed to operate similarly for all youth." So what were these folks proposing and what would it look like if it were implemented?[376]

The 40 Development Assets and the framework that it encompasses was being offered to schools, youth-serving organizations, communities, and families as a new and different form of prevention education. Up until that time, most prevention education programs were issue-specific and addressed deficits, rather than the strengths of kids. Social policy and education efforts were bouncing all over the list of dangers facing youth, whether it was illegal drug use, alcohol consumption, cigarette smoking, delinquency, early and unprotected sex, school failure... The list of risks was long, and has only expanded since then. Given the paucity of resources, including money and time to address every issue separately, proponents of the Developmental Assets Framework suggested that if we built kids' developmental assets, they would naturally avoid the ills of society that inhibit healthy development and negate the need for so many competing prevention efforts. Additionally, asset-building was good for all youth, regardless of their propensity to dabble in dangerous behaviors, so the programs and efforts that built developmental assets would be offered to everyone, not just a few high-risk kids. All of this makes a lot of sense, but it's also important to note that this work was being done before most kids were walking around with smartphones full of social media apps in their pockets or backpacks.

A list of the 40 Developmental Assets as they apply to adolescents, is included in the Appendix. If you take some time to study them, you might get the sense that they are a quaint throwback to the past, given the world of social media, 24/7 access to the internet, and a post–Covid-19 pandemic, which is now a forever-threat to society. What resonated with me then, and still does, is the insistence that humans develop inside of relationships that expose them to experiences, skills, and norms. These relationships, experiences, skills, and norms, build solid lifelines, and create resilience to adversity, the giving and accepting of support, positive family relationships, solid boundaries and behavioral restraints, strong and positive values, healthy relationships, and a commitment to lifelong learning and good citizenship.[377]

A scan through the assets (see the Appendix) suggests that every child needs frequent contact with caring people, role modeling of life skills and positive values, chances to learn, think, communicate, participate, serve, compete, and recreate. The assets also address the spiritual, emotional, and psychological dimensions of development. I remember thinking several decades ago that this was all just common sense. But that was before no one could live without a smartphone and a YouTube account. This was before we outsourced thinking and remembering. This was before most of our interactions with other humans were mediated by screens. This was before drama exploded on so many adult screens. For sure, the 40 Developmental Assets feel quaint today because, well, they are. Nowhere does it mention spending three hours a day alone in a bedroom watching short videos on TikTok. Nowhere does it reference aspiring to become famous simply by becoming famous, if that makes any sense, which it doesn't. And I'm not just thinking of youth, I'm thinking of adults who live this way, too, and if adults are living this way, who among us are going to be the ones building developmental assets for this and the next generation of kids?

Finally, too many parents care only about their own child or children's success and well-being. The 40 Developmental Assets are predicated on society-as-a-whole's responsibility for raising and supporting youth. Parents who view kids other than their own as rivals for resources they want for their kids are shortsighted because it means that our own children might end up living in a world where neglecting some kids means that the social, economic, and political climates our children grow up aren't healthy. When we embrace the mantra that "all kids are our kids,"[378] it means that we have to champion a world where not just "my" kids are nourished in rich environments, but where everyone's kids are, too. In our narcissistic society, this is a tall order for adults across the board.

It Took a Village

The story of Maurice captures the kind of boy-drama that my friend Molly Kuhl christened as "dumb stuff." She had observed that boys more often do things that are just plain stupid. The example she gave me was something a pair of boys had done in her neighborhood: capture a baby deer and bring it into a house where it ran terrified, knocking things over and probably leaving deer poop behind. Maurice was one of those fellows who lived on the edge and was always getting into scrapes. He was really good at boy drama.

The second of the three boys, Maurice was a precocious little guy with curly blond hair, blue eyes, and a huge smile. Kids and adults alike were attracted to his high energy and affinity for having fun. He was impulsive, and pushed the limits at every turn, but usually landed on his feet because there were folks looking out for him. His life started taking a serious wrong turn when he got involved in drugs in high school, but fortunately it didn't go unnoticed by a few astute adults, including the youth minister at the family's church. She alerted his parents who were highly involved in their boys' lives. Whether it was church attendance, athletics, or schoolwork, they were in it with their sons. Instead of denying there was a problem or trying to brush it under the carpet, Madeline and Jeremy reached out to other parents, family members, and lifelong friends to help address Maurice's substance use. They contacted the parents of Maurice's friends, their own friends, close family members, and concerned school personnel, and asked for help. Because Madeline and Jeremy cared about other families besides their own, and had cultivated relationships on multiple fronts, most responded and did what they could to help. Several wrote letters to Maurice encouraging him to stick to his guns and give up substance use. Another friend invited Maurice to join him in cooking a Sunday dinner for his own and Maurice's family. Maurice got the message that he was loved, valued, and important. He turned things around and left illegal drugs in the past.

One important person in Maurice's life was Cynthia, a mother of two boys who lived across the street from him. Cynthia was one of those warm, nonjudgmental parents who was good at listening. She told me that Maurice would sometimes come over just to chat with her. They would go up on the hill behind her house where she said he vented about what was going on in his life, which was usually something that flirted with danger or involved some kind of mayhem. She would ask him questions that allowed him to release his pent-up feelings and sort things out. She also noted that she kept a punching bag in her basement for any of the boys in the neighborhood to whack at when things got tense. Apparently, it got a lot of use when they were in middle and high school.

Maurice is a wonderful young man today. He's married to a special woman and is the father of three, soon to be four children. He's still bigger than life, but he is a solid citizen who might not have made it without the support he got. It had taken a village to get him where he is today.

The 40 Developmental Assets are a list of all the experiences and relationships that kids need, some more than others, to make it into adulthood successfully. Kids who find themselves devoid of these experiences, opportunities, and relationships, are less likely to make it into adulthood successfully. One thing that is clear is that one or two parents cannot do this bit of raising happy, healthy, contributing members of society alone. No matter how functional a nuclear family is, parents don't raise their kids by themselves. It takes a village, and as quaint as the assets might seem, they are the bedrock of how a healthy society perpetuates itself.

There is one vital postscript to the nurturing of assets in youth. It benefits the adults who participate. It creates connections between adults and strengthens a multigenerational community. Adults working together to bolster young people is a rewarding endeavor. In a society such as ours where loneliness is a serious problem, focusing on relationships and experiences—things we can't do alone—may be a solution to some of the depression and sadness that is affecting too many of us, children and adults alike.

CHAPTER 11
Stuck in a Funk

IT'S A LONG WAY from adolescent over-the-top episodes of social drama to social decline as evidenced by growing narcissism within the general public. A number of writers have been making the case that American civilization is on the skids, and they give plenty of evidence to back up their claims. First, we'll look at narcissism through an individualistic, close-up view, and then zoom up to thirty thousand feet. At that level, we can get a broad view of what narcissism and social drama do to a society. It helps understand how much we have gotten stuck in a funk, and it's a pretty large one, at that.

Ramani Durvasula is a practicing psychologist who specializes in helping people who live with narcissists.[379] One chapter of her book details the makeup and personality traits of narcissists. She recounts the characteristics previously enumerated: lack of empathy and entitlement, manipulation of people, projection of one's flaws on to others, lying, cheating, and gaslighting (telling someone that their reality is wrong when it is actually true and accurate). Among the personality traits of narcissists, she tells us they are superficial, jealous, envious, cheap, careless, fragile, insecure, angry, needy, entitled, passively aggressive, arrogant, sadistic, and shameless. In their relationships, narcissists are vindictive, exploitive, oppositional, paranoid, hypersensitive, lack a sense of self-awareness, don't take responsibility for their actions, and have a warped sense of what is fair and just.

Needless to say, those of us who have relationships with these folks have a rough go of life. Whether one's narcissist is a parent, sibling, child, spouse, boss, coworker, teacher, in-law, or friend, there are going to be times where the relational seas are particularly rough. Dr. Durvasula explains that we are attracted to narcissists because they are charming, charismatic, confident, attractive, successful, intelligent, and articulate.

What we usually miss are the person's darker characteristics until we are deeply involved with the person, sometimes in a relationship that lasts a lifetime, as with a parent or a child. In her work with the people trapped in narcissistic relationships, she walks a fine line between coaching them to disconnect from the person and sticking it out. Either route can be difficult and is sure to include personal and public drama.

Toward the end of her book, Durvasula makes it clear that our society has embraced toxic narcissism and is in serious trouble because of it. She sees the negative features of toxic behavior in our personal relationships seeping into our public social lives, and she is very concerned, as is Margaret Wheatley, who writes convincingly of how civilizations and societies develop and collapse in ways that are common throughout history.[380]

Wheatley explores a predictable life and death cycle of civilizations. It involves a proven pattern of behaviors that is repeated over and over in complex human societies and described by different independent researchers who have studied various human cultures that are no longer with us.[381] The process takes about 250 years and covers ten generations. Each generation advances more than the previous one because of the improved socioeconomic advancements brought on by their parents' generation. This always precipitates a march to more accumulation of wealth and material stuff, and ever higher standards of living. This is followed by generations that believe they are entitled to live better than the previous generation. As this process accelerates, there is a decrease in morality and an increase in decadence and selfishness. Greed, incivility, dishonesty, excessive individualism, social fragmentation, and entitlement cause the implosion of the society's noble norms and prosocial behaviors. Things get so bad that another group of people move in and start the process all over again. According to John Glubb,[382] what follows are the phases of a civilization's rise and fall.

It begins with the Age of Pioneers when people are strong and unified by a shared purpose that espouses strong values. These people are courageous and opportunistic as they encounter a civilization that is back on its heels and takes advantage of it. The second age is the Age of Conquest. In this phase, the Pioneers take over or conquer the society that has declined. Strong beliefs that unify the newbies creates an ideology that supplants the old one. The third development is the Age of Commerce where the newer society maintains their strong military, works hard to create new wealth that is personal as opposed to societal. During this phase, physical construction generates all kinds of infrastructure such as magnificent buildings and sprawling transportation systems. This era also sees the development of major institutions that regulate social inter-action and development. All of this highlights what we would describe as successful progress. The fourth stage is the Age of Affluence. During this time individualism trumps the collective identity and selfishness thrives. Accumulation of wealth supersedes values such as service to others and community well-being. The fifth stage is the Age of Intellect.

One would think that intellectual flourishing would ensure the longevity of a society, but instead it is a harbinger of decadence. The era of significant intellectual growth is characterized by expansion of the arts and the sciences, but while this is happening, internal conflict develops to the point where our ability to collectively solve problems for the benefit of all diminishes.

The last phase of civilizational collapse is called the Age of Decadence. During this time people have become narcissistic, materialistic, fanatical, nihilistic, and obsessed with frivolous matters. Social drama flourishes because we are living in an era of celebrity culture. Government veers toward welfarism to the point where everyone believes they are entitled to get everything for free. Being entertained is the prime occupation of most citizens. I get the feeling that some video game genius could turn these stages into an apocalyptic, "end of the world" adventure for adults, or perhaps already has. It raises a vision of millions of adults playing a video game that mirrors the outside reality but who aren't aware that "Rome is burning" until the power goes off, the battery dies, and the screens go blank. It sends chills up my spine.

This feels very harsh and terribly foreboding. Grappling with the idea that ours is a society that is ready to experience wholesale failure is terrifying. I can't help but believe that we will get our act together and change course. Margaret Wheatley offers some wise advice, about how we can sidestep this outcome when others have not, but I have wondered what societal collapse looks like in the modern era. Certainly, a society is not just put to the slaughter by some invading hoard especially in the North America of the twenty-first century, although a case can be made for Russia's invasion of Ukraine in eastern Europe, that conquest can still deliver a city to an enemy through brute force. However, consider that not all the Persians, Greeks, or Romans were sold into slavery or fed to their own lions. If the entire populations of conquered countries were exterminated, we wouldn't have countries like Iran, Greece, or Italy who claim ancestry from people who lived thousands of years ago. So why does this claim of the imminent demise of our culture feel so difficult to embrace? Who will our future "conquerors" be, as Glubb describes in his theory, which arguably, is based on solid evidence of such repeated societal collapses in the past?

One of the most perplexing aspects of the idea that we are decadent and in decline is that as a country and a global community we have achieved so many great things. We have fabulous works of art. We continue to grow our knowledge in science, technology, and medicine. We are increasing our exploration into the world of outer space. We are learning how to feed more people for less money. We are discovering and inventing ways to stop climate change. It feels as if we are riding the crest of a wave of success. But history seems to indicate that we are not where we think we are. It is terrifying to consider that what will do us in is societal polarization, accompanied by narcissism, greed, internal fighting, corruption, and all forms of drama amplified by social media and entities that lie, manipulate, and spread fear and hate.

Wheatley refers to what has been called the Progress Trap.[383] It is the optimistic belief that technology will save us, our societies, and our planet; that technology can and will fix every problem we create. The paradox though is that our innovations contribute to our degradation and impending collapse. Dr. Gloria Mark has been studying people and their interaction with screens for years, and she has found that the benefit of using computers to get work done is often displaced by the lack of productivity that is accomplished as we are constantly switching from email, to Facebook, to news, to Instagram, only to be interrupted by a phone call, that distracts us for even longer.[384] We seem oblivious to the reality that just about every advance we make has negative unintended consequences. While we are supposed to be more efficient and productive, many technological advances achieve just the opposite.[385] It seems that living in our screens may not be all it's cracked up to be.

Annalee Newitz has written a book about the disappearance of four ancient cities in different parts of the world, over long stretches of time.[386] Newitz describes research that has led her to conclude that cities can outlast their usefulness, fall apart, and are thusly abandoned by their inhabitants. In her opinion, societies don't collapse, they are transformed. All four of her examples are places that no longer exist. The reasons she cites for these failures run the gamut from climate change to bad political decisions that undermined social and governmental institutions and negatively affected the quality of people's lives. Of course, cities in the ancient world were conquered as recorded in history (think Alexandria in Egypt), but her perspective addresses the issue of internal failure due to the actions of those living in the cities, not so much because of external conquerors.

These authors and others, such as Robert Denton, Benjamin Voth,[387] and Charles Sykes,[388] are not alarmist quacks or negative Debby/Donny Downers who see disintegration and disfunction everywhere. They are thoughtful social commentators who have studied history, human social evolution, and what causes societies to fracture and fail. They are not conspiracy theorists or maniacal demagogues. They make their cases based on facts that lead to likely outcomes. They make legitimate points, and all of them suggest that our current social dysphoria is a symptom of something that is happening to all of us, and we need to figure out what to do about it—if we can, and if it's not too late.

WHAT MEDIA HYPE DOES TO US

I wasn't always a news junkie, but once our adult world devolved into adult social drama on steroids, I couldn't cope without watching as much mainstream news as possible. I was sucked in, anxious, and needed to know how much worse it would get, or conversely, that someone was going to stop the insanity so that I could turn the screen off and get back to living life. That was not to be, so for days and days I watched news while fretting and ruminating, and feeling horrified, helpless, and desperate. My mental health plummeted.

The media has exploited our sense of outrage and amplified political discord[389] that has turned many of us into ruminators. The media does this because it increases ratings and revenues. Lies sell, conspiracies sell, and intergroup discord that becomes hate, sells. When powerful people like thought leaders, media demagogues, religious manipulators, some politicians—snake oil salespersons in one guise or another—repeatedly warn people of all the bad things that are being done to them, they promote fear, anger, and a sense of having been wronged.

And they pit us against each other, deliberately. Why? To increase their ratings, influence, and market share, and hence, their profits.

Matt Taibbi has written an exposé on how and why this has happened.[390] In his history of television news, he takes us through the time when three broadcast channels reported national and international news once a day for thirty minutes, to today where there are practically more news sources than there are libraries in many states. When I was a child my parents and my friends' parents watched, heard, or read, essentially the same information every day. Back then no one could consume news all day unless they went to the library and read every newspaper on the racks of daily news' sections, of which there were quite a few.

Eventually, when cable news came around, and then social media, media owners realized that if they were going to keep their share of viewers, listeners, or readers, they would have to kick it up a notch—really several notches. Their motivation was profit. Broadcasters, radio show hosts, shock jocks, anchors and the like, were forced to move away from what had always counted as journalism and objective reporting, and become purveyors of hyped, partisan information. It was the new economic model of TV news as entertainment, and something else. News became tailored to attract consumers of particular mindsets and world views, and to paint anyone who didn't agree with these messages as the enemy. It was designed to keep consumers in a heightened sense of worry, fear, and anxiety, so that they wouldn't turn the channel, or turn off the screen, and do something like living life outside of a frenzied news media bubble. They traded real news for social drama, probably without even knowing it, and because so many of us get our news from our smartphones or computers, we have largely gotten stuck in our screens. And we get a lot of garbage thrown at us there.

BAD NEWS: MIS- AND DIS-INFORMATION

Social media provides us with multiple sources of poor-quality information and lies that portray themselves as news that is really baloney.[391] Gone are the days when what we read or saw was vetted by an editor whose job it was to make sure what was produced was accurate, factual, and truthful. Social media brought us into an era where those news sources have taken a backseat to information from places that are more interested in pushing their own ideological views, conspiracy theories, and stirring up drama than offering accurate information.[392] In June of 2024 the Pew Research Center released the findings of a national survey detailing where Americans get their news.[393] The four primary sites that Americans frequent are TikTok, X (formerly Twitter), Instagram, and Facebook. Half of Americans say they get some of their news on these and other social media sites. Journalists and news outlets are one source of information on social media sites, but so are influencers, celebrities, advocacy and nonprofit organizations, and friends, family, acquaintances, and strangers. On TikTok alone, eighty-four percent of users say they get their news from strangers.[394] *Ouch!*

The University of Washington (UW) has created what it calls "Misinformation Day" workshops and classes that help students develop critical thinking and media literacy skills.[395] Their programs address the problem of information pollution, which is not very different from the World Health Organization's term, infodemic, which is defined as too much information coming at us from all kinds of sources, some of them unreliable.[396] UW has organized and defined mis- and disinformation under the heading of "false information," which also encompasses fake news.

Misinformation is wrong, but the person spreading it doesn't know it's false. The person thinks it is true and doesn't intend to cause harm by passing the information along. Often the person is sending it on to others to inform them of something that might harm them. The intent is to protect, not harm someone. Disinformation, on the other hand, is deliberately false information that is intended to harm people and cause damage. The damage might be financial or political. It might also be directed at a person or group with the intention of ruining their reputation or their credibility. Disinformation spreads chaos and undermines public trust in experts and institutions. Regardless of whether news is mis- or disinformation, it is *bad* news.

One of the most frightening facets of consuming bad information is that people are seldom willing to change their opinions once they are fixed, and this has the effect of creating social divisions and polarization. Gary Morson and Morton Schapiro[397] have written how the certainty of individuals and groups for refusing to entertain any ideas but their own have created a culture where we can no longer even discuss information that we disagree with or opinions at odds with our own. That coupled with the Dunning-Kruger effect has made the situation more dire.

The Dunning-Kruger effect[398] is a phenomenon whereby people who aren't very knowledgeable, well-informed, or competent, think that they are very smart and are unable to recognize their own shortcomings. In various experimental conditions participants who suffer from the Dunning-Kruger effect overestimate their performance on knowledge tests on subjects such as grammar, logical reasoning,[399] scientific knowledge,[400] analytical reasoning, and political knowledge.[401] Furthermore, these folks believe strongly that their intuition is a solid source of knowledge, which makes them overly confident when it comes to what they know.[402] These individuals trust their intuition one hundred percent to guide them regardless of contradictory, expert information.[403] Welcome to the world of the flat earthers!

BELIEVING LIES: CONSPIRACY THEORIES

Conspiracy theories abound today, proliferated on social media and through internet websites and platforms, and they have been playing havoc with our sense of who we are and who we want to be.

A conspiracy theory is an attempt to explain something that is causing people to be fearful, anxious, confused, or unmoored, and then blame it on a person, a group, or an institution in order to construct a reason for the problem and then assign responsibility for it.[404] Conspiracy theories are an attempt to explain something that is unexplainable, or where the explanation given by experts is unsatisfying. Another feature of the definition of a conspiracy theory is the belief that a few powerful people are behind the scenes pulling the strings and manipulating us to achieve some evil or unlawful objective. Conspiracy theories are not new. Think of St. Joan of Arc who was burned at the stake for heresy or consider America's own version as per the Salem witch trials. More recently we have had the JFK assassination conspiracies, or the 9/11 conspiracies. At this writing there are conspiracies related to QAnon, a supposed mysterious source of information, authority, and guidance, as well as an assortment of conspiracies related to Covid-19 and vaccinations.

Those in the public health field in particular have claimed that misinformation and conspiracy theories regarding the Covid-19 epidemic, have "cost lives,"[405] mainly because people chose to believe conspiracy theories and the misinformation they promulgated instead of scientists and doctors who were trying to save lives.[406]

Jan-Willem van Pooijen has proposed an interesting idea about conspiracy theories that focuses on the presence of existential threats.[407] An existential threat is a situation that makes us feel vulnerable, out of control, helpless, and in dire fear for our safety and continued existence. Conspiracy theories manifest themselves when people are feeling anxious and insecure about themselves and the people around them encountering something life-changing like a terrorist attack, a war, economic collapse, a deadly pandemic, an unpreventable environmental catastrophe, or governmental collapse. Conspiracy theories emerge when social events are scaring people, and people don't understand what is happening and why. Van Pooijen suggests that when people are in this state, they experience intense curiosity and become highly motivated to make sense of it, especially when there is an outgroup that they perceive to be antagonistic that may be responsible for the event. This outgroup can be the government, government agencies, politicians, or experts like scientists and doctors. When the outgroup is determined to be untrustworthy, people can see these groups as threatening or adversarial and determine that they can find their own explanations and solutions—and then they embrace conspiracy theories.[408] And of course, the internet and social media are breeding grounds for all kinds of mayhem and drama when people start believing and spreading conspiracies.

Researchers have also concluded that people are especially driven to embrace what they believe they have discovered about these existential threats when they come upon information while "they are doing their own research."[409] This is especially true for people who feel that they are being preached at by the experts and being discounted as being unable to make decisions for themselves. Another problem is that conspiracy theories tend to proliferate when a country is experiencing collective narcissism.[410] Recall that collective narcissism is when people are very sensitive to how their country appears to others and may believe that other countries are trying to do them dirty or make them look bad. There is an overall belief that "my country is great" and people outside of my country should be telling us that we are great. When a society exhibits this strong sense of entitlement, they will hold outside groups or countries responsible for their own country's problems.

There is also evidence that when people and the groups they associate with possess some of the negative traits discussed previously, like being manipulative, cynical, callous, impulsive, and generally anti-social, they are more likely to believe conspiracy theories.[411] They are also more likely to have bad feelings about outgroups that don't reflect their own beliefs and opinions. Lastly, researchers know that conspiracy theories don't often satisfy people's need for knowledge on how to solve the problems that plague them, and in fact, lead to believing in more and more mis- and disinformation.[412] It's that black hole that sucks everyone into more and more drama.[413]

WE ARE GETTING DUMBER

According to Jonathan Haidt,[414] previously mentioned before, the internet has made us stupider. I agree. Americans' overall general intelligence has been on the wane for a while, but the internet and all our technological devices haven't helped. In fact, according to work done by Maryanne Wolf and fellow neuroscientists who study the "reading brain," we may be losing our ability to read deeply, think deeply, make analogies, think critically, generate new hypotheses, test them, and solve big problems.[415] Wolf theorizes that the complicated brain circuitry that allows humans to learn to read (which is not an innate ability like seeing, hearing, or speaking) requires a specific, intentional process that must be taught, rehearsed repeatedly, and nurtured from birth. She and her colleagues fear that the attention needed to develop a deep reading brain is being truncated by exposure to screens which train us to be fast, distracted skimmers and scanners of text. The list of what may be lost in our cognitive and emotional selves is frightening: the abilities to attend, focus, block distractions, follow a narrative story, understand or construct a rational argument, judge the truth of information, develop a store of background knowledge to enrich our knowing, empathize with another person, and contemplate anything from the origin of the earth to the meaning of life.

The other side of the coin of stupidity that is foreshadowing our intellectual demise, is that education can't keep up with the changes and challenges we are experiencing in our lives. The reason for this overall decline is complicated and difficult to remedy, but education that doesn't teach us how to think and how to evaluate the information imparted to us is not helpful. The founders of this country recognized the importance of an educated society, but unfortunately, they didn't leave us a great blueprint to follow to achieve that goal, especially in a world run by social media, the internet, and very soon, if not already, artificial intelligence. Who needs to learn how to think when a robot can do it better and faster than a human?[416] Frighteningly, we are moving from distraction to dystopia.

Six thousand years ago, or so, humans invented writing, reading, and numeracy, systems of symbols that have allowed our species to become advanced humans. If we are to continue to maintain our intellectual march forward, we must listen to the scientists who are telling us the best ways to educate our children: no screens until age two, and focus on reading from books that are held, touched, and placed on shelves to be read again and again. Don't let robots take over for teachers, and don't let kids use robots to do their homework.

We've worked so hard to push the STEM (science, technology, engineering, and math), agenda for the past several decades that we have shortchanged our youth's knowledge of classic civics education. As a result, many youths and a fair number of adult citizens don't understand how our government came to be, how it structures and supports our society, and why this partnership of the two keeps us functioning. Instead of honoring the common good, our narcissism and short-sightedness have led to the belief that government is no good, and that to save ourselves and our society, we have to tear it all down. The founding thinkers are rolling in their graves!

Unfortunately, education policy and spending are often the location for serious fighting in the American culture wars.[417] We fight about how to teach history, what books children can read, whether biology should include human sexuality information, and the story of race in our country. We swing from focusing on STEM, the driver of economic growth, to focusing on the soft social skills like problem solving and interpersonal communication, the tools needed to get along with each other. And, of course, somewhere in between is the issue of goodness and morality, an issue that is often claimed to be the purview of parents, families, and faith communities.

The reality is that goodness and moral behavior are not solely the purview of any religion or any group of people. Goodness and moral behaviors are vital to the success of any society and need to be modeled by adults and inculcated in youth. These qualities and behaviors are also necessary if we are to achieve the ideals ensconced in the founding documents that tell us who we are and what we stand for. The behaviors that reflect civic mindedness and the moral behavioral norms upheld by most religions are not mutually exclusive. In fact, they greatly overlap.

The separation of church and state has been used by a few religions to claim that their enactment of moral behavior, as determined by their ideology, cannot be infringed upon by the state. Some of these religions, however, have used this right to try to mandate or prohibit certain behaviors found objectionable according to their norms and beliefs.[418] The problem is that this is hypocritical. Claiming the right to engage in politics and at the same time claiming that church and state should not influence one another is incompatible. Both cannot exist at the same time.

So, too then, is the premise that goodness and moral behaviors should remain more the dictates of religion than society. Civil societies have the right to extoll the need for and articulate the moral behaviors that protect their integrity and viability. No single religion's moral code should have to mirror the set of norms that define goodness for all members of our society. Given our slide toward pervasive narcissism, it seems that America needs a moral and civic reawakening, and perhaps a refresher course on the impact of how our behaviors affect each other.

CANCEL CULTURE

Regardless of where you get your news, if you are tuned in, you have heard the term "cancel culture," or have heard of a person "being canceled."[419] Thus far, we've discussed it in terms of social media influencers, but that is not the only context where canceling goes on. So, what is it, where did it come from, why is it controversial, and what does it have to do with social drama and bad behavior?

According to Aja Romano[420] who has researched the origins of cancel culture, the meaning was first associated with breaking up with one's girlfriend. In *New Jack City*, a 1991 movie about a Harlem-based drug dealer, gangster Nino Brown loses his patience with his girlfriend who is upset about all the violence he is perpetrating and exclaims, "Cancel that b**ch. I'll buy another one." Crass and misogynistic, for sure, but quite funny, too. After that, canceling someone became connected to breaking up with a girlfriend.

Eventually, the term cancel culture became associated with the idea of political correctness and hypocrisy.[421] Back in the 1980s, if you were liberal, it was cool to embrace everything from saving the planet, to opposing cruelty to animals, to eliminating white supremacy. It was the heyday of feminism, hugging trees, fighting for clean air and water, and liberal activism of all sorts. Those on the inside, according to Ruth Perry,[422] would joke among themselves whenever anyone brought up the idea of acting in line with their beliefs. If you chose the veggie burger you were politically correct, but if you ate the Angus burger, you were politically incorrect. According to Dr. Perry, the folks on the conservative end of things, caught wind of the phrase and turned it into a weapon, believing that political correctness was a form of silencing critics or divergent opinions, and thus limiting free speech.[423]

Then along came "canceling" in Black discourse, as a gentle way to censure someone whose behavior on Twitter was incorrigible, but to do so with humor and lightheartedness.[424] When the idea of cancel culture finally emerged full-blown, it had taken on more serious and negative connotations. Canceling became a technique for smearing a prominent person in a very public way for some transgression, often one offensive to minorities.[425] Celebrities of any sort could be canceled because of their current or past behaviors that appeared to be misogynistic or racist. What might have been viewed as "calling out" someone's gaffes, or bad judgment in choosing words, became canceling, which then morphed into a cultural phenomenon called cancel culture. Essentially it was intended to be a way to publicly shame someone who had misused their power, often against a marginalized person or group of people.[426]

People who have favorable views of cancel culture see it as a way to punish people who have power and use it to engage in racist, misogynistic, ethnic, or homophobic behaviors, including past comments or misdeeds.[427] It includes actions taken by women who post to #MeToo to publicly shame sexual abusers who have never been held accountable.[428] Or by people who have demonstrated racist behavior, by doing something such as wearing blackface. Obviously, such widespread public chastisement was nearly impossible before social media. The outcome for some high profile, powerful people who have been outed for actions deemed to be hateful, criminal, or inappropriate, has resulted in campaigns to ruin these individuals' public and private reputations.[429]

Another manifestation of cancel culture has occurred when speakers who are thought to have unpalatable, antagonistic, or unsavory views are disinvited to speak in response to college students' or faculty objections. In some cases, when the college or university refused to cancel the proposed speaker's appearance, protestors have disrupted the speaker to the point of threats of violence against the guest speaker.[430]

Opinions about cancel culture range from seeing it as a form of censorship and a weapon that destroys the free exchange of ideas and is essentially a violation of the first amendment, to a powerful, positive tool to hold people accountable for anti-social actions.[431]

The history of cancel culture is clearly connected to positions people take with some rather obvious political overtones.[432] Fast forward to the present, and the idea of political correctness, whether you think it is a good thing or a bad thing, is a controversial beast that obscures problems that plague all of us, not just one group or political persuasion over another. Cancel culture is a main feature in our personalized and politicized public conversations, with dead bodies (figuratively, of course) strewn along the path of destruction.

Today, canceling someone involves destroying them on social media, exposing their bad behavior (even if it happened a long time ago), and getting them axed, from a job, an organization, or a community. In a fair number of cases, getting canceled equates to getting fired from a prominent position.[433] When social media has such a far reach, once a movement to cancel someone takes root, it's hard to stop it or wind it backwards. There is even evidence that canceling someone can be a form of vigilantism that overlaps in some cases to sadism which is joy in seeing someone suffer.[434]

We used to cancel things like magazine subscriptions or cable TV providers, often without making a big deal of it. If all we did was stop buying a product or watching a television program because we didn't like it anymore, it made little difference to anyone's personal life. Unless we took out a full page ad in *The New York Times* or *Wall Street Journal* and made a big public stink about how bad someone's cookies, laundry detergent, hair loss product, or new talk show was, our choice to boycott caused little harm to any individual.

Now we cancel each other. The act of canceling a person isn't too far off from the "feeding off each other" that goes on in reality TV and social drama. The only difference is that we don't spit the person out after we've had a chew on them, we swallow them, and they disappear. That means that some of those people get fired, and others are made to disappear. It's not passive at all. In fact, it's a very active, hostile, and aggressive response.

Cancel culture is relevant to our discussion of social drama because it is a public way of embarrassing and mortifying someone, usually someone who has celebrity status, or social prominence, often using social media. Cancel culture is about calling people out, usually someone with power who has appeared to have abused it. Social media facilitates a mob mentality. Retweeters easily and thoughtlessly click and share to the point of serious piling on and that causes drama that is damaging when facts and nuances are ignored.

The problem is that canceling people has become personal.[435] Where we once might have told a friend his or her comments were rude or insensitive, now we can go online and obliterate them in front of the masses. Kids in particular use canceling to pile on a peer who has done something embarrassing or hurtful, particularly if it is sexists, racist, or homophobic. Cancel culture involves the same behaviors as calling someone out, a practice common in online interactions with the nonpowerful. But when the person is still young, still playing with identity, still making run-of-the-mill kid mistakes, the heavy hand of public shaming, even by peers, can have serious repercussions for relationships with friends, family, and peers.

It's one thing to boycott a product, but it's another thing to take another human out. However, if we remember how people have become online productions with brands to keep shiny and polished, it isn't a long shot to see how personally canceling each other can be horribly damaging, especially when it's done for minor infractions or for something untoward that happened a long time ago. We have become mean and judgmental toward each other, and the screen has made it much easier to hurt someone who is annoying, or who is threatening our status or reputation.

Cancel culture has resulted in some pretty unsavory people getting their due, primarily because they were sexual predators who got away with it because of their power or wealth. The #MeToo movement made it harder for serial abusers to continue to get away with their sexual crimes, but in some situations canceling a person looked a lot more like bullying and cyberbullying than helping someone reexamine their words and actions.

Cancel culture has used social media as a weapon of aggression. The problem is that not everyone should be canceled for their misbehavior or indiscretion. Canceling should be a last-ditch effort to get someone to change their behavior or thinking, but it should never be used as a tool to respond to someone who has been annoying or thoughtless. And worse yet, it should never be used by someone who is too chicken to address a person directly about a troubling issue, or by someone who is too desensitized or callous to the damage it will do to the targeted person. In these cases, it's bullying, or more often cyberbullying.[436] All the personality traits that contribute to social drama—desensitization, disinhibition, rejection sensitivity, narcissism, and on and on—make it easy to maliciously attack someone when it can be done from a distance, and through a screen.

To bring this all home, it is apparent that some people use cancel culture to deal with someone they just don't like. It's mean and horrible, but it's happening more and more because we are becoming more narcissistic as individuals and as groups. There's even a term to describe it: communal narcissism.[437]

Unlike collective narcissism which describes a general phenomenon that applies equally to our society as a whole, communal narcissism is a characteristic associated with people who engage in vigilantism. It is more about everyone in a group, small or large, who share the same feelings of narcissism. When groupthink is the norm and members have disengaged from reality, or become desensitized to the extremes of emotion, vigilantism can infect the group.[438]

Vigilantes are folks who monitor what's going on in their world and act to right wrongs that they think are going unaddressed. Vigilantes may punish people whom they perceive as having harmed them, or they may become "third-party punishers" when they decide that someone has violated a norm and needs to be made aware of it.

Fan Chen and colleagues[439] have theorized that communal narcissism is a personality flaw that manifests itself in behaviors of an inflated perception of a person's prosocial attributes. In other words, the person has a sense that they are morally superior to most people, and that gives them the right to correct others for their moral failings. This sense of one's superiority extends to similar others and the people in one's ingroup. Of course, communal narcissists are grandiose and entitled, but they also have a heightened sense of psychological standing. What motivates them is not that they care about the common good but that they need to be admired for their efforts to make the world a better place. Thus, vigilantism may be construed in their minds as a positive social action. *Choke.*

But there's more to vigilantism than just making things right due to moral superiority. Some vigilantes are sadists. They enjoy making people suffer, so their punishment of people isn't about fixing a wrong, it's about inflicting pain for its own sake. According to Chen and colleagues,[440] both communal narcissists and sadists engage in vigilantism, but the difference is that the communal narcissist thinks he's doing the world a favor and isn't concerned about the target's suffering. The sadist, on the other hand, does it because he enjoys the effects of seeing someone suffer, not because he's a moral upstander. *Double choke.*

What is relevant about this is that vigilantism and cancel culture feel like identical twins that thrive in the dramatic creases of social media. It's another connection between bad behaviors like desensitization, moral disengagement, disinhibition, and narcissism, and the way we mangle and trash each other. It's that old problem of feeding off each other.

THE EPIDEMIC OF LONELINESS

We are going through a spiritual unspooling.[441] Senator Christopher Murphy has observed, when discussing the economy and how people feel about it, "[T]he challenges... are metphysical. And the sooner we understand the unspooling of identity and meaning that is happening in America today, the sooner we can come up with practical policies to address this crisis."[442]

We are going through a time as a society where we don't feel good about very much. We are alienated from our policy makers who seem obsessed with frivolous distractions. We are worried about paying our bills. We are worried about our kids, and too many of us, youth, adults, and seniors are lonely, and when we are lonely, the future looks dismal, and our prospects feel limited. Too many people feel like they are slipping backwards physically, emotionally, and psychologically. We are floundering socially. What Senator Murphy is talking about are some rather intangible things like who we are and how we are getting along as a society. It's about meaning, connection, and, as he says, identity.

Another way to think about spiritual unspooling is through the lens of loneliness, a plight that is more apparent in America than it has been in a long time. Loneliness is the difference between how much social connection one desires and how much social connection one doesn't have.[443] It's different from isolation which can be chosen if one so desires it, nor is it solitude, which is also often a chosen state. But isolation that isn't desired can be horrible and can push a person into a state of sadness and anxiety. It can cause heartache and even fear. In contrast, people who are socially connected have improved educational outcomes, are more satisfied at their jobs, are economically prosperous, live longer, feel fulfilled, and are less likely to get dementia.[444] That's a pretty good bang for the buck.

At a community level, good social connection among residents leads to better living for everyone.[445] People look out for one another and their kids and elderly parents. People are more inclined to vote, engage in service, and participate in public life. People are safer, healthier, and happier. When there is a crisis, people jump up, pitch in, and step in to fix things up and get back to normalcy.[446]

To get a flavor of why we are at this point, consider some of these research findings[447]: Trust in each other is at near historic lows. Polarization is at near historic highs. People's social networks are getting smaller. In-person contact and socialization with friends has steadily declined, especially for young folks 15 to 24 years old, and the number of our friendships has declined at the same time. As a society fewer of us go to church, synagogue, or mosque. We no longer join in community organizations the way we once did.

Another interesting point from Murthy's 2023 report on loneliness has to do with what researchers call "core discussion networks."[448] The report tells us that these are shrinking. Never having heard of core discussion networks, I did some digging. Core discussion networks are circles of people who talk about the hard topics like "politics, finances, world events, religion, health, and more."[449] These are usually people like family members and close friends. Apparently, we have fewer people in our core discussion networks now than people did years ago. When we have more people in our core discussion groups, we become more politically tolerant because in these discussion networks we become aware that there are perspectives in the world other than our own. And, of course, such shifts in thinking reduce the polarization of our society. Without these close and trusting relationships, we lose the benefits of these civilized, thoughtful, and serious dialogues. However, most of us have found that these opportunities are few and far between to nonexistent today. Today we rarely talk about these topics if we don't share the same perspective on anything like politics or religion, or even education and how to raise kids. Today, most of us test the waters to find out a person's world view before we open ourselves up for conversation on hot topics. Right now it feels like everything is a hot topic, even the weather.

Ruth Whippman, the mother of three boys and an author on how boys are doing, speaks of a "culture war-torn America,"[450] that is unhealthy for all of us, especially kids, and that includes boys who suffer more from loneliness than girls do but have fewer resources to reach for when the burden becomes unbearable. Boys are still heavily influenced by a version of masculinity that shuts them off from feelings and expressing emotions. Parents are still treating boys and girls differently when it comes to helping them develop their social-emotional selves. Boys are still getting the message that to cry is unmanly and to share deep thoughts and concerns are a sign of weakness.[451] So instead of heading out into the world finding experiences to engage in with real people, they find themselves looking for what it means to be human in online video games, pornography, and black-hole websites.[452] Yes, the boys, as well as the girls are looking for love/connection in all the wrong places, and in too many unhealthy ways. Despite their incredible online connections, many of our kids are lonely. Somehow the screen isn't a magic portal to all things wonderful.

I find it interesting that the surgeon general, Dr. Vivek Murthy, has issued three reports over the course of 2023 and 2024[453] that all touch on the theme of loneliness, or what produces loneliness. In the 2024 publication, *Parents Under Pressure*, the report includes isolation and loneliness as two of several sources of stress for parents. It also mentions "managing technology, social media, and cultural pressures"[454] as additional sources of stress. Loneliness makes us sick in greater numbers.[455] It can be worse for physical health than smoking or being obese. Loneliness is stressful and we pay a price for too much stress. That is true for people of all ages, walks of life, and demographics.

In the 2023 report, *Our Epidemic of Loneliness and Isolation*, Dr. Murthy writes:

> If we fail to [build more connected lives], we will pay an ever-increasing price in the form of our individual and collective health and well-being. And we will continue to splinter and divide until we can no longer stand as a community or a country. Instead of coming together to take on the great challenges before us, we will further retreat to our corners— angry, sick, and alone.[456]

In the fall of 2023, Senator Chris Murphy (Democrat) along with input from Governor Spencer Cox (Republican) "introduced the National Strategy for Social Connection Act, a bill to fight the epidemic of loneliness that Murphy believes has been driven by the pervasive communications technology and malignant commercialization of American life."[457] It was a short and vague bill that got little support, but Murphy did it to get the subject on the radar of politicians, not to get it passed. In discussions with policy makers, academics, and deep thinkers he has begun a conversation with people on both sides of the aisle who are exploring ideas that focus on the problems that bring societies to a cataclysmic and drama-fraught end, ones like too much narcissism, materialism, fanaticism, nihilism, entitlement, internal conflict, and too much time on our screens. I hope Margaret Wheatley[458] has been invited to join the Senator's conversation. *Amen.*

MINDLESSNESS, DISTRACTIONS, AND LOSS OF FOCUS

The mind is what the brain does. The brain isn't much more than a mass of grey gelatinous material with lots of creases and crevasses, at least that's what it looks like to the human eye, but to a neurosurgeon who looks at it microscopically, it is a magical mass of tissue that is far more sophisticated than the very best computers. It's got pathways that transport electrical impulses generated by our senses that get sent into our skull and make all manner of things happen from reading a want-ad to signing a birthday card.[459]

The mind, on the other hand, is something far less tangible. The mind is what we think, feel, and use to make sense of the world. It is memory, problem solving, desires, goals, motivation, enjoyment, and above all it is where knowledge resides and our ideas come from. When the brain stops working, so does our mind. We seldom think much about our minds, which makes living fairly easy, but sometimes we need to consider what is happening with our minds. Especially now, because it is primarily our minds that are stuck in our screens.

The screen-ubiquitous world we live in, along with the effects of Covid-19–induced isolation, has messed with our minds. Even before Covid-19 we were locked into our screens, but the epidemic forced many of us to spend far too much time on social media, at a point where we were highly vulnerable to stinking thinking and bizarre ideas. (Fear does that to a person!) We were, and still are stuck mindlessly scrolling and panning nonsense that doesn't have much value because scrolling is a bad habit we developed to address our boredom and our worry. This habit has contributed to the weakening of our ability to focus and to concentrate[460] and it is contributing to our inability to connect with one another in meaningful ways.

People think that they can multitask.[461] My daughter even put multitasking as something she was good at on one of her job applications. Somewhere along the line someone decided that we could do several things at once and be good at all of it. But that has been disproved by science. We don't multitask, we task switch.[462] We might be able to do two things relatively well like drive a car and listen to the radio, but that's because most of what it takes from our minds to do those things can be done on autopilot. Just follow someone who is texting and driving and it's obvious that they aren't doing either one particularly well. What we can no longer do is "single-task."[463] Our ability to focus, which is something our minds do, has been seriously eroded by our environment.

We are constantly buried in a consciousness that is full of distractions. Our minds are attuned to things like pings from our phones and computers, and when we hear the siren call, we attend to it. A text, an email, a Facebook/Instagram/TikTok post, a meeting reminder. Any one of those things can take us away from whatever we are supposed to be attending to, and *bam*, our focus gets shot. It can happen even when we are deep in a conversation with another human, or at least trying to be.

One of the things that the algorithms of social media does is steal our attention, and the tech companies have turned it into a multi-billion-dollar enterprise.[464] They have capitalized on the ability to use our screens to get into our minds and take control of them, or at least wear them out. Dr. Gloria Mark studies what happens when our ability to pay attention is hijacked, and she has concluded that we only have so much cognitive energy for focusing and when we spend that energy bouncing all over the internet on our screens, we get tired and have to basically take a nap before we can get back to what we were trying to do.[465] So much for productivity and efficiency.

Johann Hari, a journalist who finally cried "Uncle" when it came to being tortured by his imprisonment in social media and his cell phone screen, went on a smartphone-free hiatus.[466] As someone who writes for a living and needs to be able to focus and attend to complex ideas and thoughts, he found that living under the pressure of deadlines in a world of high-speed cerebral chaos was just too much to manage. So Hari put his cell phone in a time-locked vault, moved to a beach community and started experiencing life first hand instead of through a screen.

While the effects of addiction withdrawal were painful, he eventually managed to reconnect with himself, then with his physical environment, then with the people around him, and then with his own mind. His stress level went down. His perceptions became clearer. His thinking became deeper. He was able to write. He slept better. He felt better and he was happier.

One of the most touted avenues to better health and well-being these days is mindfulness. It is advertised as a way to reduce stress and improve one's inner sense of peace. Mindfulness is often embedded in the act of meditation, which are really two separate activities, although this is not often clear to everyone. I can attest to the fact that meditating and practicing mindfulness at the same time does reduce stress and increase one's sense of well-being. I spent five days at a Jon Kabat-Zinn retreat where I finally learned to meditate after trying to unsuccessfully teach it to myself.[467]

In the process of writing this book I began to wonder if mind*less*ness was the exact opposite of mind*ful*ness, because it had occurred to me that mindlessness was something bad and mindfulness was something good.[468] If being aware of the world and the self in a nonjudgmental way was a goal to attain, then wasn't mindlessness something to disparage and avoid? The answer turned out to be complicated, but also relevant, because of that old problem that humans tend to suffer from, narcissism, which is of course related to being stuck in our screens.

It turns out that mindlessness is really not related to mindfulness.[469] I had thought of mindlessness as cluelessness or stupidity. But it turns out that scientists see mindlessness as something akin to daydreaming, which it turns out is not a bad thing. Daydreaming alleviates the dreariness of mundane tasks and takes us to places or ideas that are tucked in the back of our minds. Daydreaming can be very creative and can result in new ideas or thinking of old ones in different ways. We are not talking about rumination of the sort discussed previously which can lead us down a black hole to depression, but the kind of thinking that is more like floating along on a cloud and focusing on how wonderful it feels.

Mindfulness comes to us from the Buddhist tradition and is generally defined as a nonjudgmental way of being very aware of what is going on around us right now.[470] Think of it as extreme perception of the external world. It is an act of seeing in a hyper-aware state of being.

What mindfulness practices taught today add to it is extreme awareness of the self and what is going on in one's mind and body. There is a heavy emphasis on the self. The purpose of practicing mindfulness in its original form[471] was to bring one into being with the universe in a way that prompted joy and gratitude for this existence, but as scholar Thomas Joiner writes, the excessive focus on the self is a perversion of the original intent and practice of mindfulness. Thus, Joiner is concerned that what people are getting from today's version of mindfulness is too much of themselves. He sees this tendency as an indication of just how narcissistic we are. It amazed me that he could write a whole book on this topic, but he brought my thinking full circle. Humans are selfish by nature, and when we spend more time thinking about ourselves during meditation, we are just growing more narcissistic. If anything, he suggests that mindfulness should make us aware of how insignificant we are in the vast creation of the universe. Mindfulness should make us humble, not more self-focused.

If mindfulness and meditation can help us get to a better place when it comes to our behavior and treatment of each other, that's all well and good. If it can improve our ability to focus and concentrate, that's good too. If it can improve our ability to think deeper and be more self-aware, then let's give it three cheers. In the end, however, I think getting our minds out of our screens might be just as good as a five-day training retreat on mindfulness-based stress reduction.

FUNCTIONING IN AND THROUGH A POST-NARCISSISTIC ERA

The years of adult bad behavior, which seem to be getting worse, not better, have taken a heavy toll on how people think about each other and treat each other. Our individual and collective behaviors have taken a nosedive. Sarcasm, insults, baiting, rudeness, entitlement, dishonesty, and denigration have filtered their way into what we accept as normative behavior, or at least tolerate, without much of a second thought. Adult drama on steroids has numbed us to the reality that we are behaving badly.

The signs of disintegration are there, but so are the answers to our problems if we choose to look for them and embrace them. We must reverse the trend toward the dehumanization of our fellow citizens that has seeped into our personal and collective identities. We need to rehumanize ourselves and change the way we see each other. Our humanness is compromised by our lack of genuine engagement with one another in relationships—those with whom we are intimate, those whom we encounter daily, those who randomly come and go in our lives, and those whom we don't know at all, but with whom we share global citizenship. Communication via computers and screens, followed by a fixation with posting pictures and performances online, mixed in with our belief that everyone should be and can be famous, these and other practices are eating our souls and making us less human. We need to have face-to-face encounters with other people who are more intentional, more thoughtful, and more genuine, if we are going survive as beings that maintain our essential humanness. We need to see ourselves in each other.

CHAPTER 12

Getting Out of the Screen

SCREENS MAY HELP US connect on some levels. They are certainly beneficial when it comes to seeing and hearing people we know and love both synchronously and asynchronously, but beyond that, when we spend hours on social media consuming or producing photos, memes, and posts, screens do more damage than good. It's especially a problem when it comes to seeing those who are not like us or who disagree with us as an adversary.[472] That's what politics in our public sphere has become.

Barbara McQuade,[473] a brilliant thinker, wise person, and kind human being has written about a fear that was expressed early in our national journey by our founding thinkers. This fear was that if our country were ever to fail as a nation, our demise would be caused by our own actions. That we would not be conquered and destroyed by an external threat, but that we would be the ones who would do ourselves in. We already experienced a Civil War that almost did cause our nation to fracture permanently, but she sees the current state of our society as one under threat from disinformation and what it can lead to. In the current case, she sees it as democracy and freedom which is what may be soon lost to us. The founders of our country realized that an educated and well-informed citizenry was essential to our success as a democratic nation. McQuade believes that lying in the cause of getting elected is destroying us, and this makes it imperative that we discuss how we come to know what we know and where our knowledge comes from, a question that interestingly has been discussed for a few centuries by philosophers, scientists, and religious thinkers.

UNDERSTANDING KNOWLEDGE
AND WHERE IT COMES FROM

Without drowning in a pool of philosophical jargon and impossibly deep logic, here's a basic summary of what knowledge is and where it comes from.[474] The basic origin of knowledge is information based in fact that has been proven or justified by empirical evidence. This means there is observable proof based on observation and experimentation. This is a scientific method of verifying that facts are accurate. It is not a method used by religions to determine what their truth or truths are, but to develop information that is reliable and confirmable in the real world that we inhabit.

Left to our own devices, we would say that we obtain knowledge through our senses which we might think of as the act of perceiving. This is a very important part of learning how to navigate the world. We make thousands of determinations based on our sensory experience of the world. For example, I can be close to one hundred percent certain that if I stick my unprotected hand into a hive full of bees, I will get stung. But perception can be wrong, as in the example of the observation that looking out to the distant horizon gives the impression that the earth is flat and we know that science has proven this to be nonfactual or false, despite the fact that 25% of the population thinks the earth is flat. Thinking that something is true doesn't make it true and accurate,[475] just as repeating a lie over and over doesn't make it true.

Another source of what we believe is factual information or knowledge is intuition, which is really a hunch based on what we perceive and what we believe.[476] The problem is that our intuition is not always correct.[477] If we don't see or perceive accurately, or if we are thrown off by beliefs or assumptions which affect how we interpret the world, then we can end up thinking something is true when it is false.[478]

In many ways adults have become hostage to their early-life education. This is particularly true when it comes to history and science. Many of us took the facts included in our basic K-12 education and decided they were all fixed in stone, and because of this, we are behind the eight ball on certain information. Good education doesn't give us a fixed set of facts by which to make decisions, it gives us the critical thinking skills to evaluate facts and new knowledge based on progress, change, and discovery. Critical thinking helps us make better assessments because it helps us sort out the junk from the authentic, and the real from the fake. Critical thinking is the primary driver of intellectual growth, which has taken a hit in recent history.[479]

Our record of history is not fixed, but is always under construction. Or better yet, history is perpetually under discovery and reevaluation. That means several things. It means that more information from the study of archeology, paleontology, anthropology, genetics, physics, and every other field of study that has been invented contributes to our total store of knowledge. This means that what might have been thought to be true and factual one hundred or one thousand years ago has shifted and been altered, because when we start learning more about ourselves and our world, we reevaluate what this knowledge means to us now. This is where interpretation comes into play. Looking backward, and forward, always nudges us to ask what x means now, even when it was thought to mean y before. The point is that knowledge is always growing, expanding, and being revised.

So what is the connection between screens and the issue of knowledge? The problem is that the screen and the information communicated to us through it is often junk, not all of it of course, but too much of it. The internet has become the primary purveyor of bad knowledge, conspiracy theories, unverified scientific garbage, and outright lies, all of which is manipulative and destructive and adds to a social environment where meanness and conflict have grown.[480]

MEANNESS AND CONFLICT

In a world where we are more fearful of the future and more likely to lash out than to lean in, meanness and conflict have increased. David Brooks,[481] writer for *The New York Times*, reports that one restaurant owner he spoke to throws a patron out once a week for bad behavior. Stories in the news about people behaving badly on airplanes have increased of late, and my husband recently related a story to me about a town council member who said that even the Democrats come in screaming and yelling at elected officials. People are in an overall snit!

Amanda Ripley,[482] a journalist who has reported on conflict all over the world, has written a book called *High Conflict* in which she maintains that high conflict has some close similarities to social drama of the steroidal sort that I have written about here. What I found most interesting and salient to this discussion is what she calls the four factors that can turn good conflict into high conflict. They are basically conflict accelerators. These are factors that throw gas on the fire.

The first is group identity. When groups are pitted against each other in a conflict, identity becomes salient. It is the old ingroup vs. outgroup phenomenon where biases and stereotypes become primary motivators and cloud out reason and common sense. The second accelerator is what she calls conflict entrepreneurs. These are people who love to see conflict get worse and generate input that divides people rather than unites them. The third is humiliation, an experience that makes the target feel that there is no option but to annihilate one's opponent, and the fourth is corruption. This is where lies, deceit, and inhumanity take over in order to get power and use it to pound the opposing party into the dust.

OUR CLASSROOMS AND WHAT CHILDREN LEARN

Classrooms today are often a microcosm of the larger world. Depending on where a child lives, there are likely to be children of recent immigrants, children who don't speak English as a first language, children who practice a variety of religions, and children of multiple races and ethnicities in their classes. Some citizens believe that children whose parents are not citizens should not be afforded a seat in our nation's public-school classrooms, but the Supreme Court has wisely said that any child who comes through the doors of our K-12 public schools must be admitted, welcomed, and treated with the same dignity as any other child.[483] All they need is proof of residency.

Every day wonderful teachers organize and manage learning for this diverse assortment of children. For this to happen smoothly and effectively, teachers set up mini societies in their classrooms. These are safe spaces where students learn with and from each other peacefully and productively, even though in the outside world, these children come from groups that may hold opposite opinions on just about everything and may dislike each other intensely.

That dislike, mistrust, and sometimes outright hate cannot infect our classrooms. In these spaces, the common good for all students dictates how children need to behave. These environments need to reflect the ideals of what it means to be American. Yet, school board meetings and policy debates have become uncivil and hostile affairs, where parents and community members vent their anger over conflicting positions on social issues and personal rights.[484] Sadly, education is often the site of tremendous social anxiety and cultural angst.

While it might be idealistic to believe that we can wrap children in a bubble of safety, equity, and kindness, shouldn't that be a goal that we strive for as a society? Afterall, we have few socializing mechanisms that are common to all of us, except K-12 education. That makes it a place where we should invest our resources and support children in becoming fully developed humans with kind hearts and sharp minds.

I bring up classrooms because they may be the one place where the bitterness of our disconnections may be able to be bridged—that is, if we get the parents out of the room and let the teachers work their magic. One of the issues that teachers have increasingly faced is helping children get along with each other as they learn and grow. One of the tools made available to educators over the past few years is social-emotional learning.[485] Having trained educators in these skills and having taught them to my own children and husband, I have concluded that not only do youth need to learn these practices, but so do the adults around them.

Depending on exposure to what is going on in schools today, you may be familiar with the term "social emotional learning."[486] Once a fringe sort of curricular topic, social emotional learning has moved mainstream and is an issue of significant concern, and of course, some controversy.[487]

Social and emotional learning (SEL) is an integral part of education and human development. SEL is the process through which all young people and adults acquire and apply the knowledge, skills, and attitudes to develop healthy identities, manage emotions and achieve personal and collective goals, feel and show empathy for others, establish and maintain supportive relationships, and make responsible and caring decisions. [488]

Social emotional learning is concerned with such abilities as knowing how to name, understand, express, and control one's emotions. It includes being able to solve problems in prosocial, nonaggressive ways. It involves learning to read others' social cues, respect people's feelings, cope with discomfort, make friends, express needs clearly and calmly, anticipate and predict the outcomes of one's decisions, understand and respect differences in people. In short, social emotional knowledge and skills promote civilized behaviors and eschew social drama (see the Appendix for the CASEL wheel). In another era we might have equated it with learning manners or going to charm school.

Adults are badly in need of some social and emotional coaching. When we see adult drama in the public sphere it is a sign that we are out of control and floundering. Flipping over tables on reality TV or its equivalent, might be entertaining on TV, but when it happens at school board meetings, we are in deep trouble.

WHAT TO LET GO OF

We need a reset. Living in this stew of drama is exhausting. Drama serves up high maintenance behaviors, and whether they take place in the world of adults or adolescents, they suck us dry. We need to figure out how to challenge drama that serves no purpose other than to wear people down. One way we can do this is to commit to civil discourse.[489] Discourse is the general tone of our public conversations and the themes that recur in these conversations. It has become harder and harder to disagree agreeably.[490] We know that when people are passionate about something, when they firmly believe they are right, when they feel that someone or something is out to get them, our ability to logically reason and consider other perspectives diminishes.

One of the favorite topics in our social discourse is blaming. When there's a problem, when something goes wrong, when someone feels aggrieved or victimized, the first response is often to ask, "Whose fault is this?" From that point on the goal becomes to lambaste an opponent, flatten anyone remotely associated with the issue, or make up a story that suits the purpose of seeking damages. I would argue that blaming is a counterproductive waste of time. We need to focus on the problems that are undermining us as functioning human beings, and how to solve them. Blaming takes up uselessly spent time that could be spent working toward a healthier and saner way of living. Whether we are trying to help a child see the world in a different way, or an angry adult mad at some injustice or slight, the best way forward is to try to reframe the problem by adding, "How can we fix this? Let's deal with this. Let's try to move on." And then move on.

While this may be an impossible ask, we need to see all of us as *us*, not an "us" and a "them."[491] So much of our conflict seems to center on our differences that have always been there and are likely to remain a part of who we are, but this acrimony and division doesn't have to define us. Part of the need here is to ask who benefits from these hostile divisions and how. What is the person's agenda? When it is embedded in self-aggrandizement or power, it's probably not going to be good for the whole of us.

WHAT TO KEEP. WHAT TO REVIVE.

We need to commit to learning how to resolve conflict peacefully and to argue our positions rationally and logically. We need to become more civil to one another. We need to do more offline sharing, talking to each other in real time, learning about critical media literacy, less whining, more serving the common good, less focusing on self-esteem, and more working toward decreasing narcissism.

Let's Talk

Having conversations and talking to each other can help us recover our connections to each other.[492] We're not talking about "gotcha" conversations, the ones that are intended to be a sarcastic attack, the kinds of opening salvos that come across more as a lobbed hand grenade than a civil opening question to start a dialogue. I distinctly remember a family member who worked on a campaign for a candidate who won the presidential election being asked by her cousin, who disliked that president, openly greeting her at a family gathering with a snide, "So how do you like the president *now*?" I don't remember what problem or situation the president was accused of causing at the time, but the question wasn't meant to start a conversation. It was meant to start an argument about politics. Sadly, many people seem to have lost interest in real conversations, instead preferring to lob one-line zingers at each other.[493] It's like the nasty tweets or asides that people use as sideways insults. Comments of this sort never lead to meaningful discussions. Perhaps we have lost how to have real conversations when so much of our interaction takes place through texts, emojis, tweets, and social media posts. Our attention spans and our abilities to conjure up sophisticated thoughts both get rusty when we don't exercise them.

Wouldn't it be wonderful if every child learned the art of debating, using rules and parameters that reflect only truthful facts that support a position? I'm not talking about debates that opposing political candidates engage in during the campaign season, which tend to be mostly theatrical (i.e., drama!). I'm talking about something that used to be taught as an academic exercise in schools. Debating was at least an afterschool activity, if not a skill included in the curriculum. In these exercises, there was no name calling, insulting, eye-rolling, or nasty asides. Just the presentation of substantiated information that built up one's own position and challenged the veracity and logic of the other's claims.

One of the most rewarding outcomes of having good conversations with someone is that it builds connections, gives us pleasure, and reduces loneliness. When conversations, even with those with whom we disagree, are thoughtful, civilized, and respectful, they fulfill a basic need to belong, to be heard, and to be valued.

As Michael Shaer[494] notes in his opinion piece, we are not about to eliminate loneliness as it relates to the problems of isolation and living through screens. The technology is here to stay, so we need to adapt. That means that we have to work at minimizing the negative effects of online existence and capitalizing on what is still available. Here are some more thoughts.

Sharing

Sharing is an antidote to loneliness, and I'm not talking about sharing on social media. I'm talking about giving things we have to other people who need them or would enjoy them, like homemade cookies or a bunch of flowers from our garden. Sharing builds connections and makes us somehow indebted to each other. In the past, sharing within a neighborhood or community was part and parcel of what brought people together and created social bonds. Today, however, many of us have so much that we no longer have to share. We may feel that we are being cheap, a burden, a nuisance, or an inconvenience when we are inclined to borrow something or ask someone for help with something.

Now we have so many ways to sidestep face-to-face connections when it comes to needing help. With do-it-yourself videos on YouTube, who needs to call up a parent or a grandparent to get advice or some specialty expertise or knowledge? Just look it up on YouTube. No need to bother the old folks for some hard-earned wisdom or expertise. Can't find grandma's old recipe? We go online and find something similar, instead of calling her up, or digging through that old box of papers we inherited from her. We are short a cup of sugar, just put in an Instacart order, instead of reaching out to a neighbor.

Sharing brings us together. It makes us feel valuable. I'm not talking about sharing online by posting photos, memes, and videos on our Facebook feed. That's not sharing; it's advertising. It's branding, and that's not real connecting. Real sharing gives us chances to talk to other humans, in real time and often face-to-face. It helps us to see each other as real and valuable, and it helps us be seen, too. It helps us see each other as useful, valuable, and needed. And when someone asks us if they can borrow a cup of sugar or a hammer, we feel useful and valued, too. We don't have enough of this anymore. It's been replaced by the screen, do-it-yourself videos, and of course, artificial intelligence.

Better Thinking

Another topic that needs resurrecting or retooling is critical media literacy. In the past, critical media literacy meant teaching kids how advertising manipulated them into buying something. Now and for the foreseeable future, this area of the curriculum needs to expand to something more akin to critical digital literacy. This area of study will explore how social media affects our thinking and behavior and how information is distorted and misrepresented. It is a growing field of study that needs to trickle down to our K-12 educational program. It is part of "critical thinking" that was discussed in a previous chapter. We need to call out bad thinking (not bad people) and learn to think better. We need to be skeptical of information and dig into it to find out who and what is behind the claims that are presented to us as facts. This is not being cynical; this is being thoughtful and thorough.

Stop Whining, Do Something for Someone Else, and Cultivate Curiosity

In the last section we dealt with the problem of blaming. To that we must add the need for all of us to take responsibility, quit whining, and do something for someone besides ourselves. This needs to be a dictum for our kids as well as for us adults. Since when did we all need someone to solve our problems for us? Where is our resilience, our common sense, and our ability to discover, create, initiate, and fix? Where is our curiosity about the world and the people in it?

Research has pointed out that over the past twenty years, our children have become less empathic.[495] It correlates with the increase in narcissism. When empathy goes by the wayside and narcissism takes over, we lose sight of how important it is to take care of each other. We have lost the ability to focus on what is good for all of us. When a society is selfish and entitled, we lose some of the social connectedness that is necessary for a healthy society.

We need to practice and celebrate service to others. Psychologists have found that people get more satisfaction and sense of well-being from doing for others than many other endeavors we engage in, including things that we do for ourselves. Perhaps it is because it makes us realize how much we have to be grateful for. Or maybe it's the reward of knowing we have contributed to another's well-being.

The psychology of self-esteem has led some of us to believe we have to practice self-congratulatory positive thinking in order to feel that we are good enough. I would argue that there might be some other things that we could do that would go a great distance to bolstering self-esteem. These include: Promoting and practicing gratitude. Seeking meaning in life outside of having status, being important, or being rich. Teaching ourselves and our children to live intentionally, not frivolously. Learning to pay attention to others and to walk in their shoes. Being humble in the face of the world we live in and the richness of the people in it. Protecting and enjoying the natural world that sustains our lives. Cultivating a spiritual life attuned to a higher form of existence. Acknowledging that happiness comes from within us. Knowing that internal motivation is always better than external motivation. Teaching, modeling, and supporting empathy for others as we parent our children or lead others. Cultivating a curiosity about the world, that manifests itself in being a thinker and a life-long learner. Choosing serious over frivolous or ignorant in all things important.

One of the manifestations of selfishness and narcissism in our society is what we do when it comes to power: getting it, having it, using it, conferring it on others, or trying to take it from someone. There are all kinds of power: personal, parental, financial, physical, social, intellectual, spiritual, military, political, religious, economic, and so it goes. You can probably think of a few more. Power needs to be used carefully. Abuse of power is a destructive force, and when we elevate those who are inclined to use power for their own ends, we risk forfeiting the glue that we need to build a strong civil society. Leadership is an act of service, and it should only be conferred on those who will exercise it carefully. We need leadership that seeks to reduce bullying and shuns aggressive management styles, across our entire society, in every kind of social organization.

Lastly, we need to revive civics education in our schools. Few people today understand the history of our country and how we came to be a democracy. Few people understand the individual and collective responsibilities required to make a free and open society work. Too few people understand the importance of civil public discourse. As we have stepped into the ever-present world of entertainment, faux news, alternative facts and nonrealities, we have lost sight of what makes societies successful. It is not possible to sustain our democracy if it is infected with social drama, fake performances, illusive truth, and excessive me-ism.

WHAT TO CHANGE PERMANENTLY

Biases keep us moored in the physical and social realities of life, but they can hinder us in detrimental ways. Howard Ross writes about what he refers to as "everyday bias."[496] Bias is a normal human psychological process that ensures that we can make decisions about our environment in an efficient and effective way. What does that mean? It means that our brain is wired so that we can make quick decisions about our environment so that we can navigate the world successfully. We learn to generalize about the world so that we can make choices quickly. Experience helps us to make predictions so that we can quickly assess our surroundings and make safe decisions without a lot of cumbersome thinking. For example, if I don't know about how stoves work and I put my hand in the gas flame or on a red glass or metal surface, I'm going to learn that it burns, that it's dangerous, and that if I see such a flame or a red glass/ metal surface in the future, I won't touch it. I will assume that it is hot and that I'll get burned if I touch it. In other words, we generalize so that decision making becomes almost automatic. It's a survival mechanism. It is an essential brain function that has kept humans from becoming extinct.

The downside of making these generalizations is that they almost guarantee that we will make decisions about people based on stereotypes.[497] For example, if I have come to believe that all young, black men in hoodies are going to hurt me, I'm going to be wary and hesitant when I am in the presence of young, black men in hoodies. The problem is that most if not all young, black men in hoodies are not going to do anything to hurt me.

When we formulate these generalizations, we are cultivating what we call biases. This natural tendency to form generalizations is not a flaw in our human reaction to our world. In fact, it would be confusing, clunky, and downright dangerous if we couldn't form biases. These biases help us make decisions and navigate the world. Biases are normal, natural, and necessary.[498]

The problem, however, is that biases are often based on stereotypes such as: All Muslims are terrorists. Republicans protect the rich. Democrats raise taxes and spend prolifically. Asians are good at math. Children with special needs get more of their share of educational resources than other students. Children whose parents have entered the US illegally should not get access to public education or health care. Wealthy parents expect special treatment for their children.

All of those statements are examples of beliefs, and beliefs are not facts, and they cannot be asserted as objective truths. Beliefs are subjective and while most people have collected enough information to generalize these beliefs as facts, they are still beliefs.[499]

Objective truth and facts have taken a big hit over the past few years, and unfortunately this misinformation and in some cases, these outright lies, have seriously affected our behaviors.[500] One of the first things that happens as drama ramps up is the scrambling of truth and facts.[501] This often happens because drama is rife with gossip. People may not be intentionally relating bad information, but as kids report, drama is like playing the old game of "telephone." Sitting in a circle, one person whispers a statement to the person to his/her/their right. That person passes it to the next person, etc. The last person to hear the message repeats it out loud to the group and compares it to the first person's original statement. Often there is no connection between the first and the last statement. The result of scrambled facts and the twisting of truth is that social interactions become adversarial and hostile, and this is exactly the kind of frightful nonsense that can happen in drama, whether it's the adolescent version or the adult version.

Adults, hence American society, are living in a psychotic world. We dance between truth and falsity attaching ourselves to both at the same time. Or at least trying to. It's unsustainable, dangerous, and speaks to a deep-seated confusion about who we are. Some people believe that the answers to our current societal disjointedness are found in the past, but no society has ever succeeded by trying to turn the clock back.

Looking backward to a better past is always dangerous because it was never as idyllic as we imagine. Nostalgia blinds us to the inequities, dangerous stereotypes, and overlooked ugliness of which we were often largely unaware. However, there are some vestiges that we might do well to revive, rethink, and relaunch with an updated worldview and open-eyed awareness of what needs to be done to build a future, without the biases of the past.

I am not a particularly global sort of person who relishes the experiences of cultures greatly different from my own. There are certain types of food, music, smells, behaviors, practices, and habits that make me uncomfortable. I make no apologies for these feelings, but I believe our behaviors toward people and their cultural norms that make us uncomfortable should be reasonably controlled. Discomfort is part of life. I used to tell my students that they didn't have to like each other, but that they had to respect each other. That meant making room for behaviors, attire, and cultural differences that they (or I) found unappealing, confusing, or annoying. Learning to cope with feelings of discomfort is part of learning to function in multiple, complex social environments.

I'm not talking about the kind of discomfort that is associated with danger, the intuition that something bad is happening whether it is people's behaviors (e.g., someone drunk getting in a car to drive); environmental threats (e.g., tornadoes); or someone coming at us with fists clenched or a pointed gun. I'm talking about people going about their daily lives, engaging in normal social behavior, at least normal as defined by their group and recognized by society as prosocial—doing something that they have a basic right to do, at a determined place and time. I'm talking about someone just being a human being.

That may sound vague, but it would include same-sex sex in a private space where only those individuals are participating. It also can extend to men dressing like women and the converse, gender reassignment, or wearing attire that may be strange to some of us, but commonplace and culturally appropriate for that person. Just because I'm uncomfortable with the idea of homosexual sex, doesn't mean that I should interfere with a person's right to have sexual contact in a consensual manner. Just because I don't find a given culture appealing doesn't mean I have the right to interfere with the rights of the people who subscribe to that culture.

When we consider the history of genocides and civil wars, it seems to me that we ought to be of the mind that anyone and everyone should be afforded a place and a space to live their lives in peace. Do I care that my progeny, if I have them, will live in a world where people don't look exactly like me or speak like me? No, I don't. I trust that my offspring, their counterparts, and all those who inhabit planet Earth will be civilized enough to extend to each other the right to live their lives respectful of each other. Trying to wipe out a cultural or ethnic group that makes me uncomfortable is not only ridiculous, futile, or impossible. It is evil.

DEVELOPING SOCIAL IDENTITIES THAT UNITE US

If we revisit adolescent drama, we recall that much of what goes on at that point in development is connected to exploring and creating an identity. Also, as noted, the drama we are experiencing as adults is also related to our uncertainty about our identity, our collective one.

Social drama can be an exercise in shallowness that seeks adulation from the audience, and very little else. In its extremes, it can reflect a lack of substance. We need to ask ourselves how we can cultivate more authenticity and what it might look like. One of the hallmarks of some personality disorders is identity confusion, the challenge of knowing who we are in a relatively stable way.[502] People in Western cultures tend toward valuing the individual as opposed to the collective, and while this characteristic is a prominent feature of our identity, we can look beyond ourselves if we are deliberate about it. We can come to see the benefit of valuing a sense of responsibility to the collective.

Covid-19 and communication using social media have increased loneliness. People no longer feel the need to gather in face-to-face situations. It may be because of the fear of contracting the virus, or it may be due to the ease of electronic communication as a substitute, or it might be that the ease of working from home is just too convenient compared with the hassles of getting to the office. Regardless, we are moving in a direction where loneliness and social isolation are affecting us as a collective. When we individually choose solitude over being with others, the world can close in on us and we can lose perspective. While we might believe it to be true, social media will not save us, nor does it really connect us in the ways that strengthen our bonds to one another. We need initiatives that bring people together in face-to-face gatherings. Community organizations can play a role in supporting activities that invite casual as well as formal connections between people. Belonging is a basic human need, making it essential for psychological health. Relationships that foster belongingness can help us develop a connection to something larger than ourselves, a sign of social and psychological health. Communities that are connected survive the divisiveness that collective narcissism fosters.[503] These communities subscribe to the position that we are in this together. None of us are the "other." Our viability is a collective task.

In the past, one problem that often brought fractured societies together was war. After the fall of the Soviet Union, Ukraine was a country that vacillated between autocratic and democratic tendencies until Russia invaded in 2022. But when threatened by a permanent return to autocracy, the country solidly united under the prospects of a democratic future. In early 2023, there was talk of a possible world war if Russia and China united against the West. If Ukraine falls to Putin, will the Western world come to its aid? Will there be another global war fought in Western Europe, this time not against Germany, but against Russia and China? It's a horrible thought that we could repeat the past, yet, during those times of death and destruction, people put aside domestic differences and work together. No one at home is "the other."[504]

Wouldn't it be wonderful if we could somehow bring that kind of unanimity into our society, but without some catastrophic destruction like war? One idea that I have toyed with is the notion of some sort of universal experience for youth or young adults across our nation. The draft and universal military service performed that function to a degree earlier in our history. In other societies, there is a year of mandatory service for all citizens. These experiences widen people's horizons and help them develop broader perspectives. My dad served in the Air Force during the Korean War, and he had the good fortune to meet a young fellow from New Jersey. In many ways, they were different, ethnically, and socio-economically, but they became fast, life-long friends. Without a way to meet and come to know "the other," he might have succumbed to negative stereotypes about this man. If only there were some ways for each of us to have experiences with those we don't know, don't like, don't trust, or are afraid of. Unless we can see ourselves in fellow citizens who are not like us, we will not solve problems. We will only create more.

One facet of this move toward each other is the realization that there will always be new challenges to meet or problems to solve. This isn't so much being negative about people and life but recognizing that we and the world are always changing. Taking on challenges and addressing them are signs of psychological health. We should expect difficulty and be prepared to meet it as a community. It's an affirmative act that celebrates our human movement toward a better world, and it could be a part of our healing as a society. It also addresses our need to have a narrative about ourselves as people who have more than an individual identity often rooted in a political or ideological agenda. Somehow, we need to set aside the righteousness and toxicity that divides us and creates high conflict[505] and drama on steroids. A United States senator even sees this problem and wants to address it. In a conversation with journalist James Pogue, Senator Chris Murphy expressed the following sentiment: "[I] do believe that we have to tell a story about what makes…people proud of being American. And [to understand] that [their American] identity is more important than their individual political identity."[506]

Lastly, I offer the wisdom of Loretta J. Ross[507] who espouses that we teach our students to call each other "in," not "out." What she is advocating is an approach that we would all do well to learn. She works with students on subjects that can lead to what we have come to know as "cancel culture." Canceling people happens when they say something biased that is offensive to a group that has experienced marginalization. Those who are offended, whether part of that group or not, react by publicly rejecting, humiliating, or denigrating the person who has behaved so. Canceling omits the possibility of repairing the damage done and building understanding. Ross views "calling out," when no harm has been intended, as contributing to our division and fragmentation. "Calling in" respects the historical entitlement and the damage that shows up in how we talk to one another, so that we can listen to and express our understanding of one another in civil ways. It reduces drama and conflict and seeks to build connection. It respects feelings, reduces the need for excessive emotionality and replaces it with genuine dialogue. It helps us move toward a healthy society, something we all need to be concerned about.

CONCLUSION
Today's World

BASED ON TODAY'S STANDARDS for social media drama, and the increasingly public lives that many youth live, the case study of adolescent social drama discussed in Chapter 3 is hardly a one-off situation. These girls used the communication tools and platforms at hand to express their frustration with someone's behavior, but experienced criticism worse than what they dished out because they had acted hypocritically. The inability to be reflective is typical of adolescent development especially when doing difficult identity work. Yes, they were narcissistic and acted entitled. Yes, they put themselves out there and put on a show. Yes, it was immature. But it wasn't fake, fabricated, or contrived. It was authentic. It caused chaos and angst, mostly because it became such a public spectacle. And it was all real, unlike what often becomes drama in our adult world today.

I now find myself wondering about a different set of questions about behavior when emotions are high, behavior is impulsive, social media is involved, and most people have access to artificial intelligence.

Is the story I am seeing real or is it fake? Is this narrative a documentary or nothing but fabrication? Is this interaction predetermined and contrived, or is it spontaneous and genuine? Is the person performing, or are they assuming an alternative identity? Can the two be blended? Does what "sells" determine which identity or portion of an identity is being performed? Does becoming a commodity mean accepting a life of constant surveillance? The answer is "yes." Is this constant exposure good, bad, or neither? What determines the value or worth of constant online commoditization? When does someone know when the real person stops and the fake one begins? Does it matter if kids play with this kind of identity development? What about adults who do this occasionally or all the time? How has social media come to figure so heavily in this process?

When someone chooses around-the-clock surveillance to become a celebrity, there is no more privacy, and there cannot be any shame. What is out there is out there. Vanessa and her friends had no shame in the beginning of the HWB-Pretty Pucksters conflict. There seemed to be little public shame for anyone discussing and commenting on social media about three people all involved in having sex, often a common theme in adolescent social drama. Eventually, Vanessa wanted "out" from the HWBs performance, but her friends didn't. So, she had a choice to make: continue to participate in the girls' hockey drama, or move away from her friends. She chose to withdraw from them, a form of passive "cancellation," in today's parlance. Later, her friends apologized and they all resumed their friendship, which continues more than a decade to today.

It's interesting to reflect on the fact that the entire saga of the girls' social drama occurred before the proliferation of a culture that condones the widespread use of canceling people for their mistakes. It could be argued that the girls' mean tweet to and about the girl who slept with their friend was an attempt to cancel the guilty girl, but it didn't work because the school community attacked them for what they saw as their hypocrisy. In the end, there was tolerance and forgiveness, and an adoption of a "let's move on" perspective. I'm not sure that could happen in today's social environment because aggressive and mean canceling of people is so accepted. The entertainment value of the drama dissipated rather quickly in this case because most of the players involved stopped throwing gasoline on the fire.

We should be deeply concerned about the blurring of entertainment, complete with its overlap of lies and fake reality with authentic reality. It seems that the desire to be one of the chosen celebrities who wield influence and get noticed, is a shallow goal. Do I really want my child to aspire to be an online celebrity who spends his, her, or their days in front of a screen, posing for the ever-present camera, and participating in aggressive or frivolous behavior? No, I don't. I want meaningful over pointless for my children. And I want serious over stupid from adults.

Collapse or Transformation?

How can we reconcile the idea of collapse with the idea of transformation? Is there a way to interpret Newitz's premises in light of Margaret

Wheatley's concerns? In rather obvious ways they seem to contradict each other. Where do they overlap? Can we save ourselves and our culture through transformation and beat the future predicted in the narrative of collapse?

Sir John Glubb[508] includes the following circumstances as signs that a society is about to collapse and be overtaken by a stronger entity (i.e., get conquered!): internal political hatreds become overwhelming, cynicism overtakes a belief in core values, and nothing important is taken seriously. Society displays traits and behaviors such as frivolity, hedonism, pessimism, narcissism, materialism, fatalism, and fanaticism. Politics is increasingly corrupt and injustice creeps into many facets of life. There is an extreme imbalance in wealth distribution. Celebrity cultures flourish where those held in highest regard are athletes, singers, and actors.

What seems to undergird the outcomes of collapse are loss of commitment to values that support human well-being and positive growth. Reading between the lines suggests that societies collapse because of a failure to adhere to values and behaviors that are life enhancing, when they ignore what is essential for everyone. This isn't a political failure alone but one that falls on the shoulders of leaders across the entire spectrum of our society—and one that falls most heavily on religious leaders and secular thought leaders, people who are respected for their willingness to listen, learn, and speak truth to power instead of seeking to amass power. The question becomes whether or not we can put leaders in place who can usher us through a period of transformation where we preserve what is good and necessary and move us toward each other.[509]

Pulling It All Together

So, what is the thread that starts with adolescent social drama and ends with society-wide social decline? I began writing this book not knowing that would be the question that I would ultimately need to answer. I didn't realize that adolescent drama, a behavioral issue that should time itself out by adulthood, would take me to a place where concerns over our societal collapse would manifest themselves. Some readers may accuse me of setting up the construct of adolescent social drama as a straw man so that I could write a book on politics. Despite this, I have tried to be objective and factual when it comes to the current state of our society and our political behaviors. Nevertheless, I do see connections between adolescent social drama and egregious bad behavior in adults, many of them displayed by politicians. If we are going to rescue ourselves, we need to sidestep politics, set aside our distrust of each other, be honest and kind, and talk to each other. I believe these are the disconnections we need to acknowledge as damaging to our sanity.

We must keep the following in mind: The internet and its accompanying platforms and applications are contributing to a less civil, less intelligent, and more poorly informed society. We are at risk of losing our ability to think deeply and attend to complex ideas and situations. Governing, parenting, educating, recreating, working, and human development itself, in a world that is being permanently changed by digital influence, has become more confusing and less certain. Relationships are being permanently altered by online consumption, digital communication, and lack of face-to-face interactions. Whether caused by, or the result of these changes, narcissism is increasing, as well as loneliness, anxiety, depression, materialism, and empathy. All of this suggests that we are at a loss for knowing who we are and what we value. In other words, we need to develop an identity that will carry us into a better and healthier future.

Social media will never meet all of our basic needs for belonging, connection, and self-fulfillment. It is more likely to interfere with our attempts to meet these needs when we primarily choose social media instead of face-to-face contact.

While these negative trends are well on their way to causing permanent dysfunction, there are ways to step up and do the identity work that will heal our society. It's not up to government to push this agenda, it's up to the members of our rank-and-file families and communities to begin discussions that will work their way up the ladder to hopefully, responsible leadership that can support these kinds of civic changes.

Logan Lane's Interview

In February of 2023, Logan Lane gave an interview to Lulu Garcia-Navarro for The New York Times Opinion broadcast, "First Person."[510] At the time Logan was a 17-year-old from Brooklyn, New York. She recounted her story of smartphone use and the effects it had on her during her adolescence.

Logan recounts her excitement at getting her first smartphone and opening an Instagram account when she was 11 years old. She recalls how she slept with it at her side. Afterall, she states that it's not possible to sleep with your computer quite the way it is with a phone.

Logan's impulse was to use her phone all the time texting her friends and mindlessly scrolling. On Instagram she joined a group of kids who were part of a popular group from another school through chat room contact. These girls were pretty, had boyfriends, and dressed well.

She says she felt weird in comparison to them because while she wanted to be popular, it didn't feel right because she didn't really care about being popular, but there was a certain high to the experience with these girls.

In seventh and eighth grades she began to post weird and unflattering selfies on Instagram and rejected the flattering aspects of the app. After a four-month hiatus from her phone because she had lost it, she says that it was nice to be without it, but at the same time when she got her phone back, she remembers feeling good about not being on the app and then the next minute missing it intensely.

During early high school, she spent a lot of time painting, knitting, and crocheting, primarily for the purpose of posting her creations online so that she would get approval from people on Instagram. When COVID-19 hit and school went online, her phone use accelerated to 24 hours a day. The effect was sleeplessness, life dysregulation, and changes in the shape of her hands and fingers, but more than that she started feeling unsatisfied with herself, doubting herself, and comparing herself to others who were prettier or more artistic. She developed "shame about who she wasn't."

At some point during COVID-19, she realized that other people were making better use of their time than she was. It made her realize that if she were going to be productive, she would have to take a step back from her smartphone. She kept her iCloud account and texting for ways to communicate with people, but closed her TikTok, Snapchat, and Instagram accounts. She got a flip phone, so she couldn't access the internet. As she expected, she pretty much lost her friends because they weren't interested in email or texting. When she ran into people she knew before, they would comment on how different she was from the person she had been when she was really plugged in.

The biggest change for Logan was that she started getting up early to be ready for her Zoom classes. She started eating lunch and looking forward to dinner with her family. She started making her own pants, and then she started *reading* [my emphasis], which she claimed was better than watching TV.

However, she was still lonely, primarily because she had no online friends. She wanted friends and knew that she needed them, but access was a serious problem. So she began to look for kids, who, like her, had ditched their smartphones in lieu of meeting together in person and talking to each other. And strangely, when in-person school resumed, all the people she had known on social media were no longer interesting or appealing to her.

Instead, she found that she really connected with people who enjoyed reading and did things like go to the farmers' market, meet for cider and donuts, or attend a concert. The problem was that this was a bit too random, so Logan founded a formal group, called the Luddite Club,[511] made up of kids like her who rejected the idea that spending all their time on screens was a good way to live. They would have regular meetings that might last twelve hours, and they would do things like go to the beach, talk about books, or hang out at a friend's pool, and of all things, they would have *a combination of a bunch of conversations* [my emphasis].

Logan makes several observations about living life on screens. "There's no premeditated Instagram knowledge, so there's no me knowing things about them [her unplugged friends] that they don't know that I know. It's made me more appreciative of people showing up [for each other]." She hopes that parents of the future "will be able to better manage kids and their technology at appropriate ages," unlike her generation.

Logan says she feels smarter than she did because she lives her life with more intentionality about what she chooses to include in her life. She says she feels more confident and has less social anxiety. She also claims she has a better grasp of reality, "whereas I was living in a sort of fantasy world before."

Lastly, Logan fears that if she ever goes back online she "fears what will become of the authentic me." She fears "that she might lose a part of myself." Not everyone is a Logan, but too many are.

Logan's story is startling, remarkable, and prescient. She speaks of inauthentic online friendships, and the tendency for people to become who they really are not. She tells a tale of addiction, overconsumption, withdrawal symptoms, ambivalent and erratic behaviors, emotional and physical exhaustion, and a fixation with the audience and her performance for the audience. She describes a life that is lonely, empty, and depressing. She considers choosing to live a life with the screen off, or on for that matter, as a life-style choice.

It makes me wonder: When did a smartphone become so essential that it could determine a lifestyle? This suggests that smartphones and the internet are very powerful tools, that for too many of us, use *us* instead of us using them. How can something that was supposed to be so good for us be so bad for some of us? What is happening to youth who get so sucked into social media and the screen that they start to suffer physically and mentally as they are unable to stop reacting to pings, rings, and dings from their phones?

I wonder if screens and social media are eating away at our humanity and purpose in life. Are some of us losing our souls to the altar of algorithms, celebrity-ism, and FoMO? What happens when nobody is looking at our performances anymore? Can we withstand the silence and stillness? Social media makes us lonelier because we forfeit real connection for adulation, and "likes." What happens when the "likes" stop? What do we do then? Who are we then? What *are* we then?

When everything that appears in front of us must be entertaining, when do we get to stop and relax, and just "be," especially when we are always the entertainment, not just the audience? Maybe that only happens when we turn off the screen and look around us. But who does that anymore? We go out to dinner and everyone at the tables stare at their phones. Families gather for holidays and half the guests are on their phones or iPads the entire time. We converse with our "audiences" online when we are in a room full of people who don't appear to us on a screen, but are blinking, breathing, laughing, and speaking in our presence? Is this preferable to a person on a screen? I hope not.

What meaning does experience have when all experience is processed through a screen? And after that, we capture it, post it, and wait for someone not physically present to us to respond to an experience they didn't have? Feels like a waste of time when authentic experience is right there beyond the screen, often in the presence of other living beings.

Have you ever had a moment when you didn't want to take a photograph of something, but just wanted to be there, in the totality of the now, the space you were in, to make sure that you savored the feeling of awe, or ecstasy, or bliss, not doing anything but enjoying and relishing the sights and sounds of the moment? Most people can't resist a selfie in those tantalizing moments that we wish could go on forever. Whenever I've taken a photo in one of those moments, the picture never captures or communicates the totality of the experience. Instead, I feel like I wasted precious time or was cheated out of the joy of the moment by distracting myself to take a photo of it.

We need more of each other, but not through screens.

A Last Word

It is important to note that as a society we are only beginning our journey into a world where electronic, mediated communication is completely inextricable from our lives. The research on how it affects our brains, our behaviors, and our relationships is in its early stages.

Communication tools, software, platforms, and the way we integrate the inevitable changes that will continue to come are not clear and not easily predicted. Likewise, the effects of these tools and how we use them are also illusive. Yet, I don't in any way suggest that we move backward in time, not that it is even possible. Too often, those who fear the present think the answers lie in a wholesale reversal to the past. That is not at all what I would want to see happen. Many of our core values are timeless, and those are the ones that we need to focus on. Drama, whether on an adolescent scale or on a society-wide scale, obscures the reality of our challenges and problems, and encourages us to look for solutions in superficial, impermanent, and sometimes regressive ways. It is time to ditch our affinity for drama, stop acting like our lives are playing out online or in the fake world of reality TV surrogacy, and reclaim our authentic selves. It's time for us to be grown-ups.

Endnotes

1   Simmons, *Odd Girl Out*; Wiseman, *Queen Bees and Wannabees*.

2   Allen, "Off the Radar," "Students' and Staff Members," "Tweeting, Texting, and Facebook Postings," "Understanding Bullying," and "We Don't Have Bullying."

3   Marwick and boyd, "It's Just Drama."

4   Postman, *Amusing Ourselves to Death*.

5   Postman, *Amusing Ourselves to Death*, 92–93.

6   Postman, *Amusing Ourselves to Death*, 155–156.

7   Words given to Justice Potter Stewart by his clerk Alan Novak in response to Justice Stewart's question about how to describe pornography.http://bleogs.wsj.com/law/2007/09/27the-origins-of-justice-stewarts-i-know-it-when-i-see-it/

8   Allen, "Off the Radar," "Students' and Staff Members," "Tweeting, Texting, and Facebook Postings," "Understanding Bullying," and "We Don't Have Bullying"; Smith et al., "'Drama' in Interpersonal."

9   Frankowski, et al., Developing and Testing a Scale, 200.

10 Frankowski, et al., Developing and Testing a Scale, 193–194.

11 Lyons, *Addicted to Drama*.

12 Lyons, *Addicted to Drama*, 3.

13 Bergner, "What Is Personality?"; Sharp, "Personality Disorders."

14 Bornovalova et al., "Stability, Change, and Heritability"; Caspi, "The Child is Father"; Caspi & Roberts, "Personality Development"; McAdams & Olson, "Personality Development"; Wanqvist et al., "Child and Adolescent Predictors."

15 Allen, "Tweeting, Texting, and Facebook"; Smith et al, "'Drama' in Interpersonal Conflict."

16 John et al., "Paradigm Shift."

17 John et al., "Paradigm Shift."

18 Mishel, *The Marshmallow Test.*

19 Allen, "Tweeting, Texting, and Facebook," "We Don't Have Bullying"; Smith et al., "Drama in Interpersonal Conflict."

20 Gunderson, "Borderline Personality Disorder"; Weston & Riolo, "Childhood and Adolescent Precursors."

21 Bender, "Mirror, Mirror on the Wall"; Thomaes et al., "When Narcissus Was a Boy."

22 Exline, "Too Proud to Let Go"; Hendrick, "Narcissism and the 'Politics of Recognition.'"

23 Reijntjes et al., "Narcissism, Bullying, and Social Dominance."

24 Derry et al., "Fearing Failure: Grandiose Narcissism"; Miller et al., "Grandiose and Vulnerable."

25 Derry et al., "Fearing Failure: Grandiose Narcissism."

26 Gore & Widiger, "Fluctuation between Grandiose and Vulnerable."

27 Bushman & Baumeister, "Threatened Egotism, Narcissism"; Fanti & Henrich, "Effects of Self-Esteem and Narcissism"; Reijntjes et al., "Narcissism, Bullying and Social Dominance"; Thomaes et al., "Trumping Shame by Blasts."

28 Derry et al., "Fearing Failure: Grandiose Narcissism"; Gore & Widiger, "Fluctuation between Grandiose and Vulnerable."

29 Baumeister et al., "Relation of Threatened Egotism"; Bushman & Baumeister, "Threatened Egotism, Narcissism, Self-Esteem."

30 Hendrick, "Narcissism and the 'Politics of Recognition.'"

31 Orth et al., "Development of Narcissism."

32 Cramer, "Young Adult Narcissism"; Thomaes, "When Narcissus was."

33 Harter, *The Construction of the Self.*

34 Farrant et al., "Perspective Taking."

35 Barnett & Womack, "Fearing, Not Loving."

36 Durvasula, *Don't You Know Who.*

37 Orth et al., "Development of Narcissism."

38 Caspi & Roberts, "Personality Development Across."

39 McAdams, "Personality Development."

40 Newton-Howes, *Personality Disorder*; Paris, *Personality Disorders*; Sharp, "Personality Disorders"; Ray et al., "All in the Mind's Eye?"

41 Hervas & Vazquez, "What Else Do You Feel"; Lyubomirsky et al., "Why Ruminators Are Poor"; Newton-Howes, *Personality Disorder.*

42 Bushman & Baumeister, "Threatened Egotism, Narcissism"; Hervas & Vazquez, "What Else Do You Feel"; Lyubomirsky et al., "Why Ruminators Are Poor"; Newton-Howes, *Personality Disorder*; Ray et al, "All in the Mind's Eye?"

43 Harter, *The Construction of the Self.*

44 Feinstein et al, "Negative Social Comparison"; Vogel et al., "Social Comparison, Social Media."

45 Feinstein et al, "Negative Social Comparison"; Vogel et al., "Social Comparison, Social Media."

46 Lyubomirsky & Nolen-Hoeksema, "Effects of Self-Focused Rumination"; Smith & Rose, "The 'Cost of Caring.'"

47 Rose, "Co-Rumination in the Friendships"; Smith & Rose, "The 'Cost of Caring.'"

48 Rose, "Co-Rumination in the Friendships."

49 Rose, "Co-Rumination in the Friendships."

50 Rose, "Co-Rumination in the Friendships"; Smith & Rose, "The 'Cost of Caring.'"

51 Rose, "Co-Rumination in the Friendships."

52 Rose, "Co-Rumination in the Friendships."

53 Rose, "Co-Rumination in the Friendships."

54 Bowker et al, "Mutual Best Friendship"; Staebler et al., "Rejection Sensitivity."

55 Bowker et al, "Mutual Best Friendship"; Staebler et al., "Rejection Sensitivity."

56 Sharp, "Personality Disorders."

57 Allen, "Students' and Staff Members' Understanding"; Lyons, *Addicted to Drama.*

58 Harter, *The Construction of the Self.*

59 Goffman, *The Presentation of Self.*

60 Milner, *Freaks, Geeks, and Cool.*

61 Duvall, *Celebrity and Youth*; Eriksson et al., "Identity Development in Early."

62 Bronfenbrenner, "Toward an Experimental Ecology"; Lerner, *Concepts and Theories.*

63 Benson, *All Kids Are Our Kids.*

64 Bronfenbrenner, "Toward an Experimental Ecology."

65 Milner, *Freaks, Geeks, and Cool.*

66   Hervas et al., "Revealing the Self in a Digital."
67   Goffman, *The Presentation of Self*; Harter, *The Construction of the Self.*
68   Rose, "Co-Rumination in the Friendships."
69   Towner et al., "Revealing the Self in a Digital."
70   Towner et al., "Revealing the Self in a Digital."
71   McInroy et al., "LGBTQ+ Youths' Community."
72   Towner et al., "Revealing the Self in a Digital."
73   Vijayakumar & Pfeifer, "Self-Disclosure during Adolescence."
74   Tamir & Mitchell, "Disclosing Information about the Self."
75   Tamir & Mitchell, "Disclosing Information about the Self."
76   Simmons, *Odd Girl Out*; Wiseman, *Queen Bees and Wannabees.*
77   Smith & Rose, "The 'Cost of Caring.'"
78   Marwick & boyd, "Networked Privacy."
79   Smith & Rose, "The 'Cost of Caring.'"
80   Ligocki, *The Drama of Reality.*
81   Goffman, *The Presentation of Self.*
82   Goffman, *The Presentation of Self.*
83   Goffman, *The Presentation of Self.*
84   The Poetry Foundation, "Speech: All the."
85   Goffman, *The Presentation of Self.*
86   Marcus, *The Drama of Celebrity*, 9.
87   Marwick & boyd, "I Tweet Honestly."
88   Milner, "Is Celebrity a New Kind."
89   Duvall, *Celebrity and Youth.*
90   Milner, "Is Celebrity a New Kind."
91   Duvall, *Celebrity and Youth*; Gamson, "The Unwatched Life"; Grin staff & Murray, "Reality Celebrity."
92   Duvall, *Celebrity and Youth*; Gamson, "The Unwatched Life"; Grin staff & Murray, "Reality Celebrity"; Lewis & Christin, "Platform Drama"; Marwick, *Status Update.*
93   Driessens, "Celebrity Capital"; Marcus, *The Drama of Celebrity.*
94   Driessens, "Celebrity Capital," 543.
95   Duvall, *Celebrity and Youth*; Ligocki, *The Drama of Reality*; Milner, "Is Celebrity a New Kind."
96   Marwick, *Status Update*; Marwick & boyd, "To See and Be Seen."
97   Ligocki, *The Drama of Reality Television.*

98   Ligocki, *The Drama of Reality Television*; Milner, "Is Celebrity a NewKind."

99   Milner, "Is Celebrity a New Kind."

100 Duvall, *Celebrity and Youth.*

101 Logocki, *The Drama of Reality*; Psarras, "'It's a Mix of Authenticity and Complete"; Grindstaff & Murray, "Reality Celebrity."

102 McIntire et al., "Tax Records Reveal."

103 Elliott & Wattanasuwan, "Brands as Symbolic"; Marwick, *Status Update*; Marwick, "Instafame: Luxury."

104 Duvall, *Celebrity and Youth. Marwick, Status Update."*

105 Elliott & Wattanasuwan, "Brands as Symbolic"; Marwick & boyd, "I Tweet Honestly"; Scolere et al., "Constructing the Platform-Specific"; Whitmer, "You Are Your Brand."

106 Elliott & Wattanasuwan, "Brands as Symbolic"; Marwick, "*Status Update*"; Marwick, "Instafame: Luxury"; Scolere et al., "Constructing the Platform-Specific'" Whitmer, "You Are Your Brand."

107 Duvall, *Celebrity and Youth.*

108 Duvall, *Celebrity and Youth*; Marwick, *Status Update.*

109 Duvall, *Celebrity and Youth*; Marwick, *Status Update.*

110 Gamson, "The Unwatched Life."

111 Garber, "We've Lost the Plot."

112 Duvall, *Celebrity and Youth.*

113 Elliott & Wattanasuwan, "Brands as Symbolic."

114 Lowry et al., "Why Do Adults Engage."

115 Lowry et al., "Why Do Adults Engage."

116 Lowry et al., "Why Do Adults Engage."

117 Baumeister & Leary, "The Need to Belong."

118 Smetana et al., "Adolescent Development."

119 Milner, "Is Celebrity a New Kind of Status Symbol?"

120 Milner, *Freaks, Geeks, and Cool Kids.*

121 Milner, *Freaks, Geeks, and Cool Kids.*

122 Milner, *Freaks, Geeks, and Cool Kids.*

123 Milner, *Freaks, Geeks, and Cool Kids.*

124 Dossey, "FOMO, Digital Dementia, Jabeen et al., "Social Media-Induced"; Prysbylski et al., "Motivational, Emotional."

125 Dossey, "FOMO, Digital Dementia, Jabeen et al., "Social

Media-Induced"; Prysbylski et al., "Motivational, Emotional."

126 Miller, "New Media, Networking."

127 Abell et al., "Fear of Missing Out."

128 Allen, "Off the Radar"; Lowry et al., "Why Do Adults Engage."

129 Duvall, Celebrity and Youth.

130 Abrams, "How to Turn Reality Star."

131 Kavka, "Reality TV," 7.

132 Kavka, "Reality TV," 7.

133 Kavka, "Reality TV," 7.

134 Kavka, "Reality TV," 7.

135 Psarras, "It's a Mix of Authenticity and Complete."

136 Abrams, "How to Turn Reality Star."

137 Hill, Reality TV.

138 Gilbert, "The Cruel Social Experiment."

139 Abrams, "How to Turn Reality Star."

140 Gilbert, "The Cruel Social Experiment"; Glascock & Preston-Schreck, "Verbal Aggression, Race, and Sex."

141 Glascock & Preston-Schreck, "Verbal Aggression, Race, and Sex"; Hill, Reality TV.

142 Glascock & Preston-Schreck, "Verbal Aggression, Race, and Sex."

143 Pozner, Reality Bites Back.

144 Ligocki, The Drama of Reality, 44.

145 Kuhne & Opree, "From Admiration to Devotion"; Ligocki, The Drama of Reality.

146 Opree & Kuhne, "Linking Adolescents' Exposure."

147 McIntire et al., "Tax Records Reveal How Fame."

148 McIntire et al., "Tax Records Reveal How Fame."

149 Marcus, The Drama of Celebrity, 21.

150 McIntire, "Tax Records Reveal How Fame."

151 Post, Dangerous Charisma.

152 Adams, "Trump and the Social Trance."

153 Marcus, The Drama of Celebrity, 23–26.

154 "Albert Bandura's Social Learning Theory," https://www.simply-psychology.org/bandura.html.

155 Lewis & Christin, "Platform Drama: 'Cancel Culture.'"

156 Lewis & Christin, "Platform Drama: 'Cancel Culture.'"

157 Lewis & Christin, "Platform Drama: 'Cancel Culture.'"

158 Kroes, "The Revenge."

159 Garber, "We've Lost the Plot"; Kroes, "The Revenge."

160 Garber, "We've Lost the Plot"; Kroes, "The Revenge."

161 Kavka, "Reality TV," 15.

162 Crawford, "Those Foolish Things."

163 Crawford, "Those Foolish Things."

164 Allen, "We Don't Have Bullying."

165 Piotrowski, "Adult Bully Syndrome."

166 Andersson & Pearson, "Tit for Tat?"

167 Hartin et al., "Bullying in Nursing."

168 Namie & Namie, *The Bully at Work.*

169 Paull & Omari, "Dignity and Respect."

170 Smith et al., "'Drama' in Interpersonal."

171 Book et al., "Adolescent Bullying"; Fanti & Henrich, "Effects of Self-Esteem"; Reijntjes et al., "Narcissism, Bullying, and Social Dominance"; Van Geel et al., "Are Youth Psychopathic Traits."

172 Van Geel et al., "Are Youth Psychopathic Traits."

173 Gore & Widiger, "Fluctuation between Grandiose"; Paris, "Modernity and Narcissistic Personality"; Twenge & Campbell, *The Narcissism Epidemic.* Sharp, "Personality Disorders."

174 Hardy & Carlo, "Moral Identity."

175 Hardy et al., "Moral Identity."

176 Hardy & Carlo, "Moral Identity."

177 Bandura, "Selective Moral Disengagement"; Bandura et al., "Mechanisms of Moral"; Bustamante & Chaux, "Reducing Moral Disengagement"; Caravita et al., "Peer Influences on Moral."

178 Bandura, "Selective Moral Disengagement"; Bandura et al., "Mechanisms of Moral"; Gini et al., "Moral Disengagement Among."

179 Caravita et al., "Peer Influences on Moral."

180 Ang et al., "From Narcissistic Exploitativeness"; Roos et al., "Emotion Regulation and Negative"; Stuewig et al., "Shaming, Blaming, and Maiming."

181 Hawley et al., "The Allure of a Mean."

182 Hardy & Carlo, "Moral Identity"; Hardy et al., "Moral Identity."

183 Spytska, "Symptoms and Main Differences."

184 Bocian et al., "Egocentrism Shapes Moral."

185 Gore & Widiger, "Fluctuation between Grandiose"; Newton-Howes, *Personality Disorder*; Sharp, "Personality Disorders"; Stuewig et al., "Shaming, Blaming, and Maiming."

186 Barkan et al., "Ethical Dissonance, Justifications."

187 Barkan et al., "Ethical Dissonance, Justifications"; Billig, "Henri Tajfel's 'Cognitive.'"

188 Bian et al., "Effects of the Presence."

189 Hawley et al., "The Allure of a Mean."

190 Hawley et al., "The Allure of a Mean."

191 Bandura, "Selective Moral Disengagement"; Bandura et al., "Mechanisms of Moral."

192 Crick & Dodge, "A Review and Reformulation"; Van Reemst et al., "Social Information Processing."

193 Crick & Dodge, "A Review and Reformulation"; Van Reemst et al., "Social Information Processing."

194 Mrug et al., "Emotional Desensitizatioin."

195 Lowry et al., "Why Do Adults"; Wu et al., "Examining the Antecedents of Online."

196 Lowry et al., "Why Do Adults"; Wu et al., "Examining the Antecedents of Online."

197 Lowry et al., "Why Do Adults"; Wu et al., "Examining the Antecedents of Online."

198 Ashmore et al., *Social Identity, Intergroup Conflict.*

199 Fine, "Review Essay: Forgotten."

200 Perlstadt, "How to Get Out of."

201 Marchlewska et al., "Superficial Ingroup Love?" Vermue et al., "Member-to-Member Generalisation"; Weisel & Bohm, "'Ingroup Love' and 'Outgroup.'"

202 Billig, "Henri Tajfel's 'Cognitive.'"

203 Anastasio & Rose, "Beyond Deserving More"; Ashmore et al., *Social Identity, Intergroup Conflict.* Billig, "Henri Tajfel's 'Cognitive'"; Buttelmann & Bohm, "The Ontogeny of the Motivation"; Weisel & Bohm, "'Ingroup Love' and 'Outgroup.'"

204 Brewer, "The Psychology of Prejudice."

205 Ross, *Everyday Bias.*

206 Stewart et al., "Do the 'Eyes' Have It?"

207 Akhmad et al., "Closed-Mindedness."

208 Spytska, "Symptoms and Main Differences."

209 Gore & Widiger, "Fluctuation between Grandiose"; Newton-Howes, *Personality Disorder*; Paris, "Modernity and Narcissistic Personality"; Sharp, "Personality Disorders."

210 Sharp, "Personality Disorders."

211 Bornovalova et al., "Stability, Change, and Heritability"; Weston & Riolo, "Childhood and Adolescent."

212 Durvasula, *Don't You Know Who?*

213 Paris, "Modernity and Narcissistic Personality"; Twenge & Campbell, *The Narcissism Epidemic*.

214 Gore & Widiger, "Fluctuation between Grandiose"; Newton-Howes, *Personality Disorder*; Sharp, "Personality Disorders."

215 Lyons, *Addicted to Drama*.

216 Sharp, "Personality Disorders."

217 Allen, "Tweeting, Texting, and Facebook"; Durvasula, *Don't You Know Who I Am*"; Lyons, *Addicted to Drama*; Sharp, "Personality Disorders."

218 Andersson, & Pearson, "Tit for Tat? The Spiraling"; DeLara, *Bullying Scars*; Lowry, et al, "Why Do Adults Engage"; Piotrowski, "Adult Bully Syndrome"; Roter, "Narcissism"; Sharp, "Personality Disorders"; Smokowski & Evans, *Bullying and Victimization*.

219 Weisel & Bohm, "'Ingroup Love' and 'Outgroup Hate.'"

220 Eriksson et al., "Identity Development"; Goffman, *The Presentation of Self*; Harter, *The Construction of the Self*.

221 Golec & Lantos, "Collective Narcissism"; Hughes & Machan, "It's a Conspiracy"; Marchlewska et al., "Superficial Ingroup Love"; Simon & Klandermans, "Politicized Collective Identity."

222 Twenge & Campbell, *The Narcissism Epidemic*.

223 Durvasula, *Don't You Know Who*; Twenge & Campbell, *The Narcissism Epidemic*.

224 Twenge & Campbell, *The Narcissism Epidemic*.

225 Twenge & Campbell, *The Narcissism Epidemic*.

226 Twenge & Campbell, *The Narcissism Epidemic*, 223.

227 Horwitz, "Politics as Victimhood"; Lukianoff & Haidt, *The Coddling of the American Mind*"; Sykes, *A Nation of Victims*.

228 Golec & Lantos, "Collective Narcissism"; Marchlewska et al., "Superficial Ingroup Love?"

229 Żemojtel-Piotrowska et al., "Communal Collective Narcissism."

230 Adams, "Trump and the Social Trance"; Trump, *Too Much and Never Enough.*

231 Sykes, *A Nation of Victims.*

232 McQuade, *Attack from Within.*

233 Adams, "Trump and the Social Trance"; Brooks, "Opinion: How to Have"; Garber, "We've Lost the Plot"; Horwitz, "Politics as Victimhood."

234 Horwitz, "Politics as Victimhood."

235 Adams, "Trump and the Social Trance"; Alberta, *The Kingdom, the Power, and the Glory*; Trump, *Too Much and Never Enough*; Post, *Dangerous Charisma.*

236 Adams, "Trump and the Social Trance"; Alberta, *The Kingdom, the Power, and the Glory.* Brooks, "Opinion: How to Have"; Du Mez, *Jesus and John Wayne*; French, "Opinion: To Save Conservatism From."

237 Adams, "Trump and the Social Trance"; Trump, *Too Much and Never Enough.*

238 Adams, "Trump and the Social Trance"; Alberta, *The Kingdom, the Power, and the Glory.*

239 PBS News. "3 Men Found."

240 Baspinar et al., "Effect of Sex Reassignment Surgery"; Bustos et al., "Regret after Gender-Affirmation"; Tang et al., "Gender-Affirming Mastectomy Trends."

241 Bem, *The Lenses of Gender.*

242 Alberta, *The Kingdom, the Power, and the Glory.*

243 French, "Opinion: To Save Conservatism."

244 Du Mez, *Jesus and John Wayne.*

245 Ross, *Everyday Bias.*

246 Dew & Foreman, *How Do We Know?*; Lamont, "The Construction of 'Critical.'"

247 Schildkraut, *Press "ONE" for English*; Schildkraut, "Boundaries of American Identity."

248 Schildkraut, *Press "ONE" for English.*

249 Schildkraut, *Press "ONE" for English.*

250 Schildkraut, *Press "ONE" for English.*

251 Schildkraut, *Press "ONE" for English.*

252 Schildkraut, *Press "ONE" for English.*

253 "The New Colossus"

254 Schildkraut, *Press "ONE" for English.*

255 David & Bar-Tal "A Sociopsychological Conception"; Schildkraut, *Press "ONE" for English*; Schildkraut, "Boundaries of American Identity."

256 Brewer, "The Psychology of Prejudice"; McQuade, *Attack from Within*; Ripley, *High Conflict.*

257 Ripley, *High Conflict.*

258 Brewer, "The Psychology of Prejudice."

259 Ho, "Agreeing to Disagree."

260 Haidt, *The Anxious Generation*; Murthy, "Our Epidemic of Loneliness"; Nesi, *Handbook of Adolescent Digital.*

261 Steiner-Adair, *The Big Disconnect.*

262 Coyne et al., "Teaching By Example"; Elphinson & Noller, "Time to Face It"; Kim & Fingerman, "Daily Social Media"; Murthy, "Social Media and Youth"; Mushquash et al., "Romance Behind."

263 Abi-Jaoude et al., "Smartphones, Social Media Use"; Keles et al., "A Systematic Review"; Nesi et al., *Handbook of Adolescent.*

264 Heitner, *Growing Up in Public.*

265 Coyne et al., "Teaching By Example"; Murthy, "Social Media and Youth."

266 Coyne et al., "Teaching By Example"; Murthy, "Social Media and Youth"; Nesi et al., *Handbook of Adolescent.*

267 Coyne et al., "Teaching By Example"; Murthy, "Social Media and Youth."

268 Coyne et al., "Teaching By Example"; Roberts & David, "On the Outside Looking."

269 Coyne et al., "Teaching By Example"; Feinstein et al., "Negative Social Comparison"; Vogel et al., "Social Comparison."

270 Coyne et al., "Teaching By Example"; Murthy, "Social Media and Youth."

271 Coyne et al., "Teaching By Example"; Feinstein et al., "Negative Social Comparison"; Vogel et al., "Social Comparison."

272 Dolev-Cohen & Ricon, "The Associations between"; McDaniel & Radesky, "Technoference: Longitudinal Associations."

273 Dolev-Cohen & Ricon, "The Associations between"; Mushquash

et al., "Romance Behind"; Rozenblatt-Perkal et al., "Infants' Physiological."

274 Rozenblatt-Perkal et al., "Infants' Physiological."

275 Rozenblatt-Perkal et al., "Infants' Physiological."

276 Dolev-Cohen & Ricon, "The Associations between."

277 McDaniel & Radesky, "Technoference: Longitudinal Associations."

278 Okuma & Tanimura, "A Preliminary Study."

279 Sundqvist et al., "Growing Up in a Digital."

280 Dolev-Cohen & Ricon, "The Associations between"; Konrad et al., "Quality of Mother-Child"; McDaniel & Radesky, "Technoference: Longitudinal Associations"; Sundqvist et al., "Growing Up in a Digital."

281 Chotpitayasunondh & Douglas; "The Effects of 'Pubbing"; Thabassum, "Phubbing: A Literature Review."

282 Komanchuk et al., "Impacts of Parental Technoference."

283 Alho et al., "Effects of Media Multitasking"; Otermans et al., "The Working Memory Costs."

284 Otermans et al., "The Working Memory Costs."

285 Otermans et al., "The Working Memory Costs."

286 Barragan-Jason & Hopfensitz, "Children with Higher Screen."

287 Shawcroft et al., "Screen-Play: An Observational."

288 Shuai et al., "Influences of Digital Media."

289 Granic et al., "The Benefits of Playing."

290 McCourt & Casey, *Our Biggest Fight*; Pezoa-Jares, "Internet Addiction."

291 Hawi & Samaha, "The Relations Among."

292 Nesi et al., *Handbook of Adolescent Digital.*

293 Nesi et al., *Handbook of Adolescent Digital.*

294 Nesi et al., *Handbook of Adolescent Digital.*

295 Hietajärvi et al., "Digital Engagement and Academic."

296 Hietajärvi et al., "Digital Engagement and Academic."

297 Morgan et al., "Risk and Protective Factors."

298 McArthur et al., "Global Prevalence"; Murthy, "Social Media and Youth"; Whiting et al., "Physical Activity, Screen Time."

299 Courage, "Screen Media and the Youngest

300 Coyne et al., "Teaching By Example"; Murthy, "Social Media and Youth."

301 Nesi et al., *Handbook of Adolescent Digital.*

302 Bexson et al., "Safety of Virtual"; Porter III & Robb, "Lingering Effects Associated."; Ronaghi, "The Effect of Reality Technology."

303 Antonovics et al., "Use of Virtual Reality."

304 Antonovics et al., "Use of Virtual Reality."

305 Shoshani, "From Virtual to Prosocial Reality."

306 Ronaghi, "The Effect of Virtual Reality."

307 Yu, "A Meta-Analysis of the Effect."

308 Porter III & Robb, "Lingering Effects Associated."

309 Porter III & Robb, "Lingering Effects Associated."

310 Bexson et al., "Safety of Virtual."

311 Porter III & Robb, "Lingering Effects Associated."

312 Zhao et al., "Persuasive Virtual Touch."

313 Zhao et al., "Persuasive Virtual Touch."

314 Dossey, "'FOMO, Digital Dementia"; Heid, "Walking and Using a Phone."

315 Barragan-Jason & Hopfensitz, "Children with Higher Screen Time."

316 Barragan-Jason & Hopfensitz, "Children with Higher Screen Time."

317 Uhls et al., "Five Days at Outdoor."

318 Prothero et al., "Which States Ban."

319 Maftei & Patrausanu, "Digital Reflections."

320 Oppong et al., "The Mediating Role of Selfitis."

321 Domingues-Montanari, "Clinical and Psychological"; Murthy, "Social Media and Youth"; Nesi et al., *Handbook of Adolescent Digital.*

322 Feinstein, "Negative Social Comparison"; Vogel et al., "Social Comparison, Social Media."

323 Feinstein, "Negative Social Comparison"; Vogel et al., "Social Comparison, Social Media."

324 Mark, *Attention Span.*

325 Coyne et al., "Teaching By Example"; *Social Studies,* Documentary.

326 Marengo et al., "Cyberbullying and Problematic."

327 Roberts & David, "On the Outside Looking."

328 Roberts et al., "The Kids Are Alright," 670.

329 Protzko & Schooler, "What I Didn't Grow Up with."

330 Protzko & Schooler, "What I Didn't Grow Up with."

331 Roberts et al., "The Kids Are Alright."

332 Twenge, *iGEN.*

333 Twenge, *Generations.*

334 Haidt, *The Anxious Generation.*

335 *Social Studies,* Documentary.

336 *Social Studies,* Documentary.

337 *Social Studies,* Documentary.

338 Webster, "Opinion: Teenagers Are Telling Us."

339 Twenge, *iGen;* Twenge, *Generations.*

340 Baumrind, "The Discipline Controversy."

341 Taylor, "David McCullough Jr. Commencement Speech."

342 Mruk, *Self-Esteem Research.*

343 Mruk, *Self-Esteem Research.*

344 Derry et al., "Fearing Failure: Grandiose Narcissism"; Gore &
    Widiger, "Fluctuation between Grandiose and Vulnerable"; Miller
    et al., "Grandiose and Vulnerable"; Taylor, "David McCullough Jr.
    Commencement Speech."

345 Thomaes et al., "When Narcissus Was a Boy."

346 Baumrind, "The Discipline Controversy."

347 Thomaes et al., "When Narcissus Was a Boy"; Thomaes et al.,
    "Reducing Narcissistic Aggression"; Twenge & Campbell, *The
    Narcissistic Epidemic.*

348 Derry et al., "Fearing Failure: Grandiose Narcissism"; Gore &
    Widiger, "Fluctuation between Grandiose and Vulnerable"; Miller
    et al., "Grandiose and Vulnerable."

349 Van Schie et al., "Narcissistic Traits in Young."

350 Baumeister et al. "Does High Self-Esteem"; Bushman &
    Baumeister, "Threatened Egotism"; Thomaes et al., "Trumping
    Shame by Blasts"; Thomaes et al., "Reducing Narcissistic Aggres-
    sion"; Brummelman et al., "Origins of Narcissism."

351 Baumeister et al., "Relation of Threatened Egotism."

352 Baumeister et al., "Does High Self-Esteem."

353 Derry et al., "Fearing Failure: Grandiose Narcissism"; Gore &
    Widiger, "Fluctuation between Grandiose and Vulnerable"; Miller
    et al., "Grandiose and Vulnerable."

354 Advice to new recruits from Inspector Armand Gamache, the main character in Louise Penny novel series.

355 Coyne et al., "Teaching By Example"; Haidt, *The Anxious Generation*; Twenge; *iGEN*.

356 Twenge, *iGen*.

357 Haidt, *The Anxious Generation*.

358 Haidt, *The Anxious Generation*.

359 Haidt, *The Anxious Generation*; https://letgrow.org/program/experience/; Gray et al., "Decline in Independent."

360 https://letgrow.org/program/experience/

361 Haidt, *The Anxious Generation*; Haidt, "End the Phone-Based."

362 Baumrind, "The Discipline Controversy."

363 Coyne et al., "Teaching By Example."

364 Garcia-Navarro, "Opinion: The Teenager Leading the Smartphone Liberation."

365 Adams, "Trump and the Social Trance"; Trump, *Too Much and Not Enough*.

366 Adams, "Trump and the Social Trance"; Trump, *Too Much and Not Enough*.

367 Bustamante & Chaux, "Reducing Moral Disengagement."

368 Paul & Elder, *Critical Thinking*.

369 Paul & Elder, *Critical Thinking*.

370 Camens, "Setting Emotional Boundaries"; confidentparentsconfidentkids, "Setting Emotional Boundaries."

371 Camens, "Setting Emotional Boundaries"; Durvasula, *Don't You Know Who*; Lyons, *Addicted to Drama*.

372 Derman & Yilman, "The Reality Paradox."

373 Goldstein & Michaels, *Empathy: Development, Training*.

374 Soares et al., "Developmental Assets Predictors of Life Satisfaction."

375 https://searchinstitute.org.

376 https://searchinstitute.org.

377 https://searchinstitute.org.

378 Benson, *All Kids Are Our Kids*.

379 Durvasula, *Don't You Know Who I Am?*

380 Wheatley, *Who Do We Choose to Be?*

381 Wheatley, *Who Do We Choose to Be?*

382 Wheatley, *Who Do We Choose to Be?* 299-304.

383 Wheatley, *Who Do We Choose to Be?* 39.

384 Mark, *Attention Span.*

385 Wheatley, *Who Do We Choose to Be?*

386 Newitz, *Four Lost Cities.*

387 Denton & Voth, *Social Fragmentation and the Decline.*

388 Sykes, *A Nation of Victims.*

389 Taibbi, *Hate Inc: Why Today's.*

390 Taibbi, *Hate Inc: Why Today's.*

391 McQuade, *Attack from Within.*

392 Jin, "Comic: Fake News Can Be Deadly."

393 Shearer et al., "How Americans Get."

394 Matsa et al., "How Americans Get."

395 "MisinfoDay 2023: Types of Misinformation."

396 Sternisko et al., "National Narcissism Predicts the Belief," 48.

397 Morson & Shapiro, *Minds Wide Shut.*

398 Dunning, "The Dunning-Kruger Effect."

399 Jansen et al., "A Rational Model of the Dunning-Kruger Effect."

400 Pennycook et al., "Science Beliefs, Political Ideology, and Cognitive."

401 Anson, "Partisanship, Political Knowledge, and the Dunning-Kruger."

402 Arroyo-Barriguete et al., "Dunning-Kruger Effect"; Jansen et al., "A Rational Model of the Dunning-Kruger"; Coutinho et al., "Dunning-Kruger Effect."

403 Pennycook et al., "Dunning-Kruger Effects in Reasoning"

404 Ariely, *Misbelief*; Hughes & Nachan, "It's a Conspiracy"; Sternisko et al., "National Narcissism Predicts the Belief."

405 Sternisko et al., "National Narcissism Predicts the Belief," 48.

406 Hughes & Machan, "It's a Conspiracy: COVID-19 Conspiracies."

407 Van Prooijen, "An Existential Threat Model of Conspiracy."

408 Van Prooijen, "An Existential Threat Model of Conspiracy."

409 Van de Cruys et al., "Insight in the Conspiracist's Mind," 1.

410 Sternisko et al., "National Narcissism Predicts the Belief."

411 Hughes & Machan., "It's a Conspiracy: COVID-19 Conspiracies."

412 Van Prooijen, "An Existential Threat Model of Conspiracy."

413 Ariely, *Misbelief.*

414 Haidt, "Why the Past 10 Years of American Life"; Haidt, "After Babel."

415 Wolf & Stoodley, *Reader, Come Home.*

416 Grose, "Opinion: A.I. Could Ruin."

417 ProPublica, "How School Board Meetings."

418 Alberta, *The Kingdom, the Power, and the Glory*; Du Mez, *Jesus and John Wayne*; French, "Opinion: To Save Conservatism."

419 Kessler, "Social Justice 101"; Tandoc, "#CancelCulture."

420 Romano, "Why We Can't Stop."

421 D. Clark, "DRAG THEM: A Brief Etymology."

422 NPR, ""How Cancel Culture Became Politicized."

423 Vogels et al., "Americans and 'Cancel Culture.'"

424 D. Clark, "DRAG THEM: A Brief Etymology."

425 Traversa et al., "Cancel Culture Can Be Collectively."

426 Traversa et al., "Cancel Culture Can Be Collectively."

427 Vogels et al., "Americans and 'Cancel Culture.'"

428 Lee & Murdie, "The Global Diffusion."

429 Vogels et al., "Americans and 'Cancel Culture'"; Rom & Mitchell, "Teaching Politics in a Call-Out"; NPR, "How Cancel Culture Became Politicized."

430 Lukianoff & Schlott, *The Canceling of the American*"; Gordon, "4 Reasons the Practice of Canceling."

431 Fahey et al., "Principled or Partisan?"

432 Fahey et al., "Principled or Partisan?"

433 Rom & Mitchell, "Teaching Politics in a Call-Out"; NPR, "How Cancel Culture Became Politicized."

434 Chen et al., "Communal Narcissism and Sadism."

435 "Is It Ever OK to Cancel Someone?"

436 Lowry et al., "Why Do Adults Engage in Cyberbullying?"

437 Chen et al., "Communal Narcissism and Sadism"; Żemojtel-Piotrowska et al., "Communal Collective Narcissism."

438 Chen et al., "Communal Narcissism and Sadism"; Żemojtel-Piotrowska et al., "Communal Collective Narcissism."

439 Chen et al., "Communal Narcissism and Sadism."

440 Chen et al., "Communal Narcissism and Sadism."

441 *The New Republic*, "The Spiritual Unspooling of America."

442 Pogue, "Opinion: The Senator Warning Democrats."

443 Shaer, "Why Is the Loneliness Epidemic"

444 Murthy, "Our Epidemic of Loneliness."

445 Page et al., "Community Belonging."

446 Murthy, "Our Epidemic of Loneliness."

447 Murthy, "Our Epidemic of Loneliness."

448 Murthy, "Our Epidemic of Loneliness," 44.

449 Murthy, "Our Epidemic of Loneliness," 44.

450 Whippman, "Opinion: Boys Get Everything Except."

451 Way et al., *The Crisis of Connection.*

452 Whippman, "Opinion: Boys Get Everything Except."

453 Murthy, "Social Media and Youth Mental Health," "Our Epidemic of Loneliness," "Parents Under Pressure."

454 Murthy, "Parents Under Pressure," 10.

455 Murthy, "Our Epidemic of Loneliness."

456 Murthy, "Our Epidemic of Loneliness," 4.

457 Pogue, "Opinion: The Senator Warning Democrats."

458 Wheatley, *Who Do We Choose To Be?*

459 Wolf & Stoodley, *Reader, Come Home.*

460 Hari, *Stolen Focus*; Mark, *Attention Span.*

461 Wang & Tuchernev, "The 'Myth' of Multitasking."

462 Hari, *Stolen Focus*; Mark, *Attention Span.*

463 Gazzaley & Rosen, *The Distracted Mind,* 112.

464 McCourt & Casey, *Our Biggest Fight Yet.*

465 Mark, *Attention Span.*

466 Hari, *Stolen Focus.*

467 Kabat-Zinn, *Full Catastrophe Living.*

468 Innovative Resources, "Mindfulness or Mindlessness."

469 Yoga Anytime, "Distracted? Why Daydreaming Is Good."

470 Kabat-Zinn, *Full Catastrophe Living.*

471 Joiner, *Mindlessness: The Corruption of Mindfulness.*

472 Ripley, *High Conflict.*

473 McQuade, *Attack from Within.*

474 Dew & Foreman, *How Do We Know?*; Lamont, "The Construction of 'Critical.'"

475 Ariely, *Misbelief*; McQuade, *Attack from Within.*

476 Lukianoff & Haidt, *The Coddling of the American Mind.*

477 Lukianoff & Haidt, *The Coddling of the American Mind.*

478 Dew & Foreman, *How Do We Know?*; Lamont, "The Construction of 'Critical.'"

479 Haidt, "Why the Past 10 Years of American Life"; Lukianoff &

Haidt, *The Coddling of the American Mind*; Lukianoff & Schlott, *The Canceling of the American Mind*.

480 Brooks, "Opinion: How to Save a Sad, Lonely, Angry and Mean Society"; Ripley, *High Conflict*.

481 Brooks, "Opinion: How to Save a Sad, Lonely, Angry and Mean Society."

482 Ripley, *High Conflict*.

483 Plyler v. Doe.

484 ProPublica, "How School Board Meetings Became Flashpoints for Anger."

485 CASEL.org.

486 CASEL.org.

487 CASEL, "Emerging Insights: Advancing Social and Emotional."

488 CASEL.org.

489 Show,' The Ezra Klein. "Opinion: How We Communicate Will."

490 "Speaking Up Without Tearing Down."

491 Ripley, *High Conflict*.

492 Duhigg, *Supercommunicators*; Morson & Shapiro, *Minds Wide Shut*; Ripley, *High Conflict*; Turkle, *Reclaiming Conversation*.

493 Ho, "Agreeing to Disagree."

494 Shaer, "Why Is the Loneliness Epidemic."

495 Durvsala, *Don't You Know Who I Am?*; Twenge, "The Evidence for Generation Me"; Twenge & Campbell, "*The Narcissistic Epidemic*"; Twenge & Foster, "Birth Cohort Increases in Narcissistic."

496 Ross, *Everyday Bias*.

497 Ross, *Everyday Bias*.

498 Ross, *Everyday Bias*.

499 Dew & Foreman, *How Do We Know?*; Ross, *Everyday Bias*.

500 McQuade, *Attack from Within*.

501 Allen, "Off the Radar," "Students' and Staff Members," "Tweeting, Texting, and Facebook Postings," "Understanding Bullying," and "We Don't Have Bullying."

502 Newton-Howes, *Personality Disorder*; Paris, *Personality Disorders*; Sharp, "Personality Disorders."

503 Page et al., "Community Belonging and Values-Based."

504 Ripley, *High Conflict*.

505 Ripley, *High Conflict*.

506 Pogue, "Opinion: The Senator Warning Democrats."

507 Ross, *Calling In*.

508 Wheatley, "Who Do We Choose to Be?" 301–303.

509 Roter, "Narcissism" *Understanding and Recognizing Dysfunctional Leadership*.

510 Garcia-Navarro, "Opinion: The Teenager Leading the Smartphone Liberation."

511 Luddites are people who reject technology. Interestingly, Logan and her Luddite Club friends only reject online phone use and social media, but still engage in phone calling, emailing, and texting.

Bibliography

Abell, Loren, Sarah L. Buglass, and Lucy R. Betts. "Fear of Missing Out and Relational Aggression on Facebook." *Cyberpsychology, Behavior, and Social Networking* 22 no. 12 (October, 2019): 799-803. https://doi.org/10.1089/cyber.2019.0071.

Abi-Jaoude, Elia, Karline Treurnicht Naylor, and Antonio Pignatiello. "Smartphones, Social Media Use and Youth Mental Health." *Canadian Medical Association Journal* 192, no. 6 (February 10, 2020): E136–41. https://doi.org/10.1503/cmaj.190434.

Abrams, Jonathan. "How to Turn Reality Star Into a Full-Time Job." *The New York Times*, August 14, 2024, sec. Arts. https://www.nytimes.com/2024/08/14/arts/television/mtv-the-challenge.html.

Adams, Kenneth Alan. "Trump and the Social Trance." *The Journal of Psychohistory* 46, no. 4 (Spring 2019): 238-258.

Akhmad, Muqtafi, Shuang Chang, and Hiroshi Deguchi. "Closed-Mindedness and Insulation in Groupthink: Their Effects and the Devil's Advocacy as a Preventive Measure." *Journal of Computational Social Science* 4, no. 2 (November 2021): 455–78. https://doi.org/10.1007/s42001-020-00083-8.

"Albert Bandura's Social Learning Theory In Psychology," February 1, 2024. https://www.simplypsychology.org/bandura.html.

Alberta, Tim. *The Kingdom, the Power, and the Glory: American Evangelicals in an Age of Extremism.* First edition. Harper, an imprint of HarperCollins Publishers, 2024.

Allen, Kathleen P. "Off the Radar and Ubiquitous: Text Messaging and Its Relationship to 'Drama' and Cyberbullying in an Affluent, Academically Rigorous US High School." *Journal of Youth Studies* 15, no. 1 (February 2012): 99–117. https://doi.org/10.1080/13676261.2011.630994.

Allen, Kathleen P. "Students' and Staff Members' Understanding of the Features, Forms, and Functions of Bullying in a High School Setting." University of Rochester ProQuest Dissertations & Theses, 2012. 3508370.

Allen, Kathleen P. "Tweeting, Texting, and Facebook Postings: Stirring the Pot with Social Media to Make Drama – Case Study and Participant Observation." *The Qualitative Report* 19, no. 2 (January 13, 2014): 1–24. https://doi.org/10.46743/2160-3715/2014.1287.

Allen, Kathleen P. "Understanding Bullying in an Affluent, Academically Rigorous U.S. High School: A Grounded Theory Analysis." *Journal of Human Behavior in the Social Environment* 23, no. 4 (May 2013): 413–36. https://doi.org/10.1080/10911359.2013.771523.

Allen, Kathleen P. "'We Don't Have Bullying, But We Have Drama': Understandings of Bullying and Related Constructs Within the Social Milieu of a U.S. High School." *Journal of Human Behavior in the Social Environment* 25, no. 3 (April 3, 2015): 159–81. https://doi.org/10.1080/10911359.2014.893857.

Alho, Kimmo, Mona Moisala, and Katariina Salmela-Aro. "Effects of Media Multitasking and Video Gaming on Cognitive Functions and Their Neural Bases in Adolescents and Young Adults." *European Psychologist* 27, no. 2 (2022): 131–140.

Anastasio, Phyllis A. and Karen C. Rose. "Beyond Deserving More: Psychological Entitlement Also Predicts Negative Attitudes Toward Personally Relevant Out-Groups." *Social Psychological and Personality Science* 5, no. 5 (July 2014): 593–600. https://doi.org/10.1177/1948550613519683.

Andersson, Lynne M. and Christine M. Pearson. "Tit for Tat? The Spiraling Effect of Incivility in the Workplace." *The Academy of Management Review* 24, no. 3 (1999): 452–71. https://doi.org/10.2307/259136.

Ang, Rebecca P., Eileen Y. L. Ong, Joylynn C. Y. Lim, and Eulindra W. Lim. "From Narcissistic Exploitativeness to Bullying Behavior: The Mediating Role of Approval-of-Aggression Beliefs." *Social Development* 19, no. 4 (November 2010): 721–35. https://doi.org/10.1111/j.1467-9507.2009.00557.x.

Anson, Ian G. "Partisanship, Political Knowledge, and the Dunning-Kruger Effect." *Political Psychology* 39, no. 5 (October 2018): 1173–92. https://doi.org/10.1111/pops.12490._

Antonovics, Emily, Grammatina Boitsios, and Thomas Saliba. "Use of Virtual Reality in Children in a Broad Range of Medical Settings: A Systematic Narrative Review of Recent Meta-Analyses." *Clinical and Experimental Pediatrics* 67, no. 6 (June 15, 2024): 274–82. https://doi.org/10.3345/cep.2023.00388.

Ariely, Dan. *Misbelief: What Makes Rational People Believe Irrational Things.* First edition. HarperCollins Publishers Inc, 2023.

Arroyo-Barrigüete, Jose Luis, Carlos Bellón Núñez-Mera, Jesús Labrador Fernández, and Victor Luis De Nicolas. "Dunning–Kruger Effect and Flat-Earthers: An Exploratory Analysis." *Public Understanding of Science* 32, no. 7 (October 2023): 835–44. https://doi.org/10.1177/09636625231166255

Ashmore, Richard D., Lee J. Jussim, and David Wilder, eds. *Social Identity, Intergroup Conflict, and Conflict Reduction.* Rutgers Series on Self and Social Identity, vol. 3. Oxford University Press, 2001.

Bandura, Albert. "Selective Moral Disengagement in the Exercise of Moral Agency." *Journal of Moral Education* 31, no. 2 (June 2002): 101–19. https://doi.org/10.1080/0305724022014322.

Bandura, Albert, Claudio Barbaranelli, Gian Vittorio Caprara, and Concetta Pastorelli. "Mechanisms of Moral Disengagement in the Exercise of Moral Agency." *Journal of Personality and Social Psychology* 71, no. 2 (August 1996): 364–74. https://doi.org/10.1037/0022-3514.71.2.364.

Barkan, Rachel, Shahar Ayal, and Dan Ariely. "Ethical Dissonance, Justifications, and Moral Behavior." *Current Opinion in Psychology* 6 (December 2015): 157–61. https://doi.org/10.1016/j.copsyc.2015.08.001.

Barnett, Michael D. and Palee M. Womack. "Fearing, Not Loving, the Reflection: Narcissism, Self-Esteem, and Self-Discrepancy Theory." *Personality and Individual Differences* 74 (February 2015): 280–84. https://doi.org/10.1016/j.paid.2014.10.032.

Barragan-Jason, Gladys and Astrid Hopfensitz. "Children with Higher Screen Time Exposure Were Less Likely to Show Patience and to Make School Friends at 4–6 Years of Age." *Acta Paediatrica* 110, no. 12 (December 2021): 3302–4. https://doi.org/10.1111/apa.16041.

Başpınar, Özge Sıla and Cennet Şafak Öztürk. "Effect of Sex Reassignment Surgery on Satisfaction and Quality of Life: A Systematic Review." *Psikiyatride Güncel Yaklaşımlar* 15, no. 1 (March 31, 2023): 161–74. https://doi.org/10.18863/pgy.1114987.

Baumeister, Roy F., Jennifer D. Campbell, Joachim I. Krueger, and Kathleen D. Vohs. "Does High Self-Esteem Cause Better Performance, Interpersonal Success, Happiness, or Healthier Lifestyles?" *Psychological Science in the Public Interest* 4, no. 1 (May 2003): 1–44.

Baumeister, Roy F. and Mark R. Leary. "The Need to Belong: Desire for Interpersonal Attachments as a Fundamental Human Motivation." *Psychological Bulletin* 117, no. 3 (1995): 497–529.

Baumeister, Roy F., Laura Smart, and Joseph M. Boden. "Relation of Threatened Egotism to Violence and Aggression: The Dark Side of High Self-Esteem." *Psychological Review* 103, no. 1 (1996): 5–33. https://doi.org/10.1037/0033-295X.103.1.5.

Baumrind, Diana. "The Discipline Controversy Revisited." *Family Relations* 45, no. 5 (1996): 405–415.

Bem, Sandra Lipsitz. *The Lenses of Gender: Transforming the Debate on Sexual Inequality.* Yale University, 1993.

Bender, Donna S. "Mirror, Mirror on the Wall: Reflecting on Narcissism." *Journal of Clinical Psychology* 68, no. 8 (August 2012): 877–85. https://doi.org/10.1002/jclp.21892.

Benson, Peter L. *All Kids Are Our Kids: What Communities Must Do to Raise Caring and Responsible Children and Adolescents.* 2nd ed. The Jossey-Bass Education Series. Jossey-Bass, a Wiley imprint, 2006.

Bergner, Raymond M. "What Is Personality? Two Myths and a Definition." *New Ideas in Psychology* 57 (April 2020): 10079. https://doi.org/10.1016/j.newideapsych.2019.100759.

Bexson, Charlotte, Geralyn Oldham, and Jo Wray. "Safety of Virtual Reality Use in Children: A Systematic Review." *European Journal of Pediatrics* 183, no. 5 (March 11, 2024): 2071–90. https://doi.org/10.1007/s00431-024-05488-5.

Bian, Junfeng, Liang Li, Xuan Xia, and Xiaolan Fu. "Effects of the Presence and Behavior of In-Group and Out-Group Strangers on Moral Hypocrisy." *Frontiers in Psychology* 11 (September 15, 2020): 551625. https://doi.org/10.3389/fpsyg.2020.551625.

Billig, Michael. "Henri Tajfel's 'Cognitive Aspects of Prejudice' and the Psychology of Bigotry." *British Journal of Social Psychology* 41, (2002): 171–188.

Bocian, Konrad, Wieslaw Baryla, and Bogdan Wojciszke. "Egocentrism Shapes Moral Judgements." *Social and Personality Psychology Compass* 14, no. 12 (December 2020): 1–14. https://doi.org/10.1111/spc3.12572.

Book, Angela S., Anthony A. Volk, and Ashley Hosker. "Adolescent Bullying and Personality: An Adaptive Approach." *Personality and In-*

dividual Differences 52, no. 2 (January 2012): 218–23. https://doi.org/10.1016/j.paid.2011.10.028.

Bornovalova, Marina A., Brian M. Hicks, William G. Iacono, and Matt McGue. "Stability, Change, and Heritability of Borderline Personality Disorder Traits from Adolescence to Adulthood: A Longitudinal Twin Study." *Development and Psychopathology* 21, no. 4 (November 2009): 1335–53. https://doi.org/10.1017/S0954579409990186

Bowker, Julie C., Katelyn K. Thomas, Kelly E. Norman, and Sarah V. Spencer. "Mutual Best Friendship Involvement, Best Friends' Rejection Sensitivity, and Psychological Maladaptation." *Journal of Youth and Adolescence* 40, no. 5 (May 2011): 545–55. https://doi.org/10.1007/s10964-010-9582-x.

Brewer, Marilynn B. "The Psychology of Prejudice: Ingroup Love and Outgroup Hate?" *Journal of Social Issues* 55, no. 3 (January 1999): 429–44. https://doi.org/10.1111/0022-4537.00126.

Bronfenbrenner, Urie. "Toward an Experimental Ecology of Human Development." *American Psychologist* 32, no. 7 (July 1977): 513–31. https://doi.org/10.1037/0003-066X.32.7.513.

Brooks, David. "Opinion | How to Save a Sad, Lonely, Angry and Mean Society." *The New York Times*, January 26, 2024, sec. Opinion. https://www.nytimes.com/2024/01/25/opinion/art-culture-politics.html.

Brummelman, Eddie, Sander Thomaes, Stefanie A. Nelemans, Bram Orobio De Castro, Geertjan Overbeek, and Brad J. Bushman. "Origins of Narcissism in Children." *Proceedings of the National Academy of Sciences* 112, no. 12 (March 24, 2015): 3659–62. https://doi.org/10.1073/pnas.1420870112.

Bushman, Brad J. and Roy F. Baumeister. "Threatened Egotism, Narcissism, and Direct and Displaced Aggression: Does Self-Love or Self-Hate Lead to Violence?" *Journal of Personality and Social Psychology* 75, no. 1 (July 1998): 219–29. https://doi.org/10.1037/0022-3514.75.1.219.

Bustamante, Andrea and Enrique Chaux. "Reducing Moral Disengagement Mechanisms: A Comparison of Two Interventions." *Journal of Latino/Latin American Studies* 6, no. 1 (2014): 52–63.

Bustos, Valeria P., Samyd S. Bustos, Andres Mascaro, Gabriel Del Corral, Antonio J. Forte, Pedro Ciudad, Esther A. Kim, Howard N. Langstein, and Oscar J. Manrique. "Regret after Gender-Affirmation Surgery: A Systematic Review and Meta-Analysis of Prevalence." *Plastic and Reconstructive Surgery - Global Open* 9, no. 3 (March 19, 2021): e3477. https://doi.org/10.1097/GOX.0000000000003477.

Buttelmann, David and Robert Böhm. "The Ontogeny of the Motivation That Underlies In-Group Bias." *Psychological Science* 25, no. 4 (April 2014): 921–27. https://doi.org/10.1177/0956797613516802.

Camins, Stephanie. "Setting Emotional Boundaries in Relationships." *Road to Growth Counseling* (blog), April 1, 2016. https://www.roadtogrowthcounseling.com/importance-boundaries-relationships/.

Caravita, Simona C. S., Jelle J. Sijtsema, J. Ashwin Rambaran, and Gianluca Gini. "Peer Influences on Moral Disengagement in Late Childhood and Early Adolescence." *Journal of Youth and Adolescence* 43, no. 2 (February 2014): 193–207. https://doi.org/10.1007/s10964-013-9953-1.

CASEL. "Emerging Insights: Advancing Social and Emotional Learning as a Lever for Equity and Excellence." Accessed June 29, 2024. https://casel.org/casel-gateway-advancing-sel-for-equity-excellence/.

Caspi, Avshalom. "The Child Is Father of the Man: Personality Continuities from Childhood to Adulthood." *Journal of Personality and Social Psychology* 78, no. 1 (2000): 158–72. https://doi.org/10.1037/0022-3514.78.1.158.

Caspi, Avshalom and Brent W. Roberts. "Personality Development Across the Life Course: The Argument for Change and Continuity." *Psychology Inquiry* 12, no. 2 (2001): 49–66.

Chen, Fan Xuan, Ekin Ok, and Karl Aquino. "Communal Narcissism and Sadism as Predictors of Everyday Vigilantism." *Personality Science* 4 (October 27, 2023): e10523. https://doi.org/10.5964/ps.10523.

Chotpitayasunondh, Varoth and Karen M. Douglas. "The Effects of 'Phubbing' on Social Interaction." *Journal of Applied Social Psychology* 48, no. 6 (June 2018): 304–16. https://doi.org/10.1111/jasp.125

confidentparentsconfidentkids. "Setting Emotional Boundaries — For Our Children and Ourselves." confident parents confident kids, March 4, 2021. https://confidentparentsconfidentkids. org/2021/03/04/setting-emotional-boundaries-for-our-children-and-ourselves/.

Courage, Mary L. "Screen Media and the Youngest Viewers: Implications for Attention and Learning." In *Cognitive Development in Digital Contexts*, 3–28. Elsevier, 2017. https://doi.org/10.1016/B978-0-12-809481-5.00001-8.

Coutinho, Mariana V. C., Justin Thomas, Alia S. M. Alsuwaidi, and Justin J. Couchman. "Dunning-Kruger Effect: Intuitive Errors Predict Overconfidence on the Cognitive Reflection Test." *Frontiers in Psychology* 12 (April 8, 2021): 603225. https://doi.org/10.3389/fpsyg.2021.603225.

Coyne, Sarah, Emily Weinstein, Spencer James, Megan Gale, and Megan Van Alfen. "Teaching By Example: Media and Parenting Practices that Are – and Are Not – Related to Adolescent Mental Health." (2022). The Wheatley Institution. https://wheatley.byu.edu/00000182-8d78-dff6-afab-8ffd11ce0001/teaching-by-example-pdf

Cramer, Phebe. "Young Adult Narcissism: A 20 Year Longitudinal Study of the Contribution of Parenting Styles, Preschool Precursors of Narcissism, and Denial." *Journal of Research in Personality* 45, no. 1 (February 2011): 19–28. https://doi.org/10.1016/j.jrp.2010.11.004.

Crawford, Kate. "Those Foolish Things: On Intimacy and Insignificance in Mobile Media," In Gerard Goggin and Larissa Hjorth, eds. *Mobile Technologies: From Telecommunications to Media*, 252–266. Routledge Research in Cultural and Media Studies 20. Routledge, 2009.

Crick, Nicki R. and Kenneth A. Dodge. "A Review and Reformulation of Social Information-Processing Mechanisms in Children's Social Adjustment." *Psychological Bulletin* 115, no. 1 (January 1994): 74–101. https://doi.org/10.1037/0033-2909.115.1.74.

D. Clark, Meredith. "DRAG THEM: A Brief Etymology of So-called 'Cancel Culture.'" *Communication and the Public* 5, no. 3–4 (September 2020): 88–92. https://doi.org/10.1177/2057047320961562.

David, Ohad and Daniel Bar-Tal. "A Sociopsychological Conception of Collective Identity: The Case of National Identity as an Example." *Personality and Social Psychology Review* 13, no. 4 (November 2009): 354–79. https://doi.org/10.1177/1088868309344412.

DeLara, Ellen. *Bullying Scars: The Impact on Adult Life and Relationships.* Oxford University Press, 2016.

Denton, Robert E. and Ben Voth. *Social Fragmentation and the Decline of American Democracy: The End of the Social Contract.* ProQuest Ebook Central https://ebookcentral-proquest-com.gate.lib.buffalo.edu, (2016).

Derman, Giray Saynur a Ozan Can Yilmaz. "The Reality Paradox: Controversies, Reflections, and Responsibilities." *International Journal of Social and Economic Sciences* 13, no. 1 (2023): 32–45. E-ISSN: 2667-4904.

Derry, Kate L., Jeneva L. Ohan, and Donna M. Bayliss. "Fearing Failure: Grandiose Narcissism, Vulnerable Narcissism, and Emotional Reactivity in Children." *Child Development* 91, no. 3 (May 2020): e581–e596. https://doi.org/10.1111/cdev.13264.

Dew, James K., and Mark W. Foreman. *How Do We Know? An Introduction to Epistemology.* Second edition. Questions in Christian Philosophy. IVP Academic, an imprint of InterVarsity Press, 2020.

Dolev-Cohen, Michal and Tsameret Ricon. "The Associations between Parents' Technoference, Their Problematic Use of Digital Technology, and the Psychological State of Their Children." *Psychology of Popular Media* 13, no. 2 (April 2024): 171–79. https://doi.org/10.1037/ppm0000444.

Domingues-Montanari, Sophie. "Clinical and Psychological Effects of Excessive Screen Time on Children." *Journal of Paediatrics and Child Health* 53, no. 4 (April 2017): 333–38. https://doi.org/10.1111/jpc.13462.

Dossey, Larry. "FOMO, Digital Dementia, and Our Dangerous Experiment." *EXPLORE* 10, no. 2 (March 2014): 69–73. https://doi.org/10.1016/j.explore.2013.12.008.

Driessens, Olivier. "Celebrity Capital: Redefining Celebrity Using Field Theory." *Theory and Society* 42, no. 5 (September 2013): 543–60. https://doi.org/10.1007/s11186-013-9202-3.

Duhigg, Charles. *Supercommunicators*. Random House, 2024.

Du Mez, Kristin Kobes. *Jesus and John Wayne: How White Evangelicals Corrupted a Faith and Fractured a Nation*. First edition. Liveright Publishing Corporation, a division of W. W. Norton & Company, 2020.

Dunning, David. "The Dunning–Kruger Effect." In *Advances in Experimental Social Psychology*, 44: 247–96. Elsevier, 2011. https://doi.org/10.1016/B978-0-12-385522-0.00005-6.

Durvasula, Ramani. *Don't You Know Who I Am?: How to Stay Sane in an Era of Narcissism, Entitlement, and Incivility*. Post Hill Press, 2021.

Duvall, Spring-Serenity, ed. *Celebrity and Youth: Mediated Audiences, Fame Aspirations, and Identity Formation*. Mediated Youth, Volume 29. Peter Lang, 2019.

Elliott, Richard and Kritsadarat Wattanasuwan. "Brands as Symbolic Resources for the Construction of Identity." *International Journal of*

Advertising 17, no. 2 (January 1998): 131–44. https://doi.org/10.1 080/02650487.1998.11104712.

Elphinston, Rachel A. and Patricia Noller. "Time to Face It! Facebook Intrusion and the Implications for Romantic Jealousy and Relationship Satisfaction." *Cyberpsychology, Behavior, and Social Networking* 14, no. 11 (November 2011): 631–35. https://doi.org/10.1089/ cyber.2010.0318.

Empowering Parents. "How to Set Healthy Boundaries with Your Child." Accessed June 29, 2024. https://www.empoweringparents. com/article/parental-roles-how-to-set-healthy-boundaries-with-your-child/.

Eriksson, Py Liv, Maria Wängqvist, Johanna Carlsson, and Ann Frisén. "Identity Development in Early Adulthood." *Developmental Psychology* 56, no. 10 (October 2020): 1968–83. https://doi.org/10.1037/ dev0001093.

Exline, Julie Juola, Roy F. Baumeister, Brad J. Bushman, W. Keith Campbell, and Eli J. Finkel. "Too Proud to Let Go: Narcissistic Entitlement as a Barrier to Forgiveness." *Journal of Personality and Social Psychology* 87, no. 6 (2004): 894–912. https://doi.org/10.1037/0022-3514.87.6.894.

Fanti, Kostas A. and Christopher C. Henrich. "Effects of Self-Esteem and Narcissism on Bullying and Victimization During Early Adolescence." *The Journal of Early Adolescence* 35, no. 1 (January 2015): 5–29. https://doi.org/10.1177/0272431613519498.

Farrant, Brad M., Tara A. J. Devine, Murray T. Maybery, and Janet Fletcher. "Perspective Taking and Prosocial Behaviour: The Importance of Parenting Practices." *Infant and Child Development* 21, no. 2 (March 2012): 175–88. https://doi.org/10.1002/icd.740.

Fahey, James J., Damon C. Roberts, and Stephen M. Utych. "Principled or Partisan? The Effect of Cancel Culture Framings on Support for Free Speech." *American Politics Research* 51, no. 1 (January 2023): 69–75. https://doi.org/10.1177/1532673X221087601.

Feinstein, Brian A., Rachel Hershenberg, Vickie Bhatia, Jessica A. Latack, Nathalie Meuwly, and Joanne Davila. "Negative Social Comparison on Facebook and Depressive Symptoms: Rumination as a Mechanism." *Psychology of Popular Media Culture* 2, no. 3 (July 2013): 161–70. https://doi.org/10.1037/a0033111.

Fine, Gary Alan. "Review Essay: Forgotten Classic: The Robbers Cave Experiment." *Sociological Forum* 19, no. 4 (December 2004): 663–66. https://doi.org/10.1007/s11206-004-0704-7.

Frankowski, Scott, Amber K. Lupo, Brandt A. Smith, Mosi Dane'El, Corin Ramos, and Osvaldo F. Morera. "Developing and Testing a Scale to Measure Need for Drama." *Personality and Individual Differences* 89 (January 2016): 192–201. https://doi.org/10.1016/j.paid.2015.10.009.

French, David. "Opinion | To Save Conservatism From Itself, I Am Voting for Harris." *The New York Times*, August 11, 2024, sec. Opinion. https://www.nytimes.com/2024/08/11/opinion/harris-trump-conservatives-abortion.html.

Gamson, Joshua. "The Unwatched Life Is Not Worth Living: The Elevation of the Ordinary in Celebrity Culture." *PMLA/Publications of the Modern Language Association of America* 126, no. 4 (October 2011): 1061–69. https://doi.org/10.1632/pmla.2011.126.4.1061.

Garber, Megan. "We've Lost the Plot." *The Atlantic*, January 30, 2023. https://www.theatlantic.com/magazine/archive/2023/03/tv-politics-entertainment-metaverse/672773/.

Garcia-Navarro, Lulu, Rhiannon Corby, Anabel Bacon, Kaari Pitkin, Stephanie Joyce, Carole Sabouraud, Isaac Jones, Sonia Herrero, and Pat McCusker. "Opinion | The Teenager Leading the Smartphone Liberation Movement." *The New York Times*, February 2, 2023, sec. Opinion. https://www.nytimes.com/2023/02/02/opinion/teen-luddite-smartphones.html.

Gazzaley, Adam and Larry D. Rosen. *The Distracted Mind: Ancient Brains in a High-Tech World*. MIT Press, 2016.

Gilbert, Sophie. "The Cruel Social Experiment of Reality TV." *The Atlantic* (blog), May 16, 2024. https://www.theatlantic.com/culture/archive/2024/05/contestant-hulu-review-allen-funt-candid-camera-reality-tv-history/678393/.

Gini, Gianluca, Tiziana Pozzoli, and Shelley Hymel. Moral Disengagement in Children and Youth: A Meta-Analytic Review of Links to Aggressive Behavior." *Aggressive Behavior* 40, no. 1 (2014): 56–68.

Glascock, Jack and Catherine Preston-Schreck. "Verbal Aggression, Race, and Sex on Reality TV: Is This Really the Way It Is?" *Journal of Broadcasting & Electronic Media* 62, no. 3 (July 3, 2018): 427–44. https://doi.org/10.1080/08838151.2018.1451859.

Goffman, Erving. *The Presentation of Self in Everyday Life*. The Overlook Press, 1973.

Goldstein, Arnold P. and Gerald Y. Michaels. *Empathy: Development, Training, and Consequences*. Routledge, 2021.

Golec De Zavala, Agnieszka and Dorottya Lantos. "Collective Narcissism and Its Social Consequences: The Bad and the Ugly." *Current Directions in Psychological Science* 29, no. 3 (June 2020): 273–78. https://doi.org/10.1177/0963721420917703.

Gordon, Mordechai. "4 Reasons the Practice of Canceling Weakens Higher Education." The Conversation, April 15, 2024. http://theconversation.com/4-reasons-the-practice-of-canceling-weakens-higher-education-227330.

Gore, Whitney L. and Thomas A. Widiger. "Fluctuation between Grandiose and Vulnerable Narcissism." *Personality Disorders: Theory, Research, and Treatment* 7, no. 4 (2016): 363–71. https://doi.org/10.1037/per0000181.

Granic, Isabela, Adam Lobel, and Rutger C. M. E. Engels. "The Benefits of Playing Video Games." *American Psychologist* 69, no. 1 (January 2014): 66–78. https://doi.org/10.1037/a0034857.

Grindstaff, Laura and Susan Murray. "Reality Celebrity: Branded Affect and the Emotion Economy." *Public Culture* 27, no. 1 (January 1, 2015): 109–35. https://doi.org/10.1215/08992363-2798367.

Gray, Peter, David F. Lancy, and David F. Bjorklund. "Decline in Independent Activity as a Cause of Decline in Children's Mental Wellbeing: Summary of the Evidence." *The Journal of Pediatrics* 260, (September 2023): 113352–113352. https://doi.org/10.1016/j.jpeds.2023.02.004

Grose, Jessica. "Opinion | A.I. Could Ruin Kids' Critical-Thinking Skills." *The New York Times*, August 14, 2024, sec. Opinion. https://www.nytimes.com/2024/08/14/opinion/ai-schools-teachers-students.html.

Gunderson, John G., Sabine C. Herpertz, Andrew E. Skodol, Svenn Torgersen, and Mary C. Zanarini. "Borderline Personality Disorder." *Nature Reviews Disease Primers* 4, no. 1 (May 24, 2018): 18029. https://doi.org/10.1038/nrdp.2018.29.

Haidt, Jonathan. "Why the Past 10 Years of American Life Have Been Uniquely Stupid." *The Atlantic*, April 11, 2022. https://www.theatlantic.com/magazine/archive/2022/05/social-media-democracy-trust-babel/629369/.

Haidt, Jonathan. *The Anxious Generation: How the Great Rewiring of Childhood Is Causing an Epidemic of Mental Illness*. Penguin Press, 2024.

Haidt, Jonathan. "End the Phone-Based Childhood Now." *The Atlantic* (blog), March 13, 2024. https://www.theatlantic.com/technology/archive/2024/03/teen-childhood-smartphone-use-mental-health-effects/677722/.

Hardy, Sam A. and Gustavo Carlo. "Moral Identity: What Is It, How Does It Develop, and Is It Linked to Moral Action?" *Child Development Perspectives* 5, no. 3 (September 2011): 212–18. https://doi.org/10.1111/j.1750-8606.2011.00189.x.

Hardy, Sam A., Lawrence J. Walker, Joseph A. Olsen, Ryan D. Woodbury, and Jacob R. Hickman. "Moral Identity as Moral Ideal Self: Links to Adolescent Outcomes." *Developmental Psychology* 50, no. 1 (2014): 45–57. https://doi.org/10.1037/a0033598.

Hari, Johann. *Stolen Focus: Why You Can't Pay Attention—and How to Think Deeply Again*. Crown trade paperback edition. Crown, 2023.

Harter, Susan. *The Construction of the Self: Developmental and Sociocultural Foundations*. 2nd ed. Guilford Press, 2012.

Hartin, Peter, Melanie Birks, and David Lindsay. "Bullying in Nursing: How Has It Changed over 4 Decades?" *Journal of Nursing Management* 28, no. 7 (October 2020): 1619–26. https://doi.org/10.1111/jonm.13117.

Hawi, Nazir S. and Maya Samaha. "The Relations Among Social Media, Self-Esteem, and Life Satisfaction in University Students." *Social Science Computer Review* 35, no. 5 (October 2017): 576–86. https://doi.org/10.1177/0894439316660340.

Hawley, Patricia H., Todd D. Little, and Noel A. Card. "The Allure of a Mean Friend: Relationship Quality and Processes of Aggressive Adolescents with Prosocial Skills." *International Journal of Behavioral Development* 31, no. 2 (March 2007): 170–80. https://doi.org/10.1177/0165025407074630.

Heid, Markham. "Walking and Using a Phone Is Bad for Your Health." *The New York Times*, January 23, 2024, sec. Well. https://www.nytimes.com/2024/01/23/well/smartphone-walking-posture-mood.html.

Heitner, Devorah. *Growing Up in Public: Coming of Age in a Digital World*. tarcherperigee, 2023.

Hendrick, Harry. "Narcissism and the 'Politics of Recognition': Concepts of the Late Modern Self." In *Narcissistic Parenting in an Insecure World: A History of Parenting Culture 1920s to Present*. 301–321. Policy Press, 2016. https://doi.org/10.51952/9781447322580.

Hervas, Gonzalo and Carmelo Vazquez. "What Else Do You Feel When You Feel Sad? Emotional Overproduction, Neuroticism and Rumination." *Emotion* 11, no. 4 (August 2011): 881–95. https://doi.org/10.1037/a0021770.

Hietajärvi, Lauri, Erika Maksniemi, and Katariina Salmela-Aro. "Digital Engagement and Academic Functioning: A Developmental-Contextual Approach." *European Psychologist* 27, no. 2 (April 2022): 102–15. https://doi.org/10.1027/1016-9040/a000480.

Hill, Annette. *Reality TV*. Key Ideas in Media and Cultural Studies. Routledge, Taylor & Francis Group, 2015.

Ho, James C. "Agreeing to Disagree: Restoring America by Resisting Cancel Culture." *Texas Review of Law and Politics* 27, no. 1 (Fall, 2022): 1–24.

Horwitz, Robert B. "Politics as Victimhood, Victimhood as Politics." *Journal of Policy History* 30, no. 3 (July 2018): 552–74. https://doi.org/10.1017/S0898030618000209.

Hughes, Sara and Laura Machan. "It's a Conspiracy: COVID-19 Conspiracies Link to Psychopathy, Machiavellianism and Collective Narcissism." *Personality and Individual Differences* 171 (2021): 110559.

"Is It Ever OK to Cancel Someone?" *Choices/Current Health*. 35, no. 7 (April 2020): 2+. *Gale Academic OneFile*, link.gale.com/apps/doc/A621580887/AONE?u=sunybuff_main&sid=bookmark-AONE&xid=6b45d6bf.

Jabeen, Fauzia, Anushree Tandon, Juthamon Sithipolvanichgul, Shalini Srivastava, and Amandeep Dhir. "Social Media-Induced Fear of Missing out (FoMO) and Social Media Fatigue: The Role of Narcissism, Comparison and Disclosure." *Journal of Business Research* 159 (April 2023): 113693. https://doi.org/10.1016/j.jbusres.2023.113693.

Jansen, Rachel A., Anna N. Rafferty, and Thomas L. Griffiths. "A Rational Model of the Dunning–Kruger Effect Supports Insensitivity to Evidence in Low Performers." *Nature Human Behaviour* 5, no. 6

(February 25, 2021): 756–63. https://doi.org/10.1038/s41562-021-01057-0.

Jin, Connie Hanzhang. "Comic: Fake News Can Be Deadly. Here's How To Spot It." Goats and Soda, April 20, 2020. https://www.npr.org/2020/04/17/837202898/comic-fake-news-can-be-deadly-heres-how-to-spot-it.

John, Oliver P., Laura P. Naumann, and Christopher J. Soto. "Paradigm Shift to the Integrative Big Five Trait Taxonomy." *Handbook of Personality: Theory and Research* 3, no. 2 (2008): 114–158.

Joiner, Thomas. *Mindlessness: The Corruption of Mindfulness in a Culture of Narcissism.* Oxford University Press, 2017.

Kabat-Zinn, Jon. *Full Catastrophe Living: Using the Wisdom of Your Body and Mind to Face Stress, Pain, and Illness.* Revised and updated edition. Bantam Books trade paperback, 2013.

Kavka, Misha. "Reality TV: Its Contents and Discontents." *Critical Quarterly* 60, no. 4 (2018): 5–18.

Keles, Betul, Niall McCrae, and Annmarie Grealish. 2020. "A Systematic Review: The Influence of Social Media on Depression, Anxiety and Psychological Distress in Adolescents." *International Journal of Adolescence and Youth* 25 (1): 79–93. https://www.tandfonline.com/doi/full/10.1080/02673843.2019.1590851.

Kessler, Steven. "Social Justice 101: Intro to Cancel Culture." *Academic Questions* 34, no. 2 (May 20, 2021). https://doi org/10.51845/34su.2.24.

Kim, Yijung K. and Karen L. Fingerman. "Daily Social Media Use, Social Ties, and Emotional Well-Being in Later Life." *Journal of Social and Personal Relationships* 39, no. 6 (June 2022): 1794–1813. https://doi.org/10.1177/02654075211067254.

Komanchuk, Jelena, Alexa J. Toews, Susanne Marshall, Lyndsay Jerusha Mackay, K. Alix Hayden, Judy L. Cameron, Linda Duffett-Leger, and Nicole Letourneau. "Impacts of Parental Technoference on

Parent–Child Relationships and Child Health and Developmental Outcomes: A Scoping Review." *Cyberpsychology, Behavior, and Social Networking* 26, no. 8 (August 1, 2023): 579–603. https://doi.org/10.1089/cyber.2022.0278.

Konrad, Carolin, Mona Hillmann, Janine Rispler, Luisa Niehaus, Lina Neuhoff, and Rachel Barr. "Quality of Mother-Child Interaction Before, During, and After Smartphone Use." *Frontiers in Psychology* 12 (March 29, 2021): 616656. https://doi.org/10.3389/fpsyg.2021.616656.

Kroes, Rob. "The Revenge of the Simulacrum: The Reality Principle Meets Reality TV." *Society* 56, no. 5 (October 2019): 419–26. https://doi.org/10.1007/s12115-019-00395-0.

Kühne, Rinaldo and Suzanna J. Opree. "From Admiration to Devotion? The Longitudinal Relation between Adolescents' Involvement with and Viewing Frequency of Reality TV." *Journal of Broadcasting & Electronic Media* 64, no. 2 (May 1, 2020): 111–30. https://doi.org/10.1080/08838151.2020.1728688.

Lamont, Peter. "The Construction of 'Critical Thinking': Between How We Think and What We Believe." *History of Psychology* 23, no. 3 (August 2020): 232–51. https://doi.org/10.1037/hop0000145.

Lee, Myunghee and Amanda Murdie. "The Global Diffusion of the #MeToo Movement." *Politics & Gender* 17, no. 4 (December 2021): 827–55. https://doi.org/10.1017/S1743923X20000148.

Lerner, Richard M. *Concepts and Theories of Human Development.* Psychology Press, 2013. https://doi.org/10.4324/9781410603517.

Lewis, Rebecca and Angèle Christin. "Platform Drama: 'Cancel Culture,' Celebrity, and the Struggle for Accountability on YouTube." *New Media & Society* 24, no. 7 (July 2022): 1632–56. https://doi.org/10.1177/14614448221099235.

Ligocki, Danielle T. *The Drama of Reality Television: Lives of Youth in Liquid Modern Times.* Constructing Knowledge: Curriculum Studies in Action, volume 17. Brill Sense, 2018.

Lim, Sun Sun. "On Mobile Communication and Youth 'Deviance': Beyond Moral, Media and Mobile Panics." *Mobile Media & Communication* 1, no. 1 (January 2013): 96–101. https://doi.org/10.1177/2050157912459503.

Lowry, Paul Benjamin, Jun Zhang, Chuang Wang, and Mikko Siponen. "Why Do Adults Engage in Cyberbullying on Social Media? An Integration of Online Disinhibition and Deindividuation Effects with the Social Structure and Social Learning Model." *Information Systems Research* 27, no. 4 (December 2016): 962–86. https://doi.org/10.1287/isre.2016.0671.

Lukianoff, Greg and Jonathan Haidt. *The Coddling of the American Mind: How Good Intentions and Bad Ideas Are Setting Up a Generation for Failure.* Penguin Books, 2019.

Lukianoff, Greg and Rikki Schlott. *The Canceling of the American Mind: Cancel Culture Undermines Trust and Threatens Us All—But There Is a Solution.* Simon & Schuster, 2023.

Lyons, Scott. *Addicted to Drama: Healing Dependency on Crisis and Chaos in Yourself and Others.* First edition. Hachette Books, 2023.

Lyubomirsky, Sonja, and Susan Nolen-Hoeksema. "Effects of Self-Focused Rumination on Negative Thinking and Interpersonal Problem Solving." *Journal of Personality and Social Psychology* 69, no. 1 (1995): 176–90. https://doi.org/10.1037/0022-3514.69.1.176.

Lyubomirsky, Sonja, Kari L. Tucker, Nicole D. Caldwell, and Kimberly Berg. "Why Ruminators Are Poor Problem Solvers: Clues from the Phenomenology of Dysphoric Rumination." *Journal of Personality and Social Psychology* 77, no. 5 (1999): 1041–60. https://doi.org/10.1037/0022-3514.77.5.1041.

Maftei, Alexandra and Acnana-Maria Pătrăușanu. "Digital Reflections: Narcissism, Stress, Social Media Addiction, and Nomophobia." *The Journal of Psychology* 158, no. 2 (February 17, 2024): 147–60. https://doi.org/10.1080/00223980.2023.2256453.

Marchlewska, Marta, Aleksandra Cichocka, Manana Jaworska, Agnieszka Golec De Zavala, and Michal Bilewicz. "Superficial Ingroup Love? Collective Narcissism Predicts Ingroup Image Defense, Outgroup Prejudice, and Lower Ingroup Loyalty." *British Journal of Social Psychology* 59, no. 4 (October 2020): 857–75. https://doi.org/10.1111/bjso.12367.

Marcus, Sharon. *The Drama of Celebrity.* First paperback printing. Princeton University Press, 2020.

Marengo, N., A. Borraccino, L. Charrier, P. Berchialla, P. Dalmasso, M. Caputo, and P. Lemma. "Cyberbullying and Problematic Social Media Use: An Insight into the Positive Role of Social Support in Adolescents—Data from the Health Behaviour in School-Aged Children Study in Italy." *Public Health* 199 (October 2021): 46–50. https://doi.org/10.1016/j.puhe.2021.08.010.

Mark, Gloria. *Attention Span: A Groundbreaking Way to Restore Balance, Happiness and Productivity.* Hanover Square Press, 2023.

Marwick, Alice Emily. *Status Update: Celebrity, Publicity, and Branding in the Social Media Age.* Yale University Press, 2013.

Marwick, Alice E. "Instafame: Luxury Selfies in the Attention Economy." *Public Culture* 27, no. 1 (January 1, 2015): 137–60. https://doi.org/10.1215/08992363-2798379.

Marwick, Alice E. "The Public Domain: Surveillance in Everyday Life." *Surveillance & Society* 9, no. 4 (2012): 378–393. http://www.surveillance-and-society.org | ISSN: 1477-7487

Marwick, Alice E. and danah boyd. "I Tweet Honestly, I Tweet Passionately: Twitter Users, Context Collapse, and the Imagined Audience." *New Media & Society* 13, no. 1 (February 2011): 114–33. https://doi.org/10.1177/1461444810365313.

Marwick, Alice and danah boyd. "To See and Be Seen: Celebrity Practice on Twitter." *Convergence: The International Journal of Research into New Media Technologies* 17, no. 2 (May 2011): 139–58. https://doi.org/10.1177/1354856510394539.

Marwick, Alice E. and danah boyd. "Networked Privacy: How Teenagers Negotiate Context in Social Media." *New Media & Society* 16, no. 7 (November 2014): 1051–67. https://doi.org/10.1177/1461444814543995.

Marwick, Alice E. and danah boyd, The Drama! Teen Conflict, Gossip, and Bullying in Networked Publics (September 12, 2011). A Decade in Internet Time: Symposium on the Dynamics of the Internet and Society, September 2011, Available at SSRN: https://ssrn.com/abstract=1926349

Marwick, Alice and danah boyd. "'It's Just Drama': Teen Perspectives on Conflict and Aggression in a Networked Era." *Journal of Youth Studies* 17, no. 9 (October 21, 2014): 1187–1204. https://doi.org/10.1080/13676261.2014.901493.

Matsa, Elisa Shearer, Sarah Naseer, Jacob Liedke, and Katerina Eva. "How Americans Get News on TikTok, X, Facebook and Instagram." *Pew Research Center* (blog), June 12, 2024. https://www.pewresearch.org/journalism/2024/06/12/how-americans-get-news-on-tiktok-x-facebook-and-instagram/.

McAdams, Dan P. and Bradley D. Olson. "Personality Development: Continuity and Change Over the Life Course." *Annual Review of Psychology* 61 (2010): 517–542.

McArthur, Brae Anne, Valeriya Volkova, Suzy Tomopoulos, and Sheri Madigan. "Global Prevalence of Meeting Screen Time Guidelines Among Children 5 Years and Younger: A Systematic Review and Meta-Analysis." *JAMA Pediatrics* 176, no. 4 (April 1, 2022): 373–383. https://doi.org/10.1001/jamapediatrics.2021.6386.

McCourt, Frank H. and Michael Casey. *Our Biggest Fight: Reclaiming Liberty, Humanity, and Dignity in the Internet Age.* First edition. Crown, 2024.

McDaniel, Brandon T. and Jenny S. Radesky. "Technoference: Longitudinal Associations between Parent Technology Use, Parenting Stress, and Child Behavior Problems." *Pediatric Research* 84, no. 2 (August 2018): 210–18. https://doi.org/10.1038/s41390-018-0052-6.

McInroy, Lauren B., Rebecca J. McCloskey, Shelley L. Craig, and Andrew D. Eaton. "LGBTQ+ Youths' Community Engagement and Resource Seeking Online versus Offline." *Journal of Technology in Human Services* 37, no. 4 (October 2, 2019): 315–33. https://doi.or g/10.1080/15228835.2019.1617823.

McIntire, Mike, Russ Buettner, and Susanne Craig. "Tax Records Reveal How Fame Gave Trump a $427 Million Lifeline." *The New York Times*, September 29, 2020, sec. U.S. https://www.nytimes.com/ interactive/2020/09/28/us/donald-trump-taxes-apprentice.html.

McQuade, Barbara. *Attack from Within: How Disinformation Is Sabotaging America.* Seven Stories Press, 2024.

Miller, Joshua D., Brian J. Hoffman, Eric T. Gaughan, Brittany Gentile, Jessica Maples, and W. Keith Campbell. "Grandiose and Vulnerable Narcissism: A Nomological Network Analysis: Variants of Narcissism." *Journal of Personality* 79, no. 5 (October 2011): 1013–42. https://doi.org/10.1111/j.1467-6494.2010.00711.x.

Miller, Vincent. "New Media, Networking and Phatic Culture." *Convergence: The International Journal of Research into New Media Technologies* 14, no. 4 (November 2008): 387–400. https://doi. org/10.1177/1354856508094659.

Milner, Murray. "Is Celebrity a New Kind of Status System?" *Society* 47, no. 5 (September 2010): 379–87. https://doi.org/10.1007/s12115-010-9347-x.

Milner, Murray. *Freaks, Geeks, and Cool Kids: American Teenagers, Schools, and the Culture of Consumption.* 1st Routledge pbk. ed. Routledge, 2006.

"Mindfulness or Mindlessness—a Battle of the Minds? – Innovative Resources." Accessed October 8, 2024. https://innovativeresources. org/mindfulness-or-mindlessness-which-is-better/.

Mischel, Walter. *The Marshmallow Test: Mastering Self-Control.* First edition. Little, Brown and Company, 2014.

"MisinfoDay 2023: Types of Misinformation \x5bPublic\x5d.Pptx." Accessed August 30, 2024. https://docs.google.com/presentation/d/12pzgk8qjczCS9B8q_fMHcxlnxCdaTArx.

Morgan, Paul L., Yangyang Wang, and Adrienne D. Woods. "Risk and Protective Factors for Frequent Electronic Device Use of Online Technologies." *Child Development* 92, no. 2 (March 2021): 704–14. https://doi.org/10.1111/cdev.13532.

Morson, Gary Saul and Morton Owen Schapiro. *Minds Wide Shut: How the New Fundamentalisms Divide Us.* First paperback edition. Princeton University Press, 2023.

Mrug, Sylvie, Anjana Madan, and Michael Windle. "Emotional Desensitization to Violence Contributes to Adolescents' Violent Behavior." *Journal of Abnormal Child Psychology* 44, no. 1 (January 2016): 75–86. https://doi.org/10.1007/s10802-015-9986-x.

Mruk, Christopher. *Self-Esteem Research, Theory, and Practice: Toward a Positive Psychology of Self-Esteem,* Third edition. Springer, 2006.

Murthy, Vivek. "Social Media and Youth Mental Health: The U. S. Surgeon General's Advisory." (2023). https://www.hhs.gov/sites/default/files/sg-youth-mental-health-social-media-advisory.pdf

Murthy, Vivek. "Our Epidemic of Loneliness and Isolation: The U. S. Surgeon General's Advisory." (2023). https://www.hhs.gov/sites/default/files/surgeon-general-social-connection-advisory.pdf

Murthy, Vivek. "Parents Under Pressure: The U.S. Surgeon General's Advisory on the Mental Health & Well-Being of Parents." (2024). https://www.hhs.gov/sites/default/files/parents-under-pressure.pdf

Mushquash, Aislin R., Jaidyn K. Charlton, Angela MacIsaac, and Kendra Ryan. "Romance Behind the Screens: Exploring the Role of Technoference on Intimacy." *Cyberpsychology, Behavior, and Social Networking* 25, no. 12 (December 1, 2022): 814–20. https://doi.org/10.1089/cyber.2022.0068.

Namie, Gary and Ruth Namie. *The Bully at Work: What You Can Do to Stop the Hurt and Reclaim Your Dignity on the Job.* Sourcebooks, 2009.

Nesi, Jacqueline, Eva H. Telzer, and Mitchell J. Prinstein, eds. *Handbook of Adolescent Digital Media Use and Mental Health.* Cambridge University Press, 2022. https://doi.org/10.1017/9781108976237.

Newitz, Annalee. *Four Lost Cities: A Secret History of the Urban Age.* First edition. W.W. Norton & Company, 2021.

New Republic, The. "The Spiritual Unspooling of America: A Case for a Political Realignment." Accessed September 17, 2024. https://newrepublic.com/article/177435/chris-murphy-case-political-realignment-economics.

Newton-Howes, Giles. *Personality Disorder.* Oxford University Press, 2015.

NPR. "How Cancel Culture Became Politicized – Just Like Political Correctness," July 26, 2021. https://www.npr org/2021/07/09/1014744289/cancel-culture-debate-has-early-90s-roots-political-correctness.

Okuma, Kanako and Masako Tanimura. "A Preliminary Study on the Relationship between Characteristics of TV Content and Delayed Speech Development in Young Children." *Infant Behavior and Development* 32, no. 3 (June 2009): 312–21. https://doi.org/10.1016/j.infbeh.2009.04.002.

Otermans, Pauldy C. J., Andrew Parton, and Andre J. Szameitat. "The Working Memory Costs of a Central Attentional Bottleneck in Multitasking." *Psychological Research* 86, no. 6 (September 2022): 1774–91. https://doi.org/10.1007/s00426-021-01615-1.

Oppong, Derek, Emma Sethina Adjaottor, Frimpong-Manso Addo, Worlali Nyaledzigbor, Amma Serwaa Ofori-Amanfo, Hsin-Pao Chen, and Daniel Kwasi Ahorsu. "The Mediating Role of Selfitis in the Associations between Self-Esteem, Problematic Social Media Use, Problematic Smartphone Use, Body-Self Appearance, and Psychological Distress Among Young Ghanaian Adults." *Healthcare* 10, no. 12 (December 10, 2022): 2500. https://doi.org/10.3390/healthcare10122500.

Opree, Suzanna J. and Rinaldo Kühne. "Linking Adolescents' Exposure to and Identification with Reality TV to Materialism, Narcissism, and Entitlement." *Psychology of Popular Media* 12, no. 4 (October 2023): 450–58. https://doi.org/10.1037/ppm0000426.

Orth, Ulrich, Samantha Krauss, and Mitja D. Back. "Development of Narcissism across the Life Span: A Meta-Analytic Review of Longitudinal Studies." *Psychological Bulletin* 150, no. 6 (June 2024): 643–65. https://doi.org/10.1037/bul0000436.

Page, M. Beth, Kathy Bishop, and Catherine Etmanski. "Community Belonging and Values-Based Leadership as the Antidote to Bullying and Incivility." *Societies* 11, no. 2 (March 29, 2021): 29. https://doi.org/10.3390/soc11020029.

Paris, Joel. *Personality Disorders: Theory, Research, and Treatment* 5, no. 2 (2014): 220–26. https://doi.org/10.1037/a0028580.

Paul, Richard and Linda Elder. *Critical Thinking: Tools for Taking Charge of Your Learning and Your Life.* 3rd ed. Pearson, 2012.

Paull, Megan and Maryam Omari. "Dignity and Respect: Important in Volunteer Settings Too!" *Equality, Diversity and Inclusion: An International Journal* 34, no. 3 (March 20, 2015): 244–55. https://doi.org/10.1108/EDI-05-2014-0033.

PBS News. "3 Men Found Not Guilty of Supporting Plot to Kidnap Michigan Gov. Whitmer," September 15, 2023. https://www.pbs.org/newshour/nation/3-men-found-not-guilty-of-supporting-plot-to-kidnap-michigan-gov-whitmer.

Pearson, Catherine. "Does Your Child Have an Unhealthy Relationship to Social Media? Here's How to Tell." *The New York Times*, May 23, 2023, sec. Well. https://www.nytimes.com/2023/05/23/well/syndrom/social-media-use-children-parents.html.

Pennycook, Gordon, Bence Bago, and Jonathon McPhetres. "Science Beliefs, Political Ideology, and Cognitive Sophistication." *Journal of Experimental Psychology: General* 152, no. 1 (January 2023): 80–97. https://doi.org/10.1037/xge0001267.

Pennycook, Gordon, Robert M. Ross, Derek J. Koehler, and Jonathan A. Fugelsang. "Dunning–Kruger Effects in Reasoning: Theoretical Implications of the Failure to Recognize Incompetence." *Psychonomic Bulletin & Review* 24, no. 6 (December 2017): 1774–84. https://doi.org/10.3758/s13423-017-1242-7.

Perlstadt, Harry. "How to Get Out of the Stanford Prison Experiment: Revisiting Social Science Research Ethics." *Current Research Journal of Social Sciences and Humanities* 1, no. 2 (December 28, 2018): 45–59. https://doi.org/10.12944/CRJSSH.1.2.01.

Pezoa-Jares, Rodolfo Eduardo. "Internet Addiction: A Review." *Journal of Addiction Research & Therapy*, 2012. https://doi.org/10.4172/2155-6105.S6-004.

Piotrowski, Chris. "Adult Bully Syndrome: An Integrative Conceptualization Based on a Personality Disorders Framework." *Psychology and Education: An Interdisciplinary Journal* 53, no. 1–2 (April 2016): 91–98.

Poetry Foundation, The. "Speech: 'All the World's a Stage.'" Accessed October 11, 2024. https://beta.poetryfoundation.org/poems/56966/speech-all-the-worlds-a-stage.

Pogue, James. "Opinion | The Senator Warning Democrats of a Crisis Unfolding Beneath Their Noses." *The New York Times*, August 19, 2024, sec. Opinion. https://www.nytimes.com/2024/08/19/opinion/chris-murphy-democrats.html.

Post, Jerrold M. *Dangerous Charisma: The Political Psychology of Donald Trump and His Followers*. Pegasus. 2019.

Postman, Neil. *Amusing Ourselves to Death: Public Discourse in the Age of Show Business*. 20th anniversary ed. Penguin Books, 2006.

Porter III, John and Andrew Robb. "Lingering Effects Associated with the Consumer Use of Virtual Reality." *Frontiers in Virtual Reality* 3 (September 29, 2022): 880634. https://doi.org/10.3389/frvir.2022.880634.

Pozner, Jennifer L. *Reality Bites Back: The Troubling Truth about Guilty Pleasure TV*. Seal Press: Distributed by Publishers Group West, 2010.

ProPublica. "How School Board Meetings Became Flashpoints for Anger and Chaos Across the Country," July 19, 2023. https://projects.propublica.org/school-board-meetings-flashpoints-for-anger-chaos/.

Prothero, Arianna, Lauraine Langreo, and Alyson Klein. "Which States Ban or Restrict Cellphones in Schools?" *Education Week*, June 28, 2024, sec. Technology, Ed-Tech Policy. https://www.edweek.org/technology/which-states-ban-or-restrict-cellphones-in-schools/2024/06.

Protzko, John and Jonathan W. Schooler. "What I Didn't Grow Up with Is Dangerous: Personal Experience with a New Technology or Societal Change Reduces the Belief That It Corrupts Youth." *Frontiers in Psychology* 14 (October 12, 2023): 1017313. https://doi.org/10.3389/fpsyg.2023.1017313.

Przybylski, Andrew K., Kou Murayama, Cody R. DeHaan, and Valerie Gladwell. "Motivational, Emotional, and Behavioral Correlates of Fear of Missing Out." *Computers in Human Behavior* 29, no. 4 (July 2013): 1841–48. https://doi.org/10.1016/j.chb.2013.02.014.

Psarras, Evie. "'It's a Mix of Authenticity and Complete Fabrication' Emotional Camping: The Cross-Platform Labor of the *Real Housewives*." *New Media & Society* 24, no. 6 (June 2022): 1382–98. https://doi.org/10.1177/1461444820975025.

Ray, Rebecca D., Frank H. Wilhelm, and James J. Gross. "All in the Mind's Eye? Anger Rumination and Reappraisal." *Journal of Personality and Social Psychology* 94, no. 1 (2008): 133–45. https://doi.org/10.1037/0022-3514.94.1.133.

Reijntjes, Albert, Marjolijn Vermande, Sander Thomaes, Frits Goossens, Tjeert Olthof, Liesbeth Aleva, and Matty Van Der Meulen. "Narcissism, Bullying, and Social Dominance in Youth: A Longitudinal Analysis." *Journal of Abnormal Child Psychology* 44, no. 1 (January 2016): 63–74. https://doi.org/10.1007/s10802-015-9974-1.

Ripley, Amanda. *High Conflict: Why We Get Trapped and How We Get Out*. First Simon&Schuster hardcover edition. Simon & Schuster, 2021.

Roberts, Brent W., Avshalom Caspi, and Terrie E. Moffitt. "The Kids Are Alright: Growth and Stability in Personality Development from Adolescence to Adulthood." *Journal of Personality and Social Psychology* 81, no. 4 (2001): 670–83. https://doi.org/10.1037/0022-3514.81.4.670.

Roberts, James A. and Meredith E. David. "On the Outside Looking in: Social Media Intensity, Social Connection, and User Well-Being: The Moderating Role of Passive Social Media Use." *Canadian Journal of Behavioural Science / Revue Canadienne Des Sciences Du Comportement* 55, no. 3 (July 2023): 240–52. https://doi.org/10.1037/cbs0000323.

Rom, Mark Carl and Kristina Mitchell. "Teaching Politics in a Call-Out and Cancel Culture." *PS: Political Science & Politics* 54, no. 3 (July 2021): 610–14. https://doi.org/10.1017/S1049096521000433.

Romano, Aja. "Why We Can't Stop Fighting about Cancel Culture." Vox, December 30, 2019. https://www.vox.com/culture/2019/12/30/20879720/what-is-cancel-culture-explained-history-debate.

Ronaghi, Mohammad Hossein. "The Effect of Virtual Reality Technology and Education on Sustainable Behavior: A Comparative Quasi-Experimental Study." *Interactive Technology and Smart Education* 20, no. 4 (November 17, 2023): 475–92. https://doi.org/10.1108/ITSE-02-2022-0025.

Roos, Sanna, Christina Salmivalli, and Ernest E. V. Hodges. "Emotion Regulation and Negative Emotionality Moderate the Effects of Moral (Dis)Engagement on Aggression." *Merrill-Palmer Quarterly* 61, no. 1 (2015): 30. https://doi.org/10.13110/merrpalmquar1982.61.1.0030.

Rose, Amanda J. "Co-Rumination in the Friendships of Girls and Boys." *Child Development* 73, no. 6 (November 2002): 1830–43. https://doi.org/10.1111/1467-8624.00509.

Ross, Howard J. *Everyday Bias: Identifying and Navigating Unconscious Judgment in Our Daily Lives.* Rowman & Littlefield, 2017.

Ross, Loretta. *Calling In: How to Start Making Change with Those You'd Rather Cancel.* [S.l.]: Simon and Schuster, 2025.

Roter, Annette B. "Narcissism." In *Understanding and Recognizing Dysfunctional Leadership: The Impact of Dysfunctional Leadership on Organizations and Followers.* 1 Edition. 75–94. Routledge, 2017.

Rozenblatt-Perkal, Yael, Michael Davidovitch, and Noa Gueron-Sela. "Infants' Physiological and Behavioral Reactivity to Maternal Mobile Phone Use – An Experimental Study." *Computers in Human Behavior* 127 (February 2022): 107038. https://doi.org/10.1016/j.chb.2021.107038.

Schildkraut, Deborah J. *Press "ONE" for English: Language Policy, Public Opinion, and American Identity.* Princeton University Press, 2013. https://doi.org/10.1515/9781400849338.

Schildkraut, Deborah J. "Boundaries of American Identity: Evolving Understandings of 'Us.'" *Annual Review of Political Science* 17, no. 1 (May 11, 2014): 441–60. https://doi.org/10.1146/annurev-polisci-080812-144642.

Scolere, Leah, Urszula Pruchniewska, and Brooke Erin Duffy. "Constructing the Platform-Specific Self-Brand: The Labor of Social Media Promotion." *Social Media + Society* 4, no. 3 (July 2018): 2056305118784768. https://doi.org/10.1177/2056305118784768.

Scribd. "CNN - Being 13 - Report PDF | Download Free PDF | Social Media | Popular Culture & Media Studies." Accessed June 26, 2024. https://www.scribd.com/document/433526896/CNN-Being-13-report-pdf.

Shaer, Matthew. "Why Is the Loneliness Epidemic So Hard to Cure?" *The New York Times*, August 27, 2024, sec. Magazine. https://www.nytimes.com/2024/08/27/magazine/loneliness-epidemic-cure.html.

Sharp, Carla. "Personality Disorders." Edited by Allan H. Ropper. *New England Journal of Medicine* 387, no. 10 (September 8, 2022): 916–23. https://doi.org/10.1056/NEJMra2120164.

Shawcroft, Jane E., Megan Gale, Katey Workman, Virginia Leiter, McKell Jorgensen-Wells, and Alexander C. Jensen. "Screen-Play: An Observational Study of the Effect of Screen Media on Children's Play in a Museum Setting." *Computers in Human Behavior* 132 (July 2022): 107254. https://doi.org/10.1016/j.chb.2022.107254.

Shearer, Elisa, Sarah Naseer, Jacob Liedke, and Katerina Eva Matsa. "How Americans Get News on TikTok, X, Facebook and Instagram." Pew Research Center, June, 2024.

Shoshani, Anat. "From Virtual to Prosocial Reality: The Effects of Prosocial Virtual Reality Games on Preschool Children's Prosocial Tendencies in Real Life Environments." *Computers in Human Behavior* 139 (February 2023): 107546. https://doi.org/10.1016/j.chb.2022.107546.

Show', The Ezra Klein. "Opinion | How We Communicate Will Decide Whether Democracy Lives or Dies." *The New York Times*, July 26, 2022, sec. Opinion. https://www.nytimes.com/2022/07/26/opinion/ezra-klein-podcast-sean-illing.html.

Shuai, Lan, Shan He, Hong Zheng, Zhouye Wang, Meihui Qiu, Weiping Xia, Xuan Cao, Lu Lu, and Jinsong Zhang. "Influences of Digital Media Use on Children and Adolescents with ADHD during COVID-19 Pandemic." *Globalization and Health* 17, no. 1 (December 2021): 48. https://doi.org/10.1186/s12992-021-00699-z.

Simon, Bernd and Bert Klandermans. "Politicized Collective Identity: A Social Psychological Analysis." *American Psychologist* 56, no. 4 (2001): 319–31. https://doi.org/10.1037/0003-066X.56.4.319.

Smetana, Judith G., Nicole Campione-Barr, and Aaron Metzger. "Adolescent Development in Interpersonal and Societal Contexts." *Annual Review of Psychology* 57, no. 1 (January 1, 2006): 255–84. https://doi.org/10.1146/annurev.psych.57.102904.190124.

Smith, Rhiannon L. and Amanda J. Rose. "The 'Cost of Caring' in Youths' Friendships: Considering Associations among Social Perspective Taking, Co-Rumination, and Empathetic Distress." *Developmental Psychology* 47, no. 6 (November 2011): 1792–1803. https://doi.org/10.1037/a0025309.

Smith, Alexandra C. G., Patti A. Timmons Fritz, and Samantha Daskaluk. "'Drama' in Interpersonal Conflict and Interactions Among Emerging Adults: A Qualitative Focus Group Study." *Emerging Adulthood* 8, no. 2 (April 2020): 133–43. https://doi.org/10.1177/2167696818792989.

Smokowski, Paul R. and Caroline B. R. Evans. *Bullying and Victimization across the Lifespan: Playground Politics and Power*. Springer, 2019.

Soares, Ana Sofia, José L. Pais-Ribeiro, and Isabel Silva. "Developmental Assets Predictors of Life Satisfaction in Adolescents." *Frontiers in Psychology* 10 (February 12, 2019): 236. https://doi.org/10.3389/fpsyg.2019.00236.

Social Studies. Documentary. Institute, Evergreen Pictures, 2024.

"Speaking Up Without Tearing Down | Learning for Justice," January 2, 2019. https://www.learningforjustice.org/magazine/spring-2019/speaking-up-without-tearing-down.

Spytska, Liana. "Symptoms and Main Differences Between a Psychopath and a Sociopath." *Journal of Nervous & Mental Disease* 212, no. 1 (January 2024): 52–56. https://doi.org/10.1097/NMD.0000000000001728.

Staebler, Katja, Esther Helbing, Charlotte Rosenbach, and Babette Renneberg. "Rejection Sensitivity and Borderline Personality Disorder." *Clinical Psychology & Psychotherapy* 18, no. 4 (July 2011): 275–83. https://doi.org/10.1002/cpp.705.

Steiner-Adair, Catherine and Teresa Barker. *The Big Disconnect: Protecting Childhood and Family Relationships in the Digital Age.* First Harper paperback. Harper, 2014.

Sternisko, Anni, Aleksandra Cichocka, Aleksandra Cislak, and Jay J. Van Bavel. "National Narcissism Predicts the Belief in and the Dissemination of Conspiracy Theories During the COVID-19 Pandemic: Evidence From 56 Countries." *Personality and Social Psychology Bulletin* 49, no. 1 (January 2023): 48–65. https://doi.org/10.1177/01 461672211054947.

Stewart, Tracie L., Jacqueline R. Laduke, Charlotte Bracht, Brooke A. M. Sweet, and Kristine E. Gamarel. "Do the 'Eyes' Have It? A Program Evaluation of Jane Elliott's 'Blue-Eyes/Brown-Eyes' Diversity Training Exercise." *Journal of Applied Social Psychology* 33, no. 9 (September 2003): 1898–1921. https://doi.org/10.1111/j.1559-1816.2003. tb02086.x.

Stuewig, Jeffrey, June P. Tangney, Caron Heigel, Laura Harty, and Laura McCloskey. "Shaming, Blaming, and Maiming: Functional Links among the Moral Emotions, Externalization of Blame, and Aggression." *Journal of Research in Personality* 44, no. 1 (February 2010): 91–102. https://doi.org/10.1016/j.jrp.2009.12.005.

Sundqvist, Annette, Felix-Sebastian Koch, Ulrika Birberg Thornberg, Rachel Barr, and Mikael Heimann. "Growing Up in a Digital World – Digital Media and the Association With the Child's Language Development at Two Years of Age." *Frontiers in Psychology* 12 (March 18, 2021): 569920. https://doi.org/10.3389/fpsyg.2021.569920.

Sykes, Charles. *A Nation of Victims: The Decay of the American Character.* St. Martin's Press. 1992.

Taibbi, Matt. *Hate Inc: Why Today's Media Makes Us Despise One Another*: With a new post-election preface. OR Books, 2021.

Tamir, Diana I. and Jason P. Mitchell. "Disclosing Information About the Self Is Intrinsically Rewarding." *Proceedings of the National Academy of Sciences* 109, no. 21 (May 22, 2012): 8038–43. https://doi.org/10.1073/pnas.1202129109.

Tandoc, Edson C, Beverly Tan Hui Ru, Gabrielle Lee Huei, Ng Min Qi Charlyn, Rachel Angeline Chua, and Zhang Hao Goh. "#CancelCulture: Examining Definitions and Motivations." *New Media & Society* 26, no. 4 (April 2024): 1944–62. https://doi.org/10.1177/14614448221077977.

Tang, Annie, J. Carlo Hojilla, Jordan E. Jackson, Kara A. Rothenberg, Rebecca C. Gologorsky, Douglas A. Stram, Colin M. Mooney, Stephanie L. Hernandez, and Karen M. Yokoo. "Gender-Affirming Mastectomy Trends and Surgical Outcomes in Adolescents." *Annals of Plastic Surgery* 88, no. 4 (May 2022): S325–31. https://doi.org/10.1097/SAP.0000000000003135.

Taylor, Ryan. "David McCullough Jr. Commencement Speech | Transcripts." Rev. Accessed June 28, 2024. https://www.rev.com/blog/transcripts/you-are-not-special-commencement-speech-transcript-by-david-mccullough-jr-at-wellesley-high-school.

Thabassum, Liyana, "Phubbing: A Literature Review of the Technological Invasion That Has Changed Lives for the Last Decade." *Psychology Research on Education and Social Sciences* 2, no.1 (June 2021): 11–18. E-ISSN:2717-7602.

"The New Colossus – Statue of Liberty National Monument (U.S. National Park Service)." Accessed October 17, 2024. https://www.nps.gov/stli/learn/historyculture/colossus.htm.

Thomaes, Sander, Eddie Brummelman, Albert Reijntjes, and Brad J. Bushman. "When Narcissus Was a Boy: Origins, Nature, and Consequences of Childhood Narcissism." *Child Development Perspectives* 7, no. 1 (March 2013): 22–26. https://doi.org/10.1111/cdep.12009.

Thomaes, Sander, Brad J. Bushman, Bram Orobio de Castro, Geoffrey L. Cohen, and Jaap J. A. Denissen. "Reducing Narcissistic Aggression by Buttressing Self-Esteem: An Experimental Field Study." *Psychological Science* 20, no. 12 (2009): 1536–1542.

Thomaes, Sander, Brad Bushman, Hedy Stegge, and Tjeert Olthof. "Trumping Shame by Blasts of Noise: Narcissism, Self-Esteem, Shame, and Aggression in Young Adolescents." *Child Development* 79, no. 6 (November/December 2008): 1792–1801.

Towner, Emily, Jennifer Grint, Tally Levy, Sarah-Jayne Blakemore, and Livia Tomova. "Revealing the Self in a Digital World: A Systematic Review of Adolescent Online and Offline Self-Disclosure." *Current Opinion in Psychology* 45 (June 2022): 101309. https://doi.org/10.1016/j.copsyc.2022.101309.

Tracy, Jessica L., Joey T. Cheng, Richard W. Robins, and Kali H. Trzesniewski. "Authentic and Hubristic Pride: The Affective Core of Self-Esteem and Narcissism." *Self and Identity* 8, no. 2–3 (April 2009): 196–213. https://doi.org/10.1080/15298860802505053.

Traversa, Marissa, Ying Tian, and Stephen C. Wright. "Cancel Culture Can Be Collectively Validating for Groups Experiencing Harm." *Frontiers in Psychology* 14 (July 20, 2023): 1181872. https://doi.org/10.3389/fpsyg.2023.1181872.

Trump, Mary L. *Too Much and Never Enough: How My Family Created the World's Most Dangerous Man.* Simon and Schuster, 2020.

Turkle, Sherry. *Reclaiming Conversation: The Power of Talk in a Digital Age.* Penguin Press, 2015.

Twenge, Jean M. "The Evidence for Generation Me and Against Generation We." *Emerging Adulthood* 1, no. 1 (March 2013): 11–16. https://doi.org/10.1177/2167696812466548.

Twenge, Jean M. *iGEN: Why Today's Super-Connected Kids Are Growing up Less Rebellious, More Tolerant, Less Happy—and Completely Unprepared for Adulthood and (What This Means for the Rest of Us).* Atria Books, 2017.

Twenge, Jean M. "More Time on Technology, Less Happiness? Associations Between Digital-Media Use and Psychological Well-Being." *Current Directions in Psychological Science* 28, no. 4 (August 2019): 372–79. https://doi.org/10.1177/0963721419838244.

Twenge, Jean M. *Generations: The Real Differences between Gen Z, Millennials, Gen X, Boomers, and Silents—And What They Mean for America's Future.* First Atria Books hardcover edition. Atria Books, 2023.

Twenge, Jean M. and William Keith Campbell. *The Narcissism Epidemic: Living in the Age of Entitlement.* Atria paperback, 2013.

Twenge, Jean M. and Joshua D. Foster. "Birth Cohort Increases in Narcissistic Personality Traits Among American College Students, 1982–2009." *Social Psychological and Personality Science* 1, no. 1 (January 2010): 99–106. https://doi.org/10.1177/1948550609355719.

Uhls, Yalda T., Minas Michikyan, Jordan Morris, Debra Garcia, Gary W. Small, Eleni Zgourou, and Patricia M. Greenfield. "Five Days at Outdoor Education Camp without Screens Improves Preteen Skills with Nonverbal Emotion Cues." *Computers in Human Behavior* 39 (October 2014): 387–92. https://doi.org/10.10 16/j.chb.2014.05.036.

Van de Cruys, Sander, Jo Bervoets, Stephen Gadsby, David Gijbels, and Karolien Poels. "Insight in the Conspiracist's Mind" *Personality and Social Psychology Review* 28, no. 3 (2024): 302–324. https://doi.org/10.1177/10888683231203145

Van Geel, Mitch, Fatih Toprak, Anouk Goemans, Wendy Zwaanswijk, and Paul Vedder. "Are Youth Psychopathic Traits Related to Bullying? Meta-Analyses on Callous-Unemotional Traits, Narcissism, and Impulsivity." *Child Psychiatry & Human Development* 48, no. 5 (October 2017): 768–77. https://doi.org/10.1007/s10578-016-0701-0.

Van Prooijen, Jan Willem. "An Existential Threat Model of Conspiracy Theories." *European Psychologist* 25, no. 1 (January 2020):16–25. doi: 10.1027/1016-9040/a000381.

Van Reemst, Lisa, Tamar F. C. Fischer, and Barbara W. C. Zwirs. "Social Information Processing Mechanisms and Victimization: A Literature Review." *Trauma, Violence, & Abuse* 17, no. 1 (January 2016): 3–25. https://doi.org/10.1177/1524838014557286.

Van Schie, Charlotte C., Heidi L. Jarman, Elizabeth Huxley, and Brin F. S. Grenyer. "Narcissistic Traits in Young People: Understanding the Role of Parenting and Maltreatment." *Borderline Personality Disorder and Emotion Dysregulation* 7, no. 1 (December 2020): 10. https://doi.org/10.1186/s40479-020-00125-7.

Varma, D. Ravi, K. Sarada, and S. Rdha Rani. "A Study on 'Selfitis,' Selfie Addiction Among Medical Students." *Journal of Dental and Medical Sciences* 19, no. 3 (March 2020): 58–61. doi:10.9790/0853-1903035861.

Vermue, Marieke, Rose Meleady, and Charles R. Seger. "Member-to-Member in Trust Behaviour: How Do Prior Experiences Inform Prosocial Behaviour towards Novel Ingroup and Outgroup Members?" *Current Psychology* 38, no. 4 (August 2019): 1003–20. https://doi.org/10.1007/s12144-019-00289-8.

Vijayakumar, Nandita and Jennifer H Pfeifer. "Self-Disclosure during Adolescence: Exploring the Means, Targets, and Types of Personal Exchanges." *Current Opinion in Psychology* 31 (February 2020): 135–40. https://doi.org/10.1016/j.copsyc.2019.08.005.

Vogel, Erin A., Jason P. Rose, Lindsay R. Roberts, and Katheryn Eckles. "Social Comparison, Social Media, and Self-Esteem." *Psychology of Popular Media Culture* 3, no. 4 (October 2014): 206–22. https://doi.org/10.1037/ppm0000047.

Vogels, Emily A, Monica Anderson, Margaret Porteus, Chris Baronavski, Sara Atske, Colleen McClain, Brooke Auxier, Andrew Perrin, and Meera Ramshankar. "Americans and 'Cancel Culture': Where Some See Calls for Accountability, Others See Censorship, Punishment." *Policy File*. Pew Research Center, 2021.

Wängqvist, Maria, Michael E. Lamb, Ann Frisén, and C. Philip Hwang. "Child and Adolescent Predictors of Personality in Early Adulthood." *Child Development* 86, no. 4 (July 2015): 1253–61. https://doi.org/10.1111/cdev.12362.

Way, Niobe, Alisha Ali, Carol Gilligan, Pedro Noguera, and David E. Kirkland, eds. *The Crisis of Connection: Roots, Consequences, and Solutions.* New York University Press, 2018.

Webster, Jamieson. "Opinion | Teenagers Are Telling Us That Something Is Wrong With America." *The New York Times*, October 11, 2022, sec. Opinion. https://www.nytimes.com/2022/10/11/opinion/teenagers-mental-health-america.html.

Weisel, Ori and Robert Böhm. "'Ingroup Love' and 'Outgroup Hate' in Intergroup Conflict between Natural Groups." *Journal of Experimental Social Psychology* 60 (September 2015): 110–20. https://doi.org/10.1016/j.jesp.2015.04.008.

Weston, Christina G. and Stephanie A. Riolo. "Childhood and Adolescent Precursors to Adult Personality Disorders." *Psychiatric Annals* 37, no. 2 (February 2007): 114–120.

Wheatley, Margaret J. *Who Do We Choose to Be? Facing Reality, Claiming Leadership, Restoring Sanity.* First edition. Berrett-Koehler Publishers Inc, 2017.

Whippman, Ruth. "Opinion | Boys Get Everything, Except the Thing That's Most Worth Having." *The New York Times*, June 5, 2024, sec. Opinion. https://www.nytimes.com/2024/06/05/opinion/boys-parenting-loneliness.html.

Whiting, Stephen, Marta Buoncristiano, Peter Gelius, Karim Abu-Omar, Mary Pattison, Jolanda Hyska, Vesselka Duleva, et al. "Physical Activity, Screen Time, and Sleep Duration of Children Aged 6–9 Years in 25 Countries: An Analysis within the WHO European Childhood Obesity Surveillance Initiative (COSI) 2015–2017." *Obesity Facts* 14, no. 1 (2021): 32–44. https://doi.org/10.1159/000511263.

Whitmer, Jennifer M. "You Are Your Brand: Self-branding and the Marketization of Self." *Sociology Compass* 13, no. 3 (March 2019): e12662. https://doi.org/10.1111/soc4.12662.

Wolf, Maryanne and Catherine J. Stoodley. *Reader, Come Home: The Reading Brain in a Digital World.* First edition. Harper, an imprint of HarperCollins Publishers, 2018.

Wu, Wenfeng, Liangrong Huang, and Fang Yang. "Social Anxiety and Problematic Social Media Use: A Systematic Review and Meta-Analysis." *Addictive Behaviors* 153 (June 2024): 107995. https://doi.org/10.1016/j.addbeh.2024.107995.

Wu, Sheng, Tung-Ching Lin, and Jou-Fan Shih. "Examining the Antecedents of Online Disinhibition." *Information Technology & People* 30, no. 1 (March 6, 2017): 189–209. https://doi.org/10.1108/ITP-07-2015-0167.

Yoga Anytime. "Distracted? Why Daydreaming Is Good for You." Accessed October 8, 2024. https://www.yogaanytime.com/blog/mindfulness/distracted-why-daydreaming-is-good-for-you.

Yu, Zhonggen. "A Meta-Analysis of the Effect of Virtual Reality Technology Use in Education." *Interactive Learning Environments* 31, no. 8 (November 17, 2023): 4956–76. https://doi.org/10.1080/10494820.2021.1989466.

Żemojtel-Piotrowska, Magdalena, Jarosław Piotrowski, Constantine Sedikides, Artur Sawicki, Anna Z. Czarna, Ramzi Fatfouta, and Tomasz Baran. "Communal Collective Narcissism." *Journal of Personality* 89, no. 5 (October 2021): 1062–80. https://doi.org/10.1111/jopy.12636.

Zhao, Yuguang, Jaap Ham, and Jurgen Van Der Vlist. "Persuasive Virtual Touch: The Effect of Artificial Social Touch on Shopping Behavior in Virtual Reality." In *Symbiotic Interaction*, edited by Jaap Ham, Anna Spagnolli, Benjamin Blankertz, Luciano Gamberini, and Giulio Jacucci, 10727:98–109. Springer International Publishing, 2018. https://doi.org/10.1007/978-3-319-91593-7_11.

Appendix

40 Developmental Assets

Search Institute has identified the following building blocks of healthy development that help young people grow up healthy, caring, and responsible. The percentages of young people who report experiencing each asset were gathered from the administration of the *Search Institute Profiles of Student Life: Attitudes and Behaviors* survey of almost 90,000 youth in the 2010 school year.

Asset type	Asset name and definition	
Support	1. **Family Support**-Family life provides high levels of love and support.	72%
	2. **Positive Family Communication**-Young person and her or his parent(s) communicate positively, and young person is willing to seek advice and counsel from parents.	32%
	3. **Other Adult Relationships**-Young person receives support from three or more nonparent adults.	50%
	4. **Caring Neighborhood**-Young person experiences caring neighbors.	40%
	5. **Caring School Climate**-School provides a caring, encouraging environment.	35%
	6. **Parent Involvement in Schooling**-Parent(s) are actively involved in helping young person succeed in school.	33%
Empowerment	7. **Community Values Youth**-Young person perceives that adults in the community value youth.	25%
	8. **Youth as Resources**-Young people are given useful roles in the community.	32%
	9. **Service to Others**-Young person serves in the community one hour or more per week.	50%
	10. **Safety**-Young person feels safe at home, school, and in the neighborhood.	54%
Boundaries & Expectations	11. **Family Boundaries**-Family has clear rules and consequences and monitors the young person's whereabouts.	47%
	12. **School Boundaries**-School provides clear rules and consequences.	56%
	13. **Neighborhood Boundaries**-Neighbors take responsibility for monitoring young people's behavior.	48%
	14. **Adult Role Models**-Parent(s) and other adults model positive, responsible behavior.	28%
	15. **Positive Peer Influence**-Young person's best friends model responsible behavior.	68%
	16. **High Expectations**-Both parent(s) and teachers encourage the young person to do well.	55%
Constructive Use of Time	17. **Creative Activities**-Young person spends three or more hours per week in lessons or practice in music, theater, or other arts.	20%
	18. **Youth Programs**-Young person spends three or more hours per week in sports, clubs, or organizations at school and/or in the community.	61%
	19. **Religious Community**-Young person spends one or more hours per week in activities in a religious institution.	51%
	20. **Time at Home**-Young person is out with friends "with nothing special to do" two or fewer nights per week.	56%
Commitment to Learning	21. **Achievement Motivation**-Young person is motivated to do well in school.	71%
	22. **School Engagement**-Young person is actively engaged in learning.	62%
	23. **Homework**-Young person reports doing at least one hour of homework every school day.	53%
	24. **Bonding to School**-Young person cares about her or his school.	61%
	25. **Reading for Pleasure**-Young person reads for pleasure three or more hours per week.	23%
Positive Values	26. **Caring**-Young person places high value on helping other people.	52%
	27. **Equality and Social Justice**-Young person places high value on promoting equality and reducing hunger and poverty.	54%
	28. **Integrity**-Young person acts on convictions and stands up for her or his beliefs.	71%
	29. **Honesty**-Young person "tells the truth even when it is not easy."	69%
	30. **Responsibility**-Young person accepts and takes personal responsibility.	67%
	31. **Restraint**-Young person believes it is important not to be sexually active or to use alcohol or other drugs.	47%
Social Competencies	32. **Planning and Decision Making**-Young person knows how to plan ahead and make choices.	33%
	33. **Interpersonal Competence**-Young person has empathy, sensitivity, and friendship skills.	48%
	34. **Cultural Competence**-Young person has knowledge of and comfort with people of different cultural/racial/ethnic backgrounds.	42%
	35. **Resistance Skills**-Young person can resist negative peer pressure and dangerous situations.	45%
	36. **Peaceful Conflict Resolution**-Young person seeks to resolve conflict nonviolently.	44%
Positive Identity	37. **Personal Power**-Young person feels he or she has control over "things that happen to me."	45%
	38. **Self-Esteem**-Young person reports having a high self-esteem.	52%
	39. **Sense of Purpose**- Young person reports that "my life has purpose."	63%
	40. **Positive view of personal future**- Young person is optimistic about her or his personal future.	75%

EXTERNAL ASSETS / **INTERNAL ASSETS**

COMMUNITIES

FAMILIES & CAREGIVERS

SCHOOLS

CLASSROOMS

Self-Awareness

Self-Management

Social & Emotional Learning

Responsible Decision-Making

Social Awareness

Relationship Skills

SEL Instruction & Classroom Climate

Schoolwide Culture, Practices & Policies

Authentic Partnerships

Aligned Learning Opportunities

CASEL.org

Index

About the Author

KATHLEEN ALLEN IS A graduate of the University of Rochester, Warner Graduate School of Education and Human Development, Rochester, NY. A lifelong educator, she worked with the Alberti Center for Bullying Abuse Prevention at the University at Buffalo, SUNY from 2012 to 2023. Dr. Allen is a program evaluator, researcher, educator, writer, parent, and grandparent. She has published several articles on adolescent social drama. *Stuck in Our Screens* is her first book.

Made in the USA
Middletown, DE
04 May 2025

75100488R00156